STEVE PARISH NATURAL HISTORY GUIDE

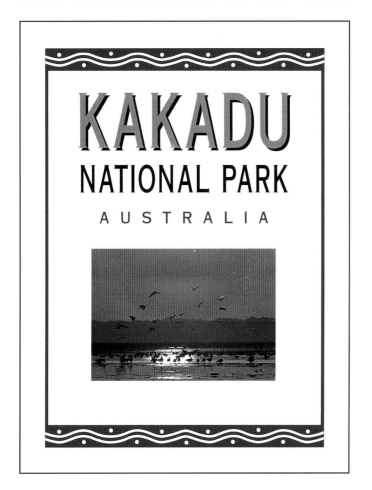

KAKADU
NATIONAL PARK
AUSTRALIA

KAKADU
NATIONAL PARK
AUSTRALIA

PHOTOGRAPHY & TEXT IAN MORRIS

Steve Parish
PUBLISHING

FOREWORD

I first visited the Alligator Rivers region with colleagues in 1962. It was a very different place then. A number of striking features were immediately apparent—the area was overrun by feral water buffaloes (then hunted as an economic resource); the numbers of waterbirds on the wetlands were astonishing; there was an abundance of mammals, especially the exquisite small ones picked up by spotlight; and, along the ancient escarpments, were galleries of truly remarkable rock paintings. Here was a paradise for researching biologists—and it would make an outstanding national park.

Access from Pine Creek by the rough old Oenpelli road was always an adventure. The white men and Aborigines in the area were centred on three safari camps, but the majority of Aboriginal people then lived at the Oenpelli Mission in the Arnhem Land Aboriginal Reserve. One family, however, Aboriginal patriarch William Alderson ("Yorky Billy"), his young wife and children, lived under a tarpaulin stretched over poles, on Woolwonga Sanctuary. It would be some years before ideas for a national park would be publicly discussed.

Kakadu National Park has had a protracted and difficult birth, much of which seems to have been forgotten or is now considered to be irrelevant. However, those who ignore history will likely have to relive it, warts and all!

In the sixties, the Northern Territory was run by an Administrator and a local administration that was part of the federal Department of the Interior. The first nature reserve in the region was declared in 1964 when the Woolwonga Aboriginal Reserve was declared to be also a Wildlife Reserve. The first move for a national park came in 1965 when the Reserves Board of the Northern Territory wrote to the Administrator recommending the proclamation of a large national park in the Alligator Rivers region. Receiving no response, the Board nevertheless continued its efforts for several years, reducing the area originally proposed, apparently to make it more palatable to departmental authorities. Those of us who know and love the park owe a great deal to the persistence of the Reserves Board, especially to its secretary, the late Tom Hare, who never gave up on things he really believed in.

At the end of 1968 the federal Department of the Interior, in an effort to offload responsibility, obtained the services of Sam Weems, a park adviser from the United States Department of the Interior and at that time first director of the NSW National Parks and Wildlife Service, to report on the area. He advised that it had all of the ingredients of a world-class national park. However, the Department apparently regarded economic development as more important than conservation and ignored his recommendation. Instead, in 1969, pastoral leases were granted for Mudginberri and Munmalary stations and mineral exploration permits were issued to several companies. As a counter, Northern Territory staff carried out a rapid survey of wildlife which kept the importance of natural values alive.

Ecology and environmental conservation in the early seventies were looked upon as subversive sciences. Few politicians considered themselves foolish enough to make decisions in these areas alone. In 1970 the Minister appointed a group to report on the proposed park and to draw up a management plan. It was led by John Bosward, chief planning officer of the NSW National Parks and Wildlife Service. I was on this team as a specialist assistant with knowledge of the Australian fauna. We were requested to exclude the pastoral leases and the Woolwonga Reserve. During our deliberations the first of the major uranium ore deposits was announced. In our report we stated that mining and national parks were incompatible and that all exploration permits should be cancelled forthwith. Copies of the report and management plan were sent to the Department and committee members in 1971, but soon after, all copies in the hands of committee members were recalled. The report was edited within the Department and the controversial parts watered down. Although the printed version is dated 1971, it was not issued until March 1972. In the same year, as an indication that at least something was happening, much of the proposed national park was declared a Wildlife Sanctuary.

By 1972, all uranium ore deposits had been found and mapped. In that year the federal government and the mining industry set up a fund to carry out an Environmental Fact-Finding Study. My division of CSIRO was given the task of surveying the land vertebrate fauna. We had already begun such a study in 1971, and continued our work in all seasons until 1975. Following the publication of the second Fox Report on the Ranger Environmental Enquiry of 1976–7 (enquiring into the potential uranium mining industry) the Prime Minister, Malcolm Fraser, formally announced that the Kakadu National Park was to be established. But it was not until 1979 that Stage 1 was declared in a package of four Bills which also established the Ranger Uranium Mine and strategies for its control and management, as well as joint Aboriginal and Australian National Parks and Wildlife Service management for the park. In two later stages the pastoral leases of Mudginberri, Munmalary, Goodparla and Gimbat have been added. Lands of the Woolwonga Reserve are part of the Kakadu National Park.

It was during the period of our fauna survey that I met Ian Morris, but knowledge of his deep understanding of the area and his wonderful photography had preceded him. Ian has written a great book. It tells of the annual cycle in weather and the flora and fauna from an Aboriginal viewpoint. He emphasises the profound spiritual attachment of the people to the land and its non-human inhabitants. Aboriginal views of ecology are rarely written, and by writing this book Ian (with his publisher) has performed a great service for the local people and indeed for all Australians.

John Calaby, Order of Australia (AO), for services to science and Australian wildlife; Hon. DSc (ANU); Honorary Member of the American Society of Mammologists; Honorary Member of the Mammal Society of Australia

THE SIX BININJ SEASONS OF KAKADU

MONSOON SEASON
GUDJEWG
(DECEMBER TO MARCH)

- Monsoon time
- Continuous low cloud from northwest
- The heaviest rain; rivers flood
- Floodplain wildlife moves to high ground
- Yam vines festoon the trees
- Spear grass reaches full height
- Main frog breeding season

HARVEST TIME
BANGGERRENG
(MARCH TO MAY)

- Last storms from the east ('knock-em-down' rain)
- Humidity remains high
- Rivers falling
- Spear grass seeding
- Geese and Estuarine Crocodiles nest
- Yamitj the grasshopper is calling

COOL WEATHER TIME
YEGGE
(MAY TO JUNE)

- Clear weather getting cooler
- Humidity drops
- Harvest time for many bush foods
- Water lilies at their best
- Grass yellowing; early burning begins
- Estuarine Crocodiles moving from wetlands back to main river channels

EARLY DRY SEASON
WURRGENG
(JUNE TO AUGUST)

- Cool nights
- Morning mists
- Marsupials and Spiny Anteater most active
- Rats and pythons move back on to the plains
- Nights become hotter once more

HOT DRY SEASON
GURRUNG
(AUGUST TO OCTOBER)

- The hottest driest period before the rains
- Almost cloudless skies
- Floodplains drying out
- Waterbirds congregate on available water
- Freshwater Crocodiles and Pig-nosed Turtles laying eggs
- Variety of wild fruits

PRE-MONSOON SEASON
GUNUMELENG
(OCTOBER TO DECEMBER)

- Irregular easterly storms in the afternoon
- Spear grass germinates
- Land changes from brown to green
- Animals become more active and visible
- Creeks begin to run; water plants grow
- Fish migrate upstream; frogs call
- Migratory birds arrive

CONTENTS

BILL NEIDJIE   TOBY GANGELE   MICK ALDERSON

BLUEY ILKIRR   FELIX HOLMES   NIPPER GABIRRIKI

DOLLY YANMALU   DIAMOND & GUNBUNUKA   CARLA NGALYURRUM

ACKNOWLEDGEMENTS

The accumulated information for a book of this nature flows constantly from all directions.

I am indebted to the Yolngu people of northeast Arnhem Land for many years of environmental instruction which subsequently helped me to come to grips with the natural systems of the Kakadu region. Allan Fox encouraged me to become involved in the Kakadu Project and constantly shared his unique world view. Some of his fine, hand-drawn perspective maps appear in the final chapter.

Much of this traditional information came to light when I was working with various ranger training groups, who individually had much to share. In particular I would like to thank Violet Lawson, Kevin Buliwana, Victor Cooper, James Wauchope, Nellie Bain, Jacky Godjbalk Namandali, Jonathon Yarrmarna, Mary Blyth and Eddie Hardy. Theirs is a great responsibility as they assume the roles of senior advisors in Kakadu.

Greg and Jane Miles freely shared over three decades their deep enthusiasm and enjoyment of all that is special about Kakadu. Together with Steve Parish, who regularly charged my enthusiasm for nature photography, their generosity and constant encouragement to put pen to paper has eventually produced this book.

Many other people made my Kakadu experience a pleasant one, both professionally and socially, including Mike Hill, Peter Wellings, Peter Butler, Wendy Murray, Bruce Lawson, Andrew Pickering, Terry Piper and other staff members of the Australian National Parks and Wildlife Service as it was, members of the Gunbalanya Community, Alf and Helen Wilson, Brian and Kaye Jukes, Stan Breeden and Belinda Wright, Peter Carroll, Jeremy Russell-Smith and Di Lucas, John Brock, Pat Shaunessy, Kate Duigan, John Woinarski, Mike Ridpath, Dick Braithwaite, Alan Andersen, Lee Moyes, Terry Barnes, Dave Irwin, Dave Wilson, Billie Gill, John Wombey and many more.

The Australian Nature Conservation Agency (ANCA) kindly gave permission to reproduce Park information from their visitor guides.

The friendly staff of Steve Parish Publishing made the long and tedious process of assembling this guide an enjoyable experience. Special thanks to editor Diane Furness and graphic designer Pip McConnel.

I would like to dedicate this book to the senior instructors of Kakadu, many of whom are no longer with us, who suffered the traumas of the negotiation and establishment of the Park because they had a vision of sharing their culture with the wider world. In particular, Bill Neidjie, Nipper Gabirriki, Toby Gangele, Carla Ngalyurrum, Felix Holmes, Little Dolly Yanmalu, Bluey Ilkirr and Susie Aladjinggu, Mick Alderson, Minnie Alderson, Billy Miyaku, Jimmy Waukwauk and Talkinbilly Gununbunka.

Ian Morris

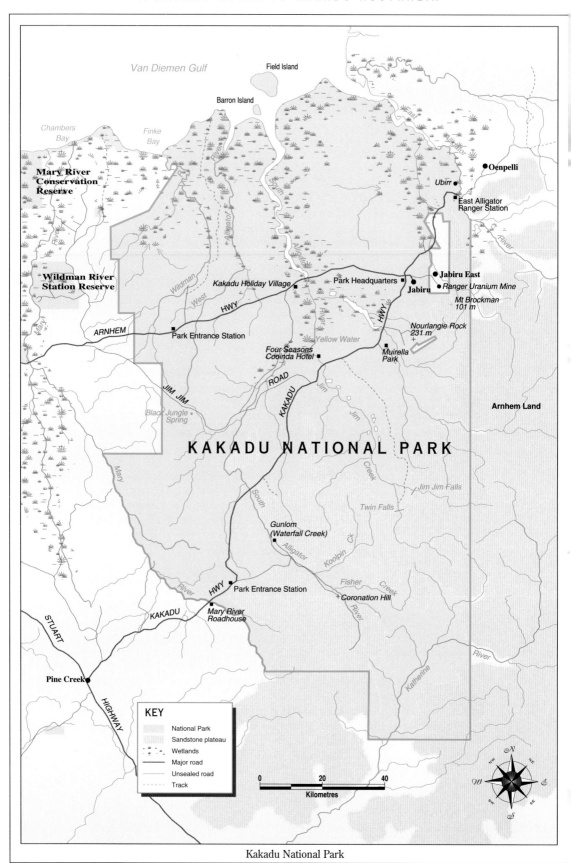

Kakadu National Park

HOW TO USE THIS BOOK

Chapter heading/season

Habitat

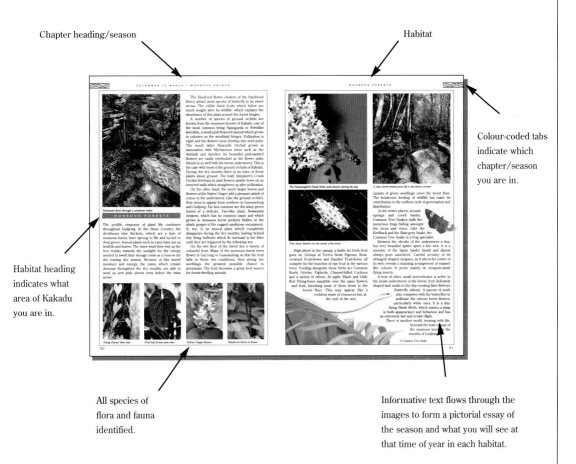

Colour-coded tabs indicate which chapter/season you are in.

Habitat heading indicates what area of Kakadu you are in.

All species of flora and fauna identified.

Informative text flows through the images to form a pictorial essay of the season and what you will see at that time of year in each habitat.

This guide is designed to help you make the most of your visit to Kakadu National Park. It is also a detailed resource for those who wish to enrich their knowledge of one of the world's great natural systems.

The **Introduction** gives an orientation to the Park and explains the distinctive seasonal organisation of the book. The variations from season to season are many; they are often dramatic and sometimes extremely subtle. With each chapter focussing on a particular season, **Chapters 1-6** provide detailed descriptions of wildlife, vegetation and the landscape. The yearly cycle begins in Chapter 1 with <u>Gudjewg</u>, the monsoon season which occurs between December and March; it concludes in Chapter 6 with <u>Gunumeleng</u>, the pre-monsoon season which is experienced between October and December. **Chapter 7** features the Park's special

endemic species while **Chapter 8**, <u>Using the Park,</u> is devoted to describing, region by region, some of the Park's best locations and walks. It guides you through the landscape, highlighting the wildlife and other natural features that are there. Maps, illustrations and special boxed features provide additional invaluable information.

<u>Wildlife Terminology</u> provides scientific and Aboriginal names for Kakadu's native animals. A simple guide to the language system of Kakadu follows. Aboriginal names are used freely throughout the text, with their English equivalents provided. Increasingly Park Headquarters is using Aboriginal names in its literature and signage. The author's spelling of Aboriginal names differs occasionally from Park usage.

INTRODUCTION

Kakadu is God's own country. To spend time there, and enjoy its moods, its seasons, its people and its spirit, is a privilege. If you let it, Kakadu imparts a spiritual quality that stays with you—it is a part of the original Australia. This book is an attempt to help you, the visitor, to appreciate this amazing landscape. Coming to terms with its spiritual dimension is a very personal affair, something that can be gained only from your experience with the Park and its people. Hopefully you will find this book a useful stepping-stone.

East Alligator River region to describe the dominant language of that time.

During preliminary ecological research in the 1960s, renowned Australian zoologist Dr John Calaby saw the region's potential to become one of Australia's premier national parks. He felt that the park should bear a title synonymous with its people and his vision became a reality on 5 April 1979, with the declaration by Federal Parliament of Kakadu National Park.

Outstanding biological diversity in an unspoiled and breathtaking landscape, and a cultural heritage

LOCATION

Kakadu National Park is situated at the top end of Australia's Northern Territory about 200 kilometres east of Darwin. Kakadu covers almost 20 000 square kilometres of the Alligator Rivers region in the tropical north of Australia. It is unique in that almost the entire catchment of the South Alligator River lies within its boundaries.

THE BEGINNING

In a very short period, the name 'Kakadu' has gained international significance. It was chosen from three words (Gagadu, Gagudju and Kakadu) recorded by anthropologist Baldwin Spencer in 1911. The words were given to Spencer by Aboriginal residents of the

which continues to reflect the unique relationship that has always existed between Aboriginal custodians and the land itself, have combined to make this place a treasure house of natural information typical of unspoiled Australia.

THE ABORIGINAL CUSTODIANS

The natural systems of northern Australia are enormously exciting, but poorly understood by western science. Yet they are well known and central to the lives of the Aboriginal custodians of the land – the 'Bininj' as they call themselves. Over the past centuries, managing the land has been critical to maintaining a satisfying standard of living, as well as being an inherited responsibility of the people.

With this responsibility comes a complex and life-long social learning system which teaches that you the human are but a part of this dynamic landscape. This responsibility is woven into the fabric of life itself and cannot be separated. It is the basis of all human activities and directly relates human beings to the other living species. This comes about because there is also a 'spiritual' landscape which overlays the physical, providing the means for a human link with the other species.

In order to manage natural landscape effectively, it is necessary not only to know what is there, but how it all interrelates. This profound ecological knowledge, developed by Bininj over centuries, has largely been dismissed by the western world. Now we are seeing the error of our ways and the value of that traditional knowledge.

Non-Aboriginal people will always have difficulty understanding the relationship of Bininj to their land, just as Bininj have great difficulty in explaining this relationship cross-culturally. We need simply to accept that it exists, be supportive and enjoy the richness of knowledge that flows from it. Kakadu National Park is a place where this can happen, owing to the generosity of the traditional owners. It must also be remembered that this diverse landscape was the traditional hunting ground of Bininj up until the declaration of the Park. Park legislation based on the National Parks and Wildlife Conservation Act of 1975 now provides for a continuation of this important aspect of their lifestyle.

Kakadu National Park has recently been classified as World Heritage landscape. This in part is because it is one of the last remaining examples of Aboriginal Australia. The remarkable landscape, shaped by many thousands of years of Aboriginal land management, is now judged as world class.

THE SEASONS

While a book of this size can only begin to describe what really happens throughout the Kakadu seasons, it attempts to explain to the reader, in broad terms, what is there; if, when and where it may be seen; and, briefly, how it fits into the ecological scheme of things. It is based on the Bininj calendar, as species availability is always discussed in relation to season. Unlike the fixed western calendar months, the natural seasons may start and finish at different times from year to year. Through long association with the land, Bininj have learned to read the signs which give advanced knowledge of when the changes are going to occur. These seasonal indicators may take the form of a certain species of plant blooming, caterpillars moving up tree trunks, a change in wind direction, or the call of a grasshopper.

For a variety of reasons, most people visit Kakadu between the months of May and August, avoiding both the main dry season and the entire wet season. Yet each season offers a variety of worthwhile experiences. The seasonal organisation of this text is an attempt to provide a greater range of information on which to base your next visit.

Almost every species of edible plant and animal has a time on the seasonal cycle when it reaches a peak in condition – either fruiting or carrying large amounts of body fat or eggs, or in the case of root crops such as yams, reaching a peak in storage capacity. This is when the species becomes important to Bininj and there are many natural indicators which tell the people when these individual species are suitable for harvest. The timing of natural events is difficult to predict by any other technique and over time these indicators have proved accurate.

The movement of people around their clan estates from season to season has always been determined by the condition of the wildlife. Because species are exploited only at the peak of their seasonal cycle and not for the rest of the year, an efficient form of conservation has prevailed. Traditionally, Magpie Goose eggs were collected in the late wet, File Snakes were collected later in the dry, while Barramundi were speared even later in the season, after they had been gorging on smaller fish in the drying billabongs and developed large fat reserves. Each species had its specific time for harvesting and outside that time was left alone. This is probably the reason that such a diverse range of natural species was preserved here while such a large population of people was harvesting them.

Artist Bluey Ilkirr's graphic representation of the Bininj seasons at the Bowali Visitors Centre

RECORD OF THE FIRST EUROPEAN EXPLORER

THE FIRST EUROPEAN EXPLORER TO TRAVERSE THIS AREA, LUDWIG LEICHHARDT, COMMENTED IN HIS DIARY ON THE LARGE NUMBERS OF VERY FRIENDLY BININJ AND THE AMAZING ABUNDANCE OF WILDLIFE IN ALL DIRECTIONS AS HE AND HIS PARTY PASSED THROUGH THE COUNTRY BETWEEN THE SOUTH AND EAST ALLIGATOR RIVERS

Nov 27th, 1845

"...The natives were very numerous, and employing themselves in either fishing or burning the grass on the plains, or digging for roots. I saw here a noble fig-tree, under the shade of which seemed to have been the camping place of the natives for the last century. It was growing at the place where we first came to the broad outlet of the swamp. About two miles to the eastward, this swamp extended beyond the reach of sight, and seemed to form the whole country, of the remarkable and picturesque character of which it will be difficult to convey a correct idea to the reader. . .We encamped at this pool, and the natives flocked round us from every direction. Boys of every age, lads, young men and old men too, came, every one armed with his bundle of goose spears, and his throwing stick. . .

Nov 28th

...After having guided us over the remaining part of the swamp to the firm land, during which they gave us the most evident proofs of their skill in spearing geese – they took their leave of us and returned ...The country was most beautifully grassed: and a new species of Crinum, and several species of leguminous plants, diversified with their pretty blossoms the pleasing green of the flats and the forest.

Since the 23rd of November, not a night had passed without long files and phalanxes of geese taking their flight up and down the river, and they often passed so low, that the heavy flappng of their wings was distinctly heard. Whistling ducks, in close flocks, flew generally much higher, and with great rapidity. No part of the country we had passed, was so well provided with game as this; and of which we could have easily obtained an abundance, had not our shot been all expended. The cackling of geese, the quacking of ducks, the sonorous note of the native companion, and the noises of the black and white cockatoos, and a great variety of other birds, gave to the country, both night and day, an extraordinary appearance of animation. . ."

Journal of an Overland Expedition in Australia
Dr Ludwig Leichhardt

CONSERVING THE WILDLIFE

So far, the region has been spared the gross alterations of the western world that have marred so much of the rest of Australia, although change is now occurring here too. New highways, which give access to many thousands of interested and well-meaning tourists each year, take a massive toll on native species. Some of these species, such as the Partridge Pigeon, Brush-tailed Phascogale and the Northern Quoll, common when the Park was first declared, are becoming less common. A timely warning perhaps. Two relatives of the Northern Quoll once lived in the Park, but today are known only from bone fragments and the rock art record. These are the Thylacine *Thylacinus cynocephalus* and the Tasmanian Devil *Sarcophilus harrisii*. They are both thought to have been outcompeted as tropical predators several thousand years back when the Dingo came in from the north and quickly took up the role of dominant carnivore.

We still need to find better ways of fitting in with our natural environment, in order to follow the example set by those who managed Kakadu first. At the signing by the traditional owners of the lease agreement with the Commonwealth Government, the Park was opened to the world in good ecological order. Environmental damage caused by the introduction by the British of Asian Water Buffalo from the early British settlement of Victoria, on the Cobourg Peninsula north of Kakadu, has now been reversed. More recent issues such as feral pigs, weed invasion and the pressure of high visitor numbers are still being dealt with through Park management. Commercial net fishing, which was being carried out in the major rivers at the time of declaration, has now ceased.

ENDEMIC SPECIES

Today there are no native species in the Park which are considered 'threatened' or 'endangered', although there appears to be a recent downward trend in the frequency of sightings with several species. Some of the endemic plants and animals have a very limited geographical distribution. Some animals are shy and rarely seen, many are nocturnal or inhabit rugged and remote areas, and all but a few avoid the extremes of heat and strong light. As a result, it may be very difficult to spot wildlife while visiting the Park, but animal and plant diversity here is surprisingly high by Australian standards and, to seek out these animals here, it is just a matter of knowing when and where to look. As time progresses, native species are slowly adjusting to the large numbers of daytime visitors and are becoming more visible. Endemic species such as the Chestnut-quilled Rock-pigeon and Black Wallaroo are now regularly sighted during daylight hours in rock-art viewing areas. Nevertheless, the keen naturalist needs to venture out at night armed with a good torch in order to spot many of the shyer species. It is never necessary to wander far in order to see interesting things in Kakadu. The creatures of Kakadu are both restricted to certain habitats and very seasonal in their activities. Knowing this may help to locate and observe them.

KAKADU'S EIGHT HABITATS

The natural landscape of Kakadu can be divided into eight discrete components, or habitats, as follows: stone country, monsoon forests, rivers and billabongs, floodplains, paperbark swamps, tropical woodlands, mangrove forests and shorelines. The most extensive habitat is tropical woodland, occupying more than 75 per cent of the Park, while mangroves and monsoon forests are the most fragile and restricted.

Nevertheless, the latter two are very productive in terms of natural resources. Rivers, billabongs, floodplains and paperbark swamps become one entity during the wet season, linked by floodwater and sharing the same wildlife species. This group of habitats is collectively known as 'wetlands'. In the dry months, however, they become isolated and are frequented by different sets of animals and for this reason they are treated separately in the text. The eight broad habitats occur in each seasonal chapter of this book in the following order:

Stone Country

Stone country is a broadly translated term used by Bininj to cover a variety of rocky situations. The major geological feature in Kakadu is the Arnhem Plateau, an ancient sandstone formation which has its western edge inside the eastern boundary of Kakadu National Park. Its bulk takes up about one-third of Arnhem Land. This imposing rock face has become known as 'the Escarpment', and this is where most of the unusual plant and animal life of Kakadu is found.

Endemic species such as Gurrbelak, the Chestnut-quilled Rock-pigeon, Adjmu, the Banded Fruit-dove, Nawaran, the Oenpelli Rock Python, and Barrk, the Black Wallaroo, exist only in this limited zone. Anbinik is a very large and ancient Gondwanan tree which is restricted to the slopes and valleys of the northern and western Arnhem Plateau. In places with deep, sandy soils, almost pure stands of Anbinik form unique, closed-canopy forests which then become refuges for other unusual plants and animals. It all adds up to a very special place.

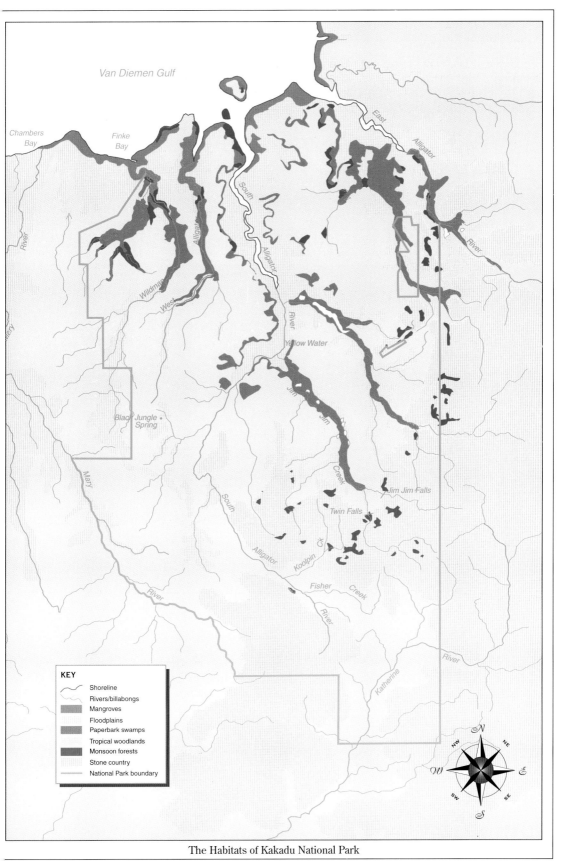

The Habitats of Kakadu National Park

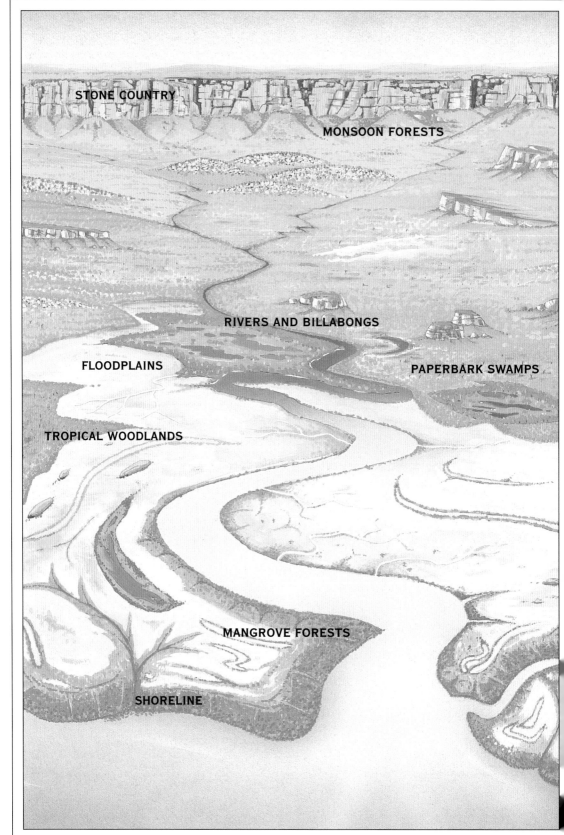

Artist's representation of Kakadu's habitats

Monsoon Forest

Monsoon forest is a variety of rainforest which has specialised in a harsh climate of extreme wet and extreme dry. It is a selection of 'tough' species from families which are represented in rainforests throughout the tropical world, particularly in South-East Asia and Papua New Guinea. In Kakadu, there are a number of varieties of monsoon forest. Those growing in rocky, dry places largely consist of deciduous species while those growing on permanent spring-fed creeks and rivers are more complex and support more delicate species. In the late dry season, the added cool and shade of monsoon forest is an important refuge for animal species from other habitats.

Rivers and Billabongs

In terms of natural importance, as well as importance to Bininj residents, the famous wetlands of Kakadu form the most productive of these habitats. They consist of the floodplains of the East, South and West Alligator Rivers, as well as part of the Wildman River system. The rivers feed the wetlands with nutrients each year. Numerous billabongs are a feature of the constant alterations in the courses of these rivers over the flat lowland country. Billabongs represent sections of river channel that have been isolated from the main river flow. Only during floods are they rejoined to the parent river. They hold deep, usually permanent, water and thus are important in sustaining life during the dry months.

The flat nature of the lowlands means that salt water reaches way inland around one hundred river kilometres on the East and South Alligator Rivers. The time difference between high tide at the coast and the upper tidal reaches of the big rivers can be as much as five and a half hours.

Floodplains

Floodplains form the basis of the Kakadu wetlands. They represent a silt load laid down over thousands of years in a process that continues today. During Gudjewg, the rivers are unable to cope with the huge volume of water which then spills over the levee banks and across the lowlands, submerging many hundreds of square kilometres. A unique ecology has developed under this seasonal regime.

Paperbark Swamps

Paperbark swamps occur in wetland areas where drainage is poor. Stands and often forests of the Giant Paperbark develop around these shallow water bodies, creating a unique and beautiful habitat for both plants and animals. Unlike billabongs, however, these areas eventually dry out completely, causing the wildlife to adopt some unique survival strategies.

Tropical Woodlands

Tropical woodland, or open woodland, is the most obvious and widespread of all the habitats. It is dominated by eucalypts with shrubs and grasses in the understorey and comes in a variety of forms, depending on geology, soil type and drainage. To the visitor this habitat may appear to be devoid of wildlife, however the reverse is true. Fauna surveys have shown that these areas have a wildlife diversity equal to comparable habitat anywhere else in Australia. It has many secrets yet to be revealed.

Mangrove Forests

Mangrove forests in this part of Australia are well developed and quite extensive in places. Over 30 species of mangrove trees have been identified here and each of these grows in its own special zone. These forests are stabilising the vast amounts of silt which are being carried down by the big rivers each season and deposited along the coastline and estuaries. This constant process is steadily increasing the land surface of Kakadu.

Shoreline

Shoreline in Kakadu is dominated for the most part by mudflats and mangrove forests, which are part of a land-building process. In a few places, sandy beaches have formed and these are important nesting sites for the endemic Flatback Turtle. At present it is difficult for the visitor to gain access to shorelines or mangrove forests without specialised equipment, but in the following chapters you will gain a deeper insight to the structure and ecology of these fascinating areas.

Kakadu's diverse habitats are subdued and revived each year by a wildly oscillating climate. It is very dry in the dry season and very wet for the remainder. Each living thing, plant and animal, has learned to cope with these annual extremes.

Today, the Park is jointly managed by the traditional owners and the Australian Nature Conservation Agency under a lease agreement between the two. Quite a number of the senior custodians involved in the initial negotiations for the development of the Park have since passed on, highlighting the urgency of gathering, understanding and implementing the fading traditional knowledge of this area. It has been their hope that people from the rest of Australia, and indeed the world, will visit, enjoy and learn from their land and lifestyles and support their heritage.

Bininj lifestyle and land management have brought this landscape and its ecology thus far, preserving the amazing diversity we see today. It has now become a joint effort, which requires additional understanding and support from the outside world.

Enjoy and be proud of Kakadu.

DECEMBER TO MARCH

MONSOON SEASON

GUDJEWG

CHAPTER 1

MONSOON SEASON – GUDJEWG

Gudjewg is all about rain. It is the very centre of what non-Aboriginal people call 'the wet season'. In the ecosystem, it is 'action time' whereby conditions have shifted dramatically to one extreme of the seasonal spectrum.

By late December or early January, the Top End weather pattern changes completely. The violent but brief easterly afternoon storms of Gunumeleng, which brought refreshing rain showers to a parched landscape and marked the beginning of the wet, are now pushed out of the way by a much stronger system from South-East Asia. In Arnhem Land, this is known across the language groups as 'Barra', the northwest monsoon. This term is itself derived from the languages of South-East Asia.

A dense blanket of low cumulus cloud, often less than 400 metres above the earth's surface, rolls in from the Timor Sea and the sun may not be seen for up to six weeks. A strong, salt-laden wind blows constantly from the sea, driving the heavy showers almost horizontally at times and browning off the foliage of the coastal trees. The murky sea pounds against the coastline. Waterfalls thunder, frog choruses saturate the night and the watertable is replenished for another year. This is one part of the Australian continent where annual rainfall is virtually guaranteed.

While Gudjewg includes the three wettest months of the wet season, there are usually some dry weeks which create pauses within the systems. Cloudless skies and sunny days with no rain at all are not uncommon during the wet season. The heat and humidity can then be quite oppressive to those who are unacclimatised. This happens particularly when the monsoon is forming over South-East Asia or when it contracts back to the northwest. Passing cyclones, while they may deposit a lot of rain at the time, are likely to drag all the wet weather away with them as they go past. If this occurs towards the end of Gudjewg, it can cause an abrupt end to the wet season. Each wet season has its own peculiar characteristics and total rainfall may vary greatly.

On the first sunny day after a prolonged monsoon, Fork-tailed Swifts suddenly appear in the skies to dine on the sudden release of insects. These momentary breaks after a period of intense rain throw light on a greatly changed landscape—inundated, sparkling, fresh and vibrant. Birds and insects are free to fly again as the river systems work to capacity.

Left and above: Driving monsoon rain on the sandstone plateau generates a vast run-off that floods the lowlands

WET SEASON VISITORS

Indonesian fishermen the Celebes Islands (known today as Sulawesi) have been visiting the northern Australian coastline each wet season for at least 400 years. Their main objective was to gather as much Trepang or Sea Cucumber as possible, before the southeast trade winds returned at the end of the wet to bear them home. This product was in turn traded to the Chinese who, even today, regard it as a delicacy.

To the Aboriginal residents of western Arnhem Land, these people were known as 'Mangatjarra'. There was a great deal of cultural exchange between the two groups and, during each wet season, considerable trade took place. Aboriginal divers worked for the Macassan crews. Long before the arrival of Europeans, Aboriginal groups in the Kakadu area were familiar with foreign products such as alcohol, rice, steel implements, glass and pottery. Much of this historical contact was recorded in the rock art records of Arnhem Land, some of which are still preserved today. Many words in the Kakadu languages have their origin in Indonesia.

Twin Falls

Jim Jim Falls

STONE COUNTRY

Much of the water flowing through the wetland systems of Kakadu is channelled off the rugged sandstone surface of the Arnhem Plateau. The rain falling there is instantly converted to fast-flowing run-off. Rocky streams converge into rivers which spill over the edge of the escarpment, only to bank up and spread over the lowlands. This water is the lifeblood of the Kakadu ecosystems.

Back on the Plateau, plants have sprung to life. Many are flowering, and some are already fruiting. Giant mosses have turned from a brown mat to a vibrant green carpet. The insectivorous sundews and bladderworts appear from nowhere and bloom in bright clusters while the showy Mount Brockman Grevillea sprawls across the sandstone boulders and ledges trailing its large bright yellow flowers across the rock surface. This means that birds such as Red-collared Lorikeets and Sandstone Friarbirds must land on the ground and walk from flower to flower in order to access the prolific nectar.

Upper Jim Jim Falls

Red-collared Lorikeets

Run-off on a lesser scale reaches the foot of the scarp

Mount Brockman Grevillea flowers at the height of the monsoon

The sandstone animals are enjoying the new abundance of food resources. Over the next few months they will put on condition, leading up to the main breeding season in Wurrgeng, the early dry season.

The Ghost Bat, called Malambipi by Bininj, is a large carnivorous bat. It roosts in colonies in the sandstone caves by day, and ranges widely at night through the lowland forests in search of prey. The characteristic sonic calls of these hunting bats are regularly heard in the woodlands at night. Large insects, frogs, lizards, roosting birds and even other bats form the bulk of their diet. Once the prey has been captured and killed, it is carried on the wing back to a regular 'dining table', which may be a flat rock in a cave or

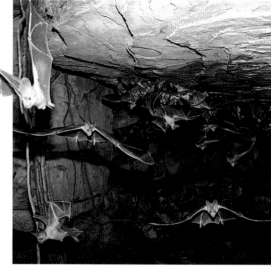

Unlike the other carnivorous bats, Ghost Bats have large eyes

Ghost Bats roost in caves in colonies, emerging after dark to hunt

the top of a large log or, in one instance, the wing of an aircraft in a hangar at the Oenpelli Airstrip. There the prey is dismembered and devoured, leaving wings, legs, feathers and other discarded remains on show the following morning.

Ghost Bats have good eyesight as well as sophisticated echolocation. Quite harmless to humans, they are surprisingly gentle to handle.

Though they have disappeared from many parts of Australia, they remain plentiful in the Arnhem Land region. They actively hunt through the art-sites of Kakadu each night.

For the herbivores, there is once more an abundance of leafy plants, fruits and grasses. Animals like the Short-eared Rock-wallaby and the endemic Black Wallaroo no longer need to move to the foot of the escarpment at night in search of green pick. As a result of the abundant resources available to them at this time of year, they remain in the more rugged areas. They are not as easily observable now as they are in the dry months.

A young male Black Wallaroo

A Merten's Water Monitor awaits an easy meal of fish above the rapids

At intervals along the rocky streams, large Merten's Water Monitors position themselves to catch the numerous small fish forcing their way upstream. The fish, which include Spangled Grunters, Eel-tailed Catfish and Purple-spotted Gudgeons, face strong competition to reach newly created feeding grounds upstream. As they hurl themselves up the rapids and rock ledges, some of them land on bare rock. And this is where the water monitors like to be. They just sit back and let the food come to them.

Another reptile which feeds in this manner is the endemic Nawuran or Oenpelli Python. Relaxing by day among the cool crevices and caves of the escarpment, this shy predator moves stealthily amongst the boulders at night in search of mammals and birds. It prefers to set up in ambush beside well-used pathways or scent-trails and surprise the victim. Though it is rarely seen anywhere within its limited range, it is nevertheless present in reasonable numbers.

Up on the rocky slopes, the tiny Firetail Skink can be seen darting between patches of shade over the hot rock surfaces. While showing a remarkable tolerance to the hot rocks, the tiny skink constantly maintains the delicate balance of its body temperature as it searches for tiny invertebrates in the crevices. These skinks are commonly seen around the rock art sites of Kakadu.

Firetail Skink

Oenpelli Rock Python at rest during daylight hours

Gudjewg rain creates breeding sites for sandstone frogs

Male Copland's Rock Frog calling at night after rain

Male Masked Rock-frog calling at night beside a stream

Even the smallest sandstone pools seem to have tadpoles in them and these pools heat up during the day until the water is quite hot. The tadpoles of sandstone frogs can tolerate extremely high water temperatures without any apparent ill effects. They also have rapid development rates, similar to those of arid zone frogs.

At night, frogs can be heard calling wherever water is standing or flowing. The four main frogs breeding in the sandstone pools are the endemic Masked Rock-frog, the tiny Rockhole Frog, Copland's Rock Frog and the much larger and distinctive Carpenter Frog.

Male Rockhole Frog

The fruit of several trees, which flowered some months ago in Gurrung, are now falling into the fast-flowing streams to be carried away downstream. They are Anboiberre, the White Apple, and Anbungbung, the Water Apple. These and other fallen fruits become food for fish such as the Sooty Grunter and Arderrhwu, the Snapping Turtle. The seeds, however, remain intact after passing through the host animal and eventually settle to germinate on a riverbank lower down.

The charming territorial song of the male White-throated Grasswren can be heard in the mornings and evenings from the sandstone slopes as the females incubate eggs well hidden amongst spinifex clumps. In the nearby gorges, the enchanting half-tone whistles of the White-lined Honeyeater echo down the watercourses, epitomising the spirit of the sandstone. The old people say that this bird communicates with the Mimi spirits and informs them of human movement.

Towards the end of Gudjewg the ripening spinifex seed-heads make an impressive display of gold in the morning sunlight. The crop of seed will provide a valuable food source for numerous sandstone creatures in the coming months. Other common plateau plants flowering in Gudjewg include a sweet-smelling, scrambling Hoya and *Calytrix decussata*, a delicate red and pink member of the Turkey Bush family.

The delicate flowers of a tough little bush, Calytrix decussata

Male White-throated Grasswrens frequently call from high points

Rainwater flows through a sandstone valley

MONSOON FORESTS

The prolific response of plant life continues throughout Gudjewg. In the Stone Country, the deciduous vine thickets, which are a type of monsoon forest, have sprung to life and turned to deep green. Annual plants such as yams have put up tendrils and leaves. The vines wind their way up the tree trunks towards the sunlight for the energy needed to swell their storage roots as a reserve for the coming dry season. Because of this stored moisture and energy, the yams, which remain dormant throughout the dry months, are able to send up new pink shoots even before the rains arrive.

The blood-red flower clusters of the Bandicoot Berry attract most species of butterfly to its sweet nectar. The edible black fruits which follow are much sought after by wildlife, which explains the abundance of this plant around the forest fringes.

A number of species of ground orchids are known from the monsoon forests of Kakadu, one of the most common being Ngangarda or *Nervillea holochila*, a small pink-flowered annual which grows in colonies on the woodland fringes. Pollination is rapid and the flowers soon develop into seed pods. The much taller Hyacinth Orchid grows in association with Myrtaceous trees such as the Anbinik and Anrebel. Its beautiful pink-spotted flowers are easily overlooked as the flower spike blends in so well with the forest understorey. This is the case with most of the ground orchids of Kakadu. During the dry months there is no trace of these plants above ground. The leafy Shepherd's Crook Orchid develops its pink flowers upside down on an inverted stalk which straightens up after pollination.

On the other hand, the much larger leaves and flowers of the Native Ginger add a pleasant splash of colour to the understorey. Like the ground orchids, they seem to appear from nowhere in Gunumeleng and Gudjewg. Far less common are the shiny green leaves of a delicate, Taro-like plant, *Remusatia vivipera*, which has no common name and which grows in monsoon forest pockets hidden in the shady gorges of the rugged sandstone escarpment. It, too, is an annual plant which completely disappears during the dry months, leaving behind tiny living bulbules which lie dormant in the litter until they are triggered by the following wet.

On the wet floor of the forest lies a variety of colourful fruit. Many of the monsoon forest trees flower in Gurrung or Gunumeleng so that the fruit falls in these wet conditions, thus giving the seedlings the greatest possible chance to germinate. The fruit becomes a great food source for forest-dwelling animals.

Young Round Yam vine

First leaf of new yam vine

Native Ginger flowers

Bandicoot Berry in flower

The Hummingbird Hawk Moth visits flowers during the day.

A clear forest stream gives life to the forest corridor

Tiny Spiny Spiders are the jewels of the forest

High above in the canopy, a battle for fresh fruit goes on. Groups of Torres Strait Pigeons, Rose-crowned Fruit-doves and Banded Fruit-doves all compete for the bunches of ripe fruit in the various trees. Feeding alongside these birds are Common Koels, Orioles, Figbirds, Channel-billed Cuckoos and a variety of others. At night, Black and Little Red Flying-foxes squabble over the same flowers and fruit, knocking most of them down to the forest floor. This may appear like a reckless waste of resources but, at the end of the wet,

carpets of green seedlings cover the forest floor. The boisterous feeding of wildlife has made its contribution to the endless cycle of germination and distribution.

In the wetter places, around springs and creek banks, Common Tree Snakes stalk the numerous frogs hiding amongst the ferns and vines. Like the Keelback and the Slate-grey Snake, the Common Tree Snake is a frog specialist.

Between the shrubs of the understorey a tiny, but very beautiful spider spins a fine web. It is a member of the Spiny Spider family and almost always goes unnoticed. Careful scrutiny of its strangely shaped carapace, as it sits at the centre of its web, reveals a stunning arrangement of enamel-like colours. It preys mainly on mosquito-sized flying insects.

A host of other small invertebrates is active in the moist understorey of the forest, from delicately shaped land snails to the day-roosting Rare Red-eye Butterfly (*above*). A species of moth also competes with the butterflies to pollinate the various forest flowers, particularly white ones. It is a day-flying Hawk Moth, which mimics a wasp in both apppearance and behaviour and has an extremely fast and erratic flight.

There is another world, teeming with life, beneath the leafy canopy of the monsoon forest in the months of Gudjewg.

A Common Tree Snake

RIVERS & BILLABONGS

As the rushing floodwaters from the Stone Country empty into the main river systems, the narrow river channels are unable to cope with the surging volume. The water rises over the levee banks spilling out onto the floodplains, where it may reach a depth of over three metres. This floodwater effectively connects the billabongs and paperbark swamps, not only to the river itself but also to the sea. This important feature allows species such as the Barramundi, the Ox-eye Herring and the Salmon Catfish to return from the billabongs to the saltwater to breed or feed and young Barramundi to move from the mangroves up into the billabongs to feed and grow to adulthood.

As the floodwater fills the billabongs, Salmon Catfish and Ox-eye Herring can be seen in tight schools frolicking at the surface. They project their fins and tails above the surface as they play. Above the water surface, beautifully coloured Shining Flycatchers frequent the billabongs and creeks. The males regularly challenge and display to each other over the water in preparation for the breeding season which follows the floods. The raspy calls and crest-raising displays play an important part in reinforcing territory for each pair.

Azure Kingfishers are also more vocal and visible during the floods as they raise young in a nest tunnel situated well back from the reach of the floodwaters. This can involve much flying between the nest and the water when feeding the voracious chicks. They sometimes select a bank or termite mound many hundreds of metres into the bush as a nest-site. The high-pitched whistle followed by a brilliant flash of blue and orange at water level announces the passing of a kingfisher on a mission.

With the rising waters, Estuarine Crocodiles, which have spent the dry months in the main river channel, move out on to the plains and follow the fish into shallower waters. Those involved with nest-building, however, remain near the river channel where the females begin nest construction as soon as the floodwaters begin to fall. The main Estuarine Crocodile breeding period is between March and June, although individual females may begin building their nests as early as the first rains. Late floods may catch the nesting crocodiles out and inundate the nests, which causes the eggs to die both from cold and lack of oxygen. If this is the case, the female will usually nest again before the season finishes.

Often the only sign of the billabongs during flood times is the treetops of the fringing vegetation rising above the waterline of the inland sea.

East Alligator River and surrounding floodplain during monsoon inundation. Inset above: Dwarf Green Tree-frog

Wet season view of Island Billabong on Magela Creek

Lower East Alligator River prior to the arrival of the floodwater

Ghost Gums on the floodplain fringe experience seasonal flooding

Clustered on the vegetation above the water level are hundreds of frogs, particularly Dwarf Green Tree-frogs, Rocket Frogs and Wotjulum Frogs. They are extremely vulnerable at this time to predatory fish, snakes and waterbirds. Their large numbers ensure their survival.

The small and insignificant Mitchell's Water Monitor is also more easily seen during the floods as it is forced on to rafts of debris or on to exposed rocks or branches. Under drier conditions, these small members of the goanna family live around the edges of billabongs and creek tributaries, sunning themselves on overhanging limbs or pursuing tadpoles, frogs and small fish. Shy of humans, they quickly vanish—into the water, holes in the ground or tree hollows—until the coast is clear.

Further downstream of the flooded central section, towards the estuaries, the increased width of the rivers is able to accommodate the extra water. In the fringing mangroves, waterbird rookeries are once again noisy with the sound of squabbling egrets, herons and ibis. Constant displays between rival males, thieving of nesting materials, boundary disputes and trespassing all tend to magnify the hoarse croaks of these waterbirds into one giant cacophony. Down below, on the darkened floor of the

mangrove forest, beautifully marked Mangrove Monitors search for fallen eggs and young. When the tide comes in, or as night falls, this patrol is taken over by Estuarine Crocodiles.

Kakadu Park staff have conducted surveys of crocodile activity on the region's major rivers. These have indicated that, throughout Gurrung and Gunumeleng (between August and December), Estuarine Crocodile numbers steadily increase in the rivers adjacent to the floodplains, until the river level rises to cover the floodplains in Gunumeleng. The bulk of the population (all the non-breeding individuals) then moves away from the river channels and on to the wetlands to feed. After the wet, this pattern slowly reverses as the wetlands dry up.

The highly aquatic Mitchell's Water Monitor

FLOODPLAINS

Having survived the hardships of the previous dry months, the Magpie Geese are feeding hungrily on the explosion of aquatic plants. As a result, they will gain enough condition to begin nesting after the monsoon. Nesting geese are a feature of late Gudjewg and early Banggerreng.

At this time of year the floodplains become inundated. The storms of Gunumeleng have given way to the driving monsoon rains of Gudjewg. The floodplains turn into a vast inland sea. The extent of flooding depends upon the strength and endurance of the monsoon. A week or two of monsoon rain can cause a flood, as can the occasional passing of a cyclonic depression, but some wet seasons pass

A carpet of red flowers at sunrise beneath a Freshwater Mangrove

The beautiful pink blooms of the Lotus Lily

without sufficient concentrated rain to cause a river to break its banks. If the monsoon fails, or is weak, floodplain inundation from storm rains may only amount to ten centimetres rather than the three metres or so of a good monsoon.

During the floods, the vast beds of Lotus Lilies (which have been steadily building up again since the numbers of feral buffalo have been brought under control) become completely submerged. This causes little damage to the plants which quickly regenerate from root stock after the water goes down. The main flowering period for these and other water plants occurs during Banggerreng (harvest time) and the cooler weather of Yegge.

Most vegetation that grows on the floodplains can tolerate submersion for several months. Large trees normally grow only on the rich silt deposits of the levee banks, creating a skeleton outline to the river in flood times. These trees, mainly Kapok, River Almond, Leichhardt Tree, Cluster Fig and Beach Hibiscus, become important refuges for

floodplain wildlife during the floods. Traditional enemies like snakes, rats, goannas and grasshoppers may all end up sharing the same branches in collective misery until the water subsides. On the floodplains themselves, Angangki, the Freshwater Mangrove, and a large legume, Ganadjulinj, stand in isolation, or sometimes in small thickets. These trees not only provide shelter for larger floodplains fauna such as the Agile Wallaby, but the taller individuals are also strategic refuges for all wildlife in times of flood.

Under normal circumstances floods only last for about a week, and appear to cause most terrestrial wildlife at least some discomfort. However, there are two floodplain dwellers which definitely capitalise on a flood.

A passing storm leaves small pools on the Lotus pads

The lower South Alligator River and surrounding floodplain featuring the Arnhem Highway crossing

Water Python in defensive mode

A Dusky Rat stranded in vegetation above the floods

Dusky Rat clinging to submerged vines at the height of the flood

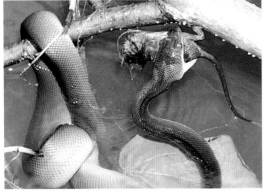

A young Water Python eating a stranded planigale

First of these opportunists are Water Pythons, large and common predators of small mammals, birds and reptiles on the floodplains. They gorge themselves on the wide range of stranded wildlife as they swim between the exposed treetops. As many as six or eight engorged pythons may be found sleeping their meals off in the same tree.

The bulk of the Water Python population moves off the plains behind the fleeing Dusky Rats as the waters rise. This is one of the rare examples of reptiles following a prey species from one habitat to another and back again. The pythons feed on a wide variety of birds, mammals and reptiles, but rely heavily on the abundant Dusky Rats as their staple diet. In the dry months, they both inhabit the deep cracks in the blacksoil of the floodplains.

In areas of floodplain adjacent to mangroves, it is possible to observe marine creatures like the Mud Crab and freshwater creatures like the Northern Long-necked Turtle swimming together. Many marine animals appear to be able to tolerate the fresh floodwater as it replaces the saltwater in the estuaries.

The Estuarine Crocodile is also aware that stranded animals will be attempting to swim to higher ground and, if the flood occurs late in Gudjewg, many young Magpie Geese will be marooned by rising floodwater before they can fly. The parent geese stay with their brood and attempt to swim them to safety, but this may entail traversing several kilometres of open water. It is not uncommon to see a crocodile tailing such a family group and leisurely taking the slower birds. In these circumstances, the parent geese display amazing bravery and may be eaten themselves.

Towards the end of Gudjewg, the sweet smell of the wild rice seed-heads is rapidly replaced with the stale smell of decomposing water plants which have fulfilled their purpose and now begun to die back in bulk. This is all part of the great annual wetlands nutrient cycle.

Magpie Geese enjoy the inundated grasslands

Intermediate Egrets performing territorial threat displays at the rookery

The high temperature of the shallow water greatly exaggerates this decomposition process. It gives rise to a powerful product referred to locally as 'swamp gas'.

As the water level on the plains begins to drop, the shallower areas become a haven for waterbirds, both those which feed on vegetation and those which feed on aquatic invertebrates and fish. For many months to come there will be shallow areas on the floodplains for these waterbirds to visit, and each in turn will be the focus of a thorough exploitation by mixed flocks of birds. Cormorants, pelicans, egrets, spoonbills, herons and ibises all join forces to harvest the fish bounty. It is an amazing sight to see such an aggregation in action.

Whistling Kites circle overhead to snatch struggling fish from the beaks of the industrious waterbirds, often losing the prize themselves to other kites. Other species, such as Jabiru and White-bellied Sea-Eagles, keep a careful eye on the activity in case a larger creature is disturbed.

Rising floodwaters on the South Alligator floodplain

Brolgas pair up and begin nesting on floodplains at this time

Mirrored reflections of an inundated Paperbark forest

PAPERBARK SWAMPS

It may be a distance of several kilometres across the floodplains from the river to the woodland edge. Along these landward edges of the plains there are areas of poorly drained black soil which retain floodwater well into the dry season. These are the paperbark swamps. They resemble shallow billabongs but cannot retain water for the entire dry season. The plants and animals of the paperbark swamps all have survival strategies to cope with the loss of surface water each year.

The unusual feature of paperbark swamps is the

Magpie Geese harvest grass seeds and bulbs

dominance of a single species of tree, Birriyalang or the Giant Paperbark. It forms dense stands around these bodies of water, creating a unique habitat. Like mangrove trees, these paperbarks not only tolerate having their root systems immersed in water for half the year, but actually flower prolifically during that time. This habitat seems to exclude almost all other terrestrial trees, with the exception of Angangki, the Freshwater Mangrove.

Weeping Paperbarks are also found along rivers and watercourses as well, but only around paperbark swamps do they have the opportunity to develop into extensive forests.

Rainbow Bee-eaters hunt dragonflies above the waterlilies

Lilies and other aquatic plants appear after the inundation

leaves can completely cover the water surface for large areas and this helps cut down the evaporation later in the year. The lily pads are jealously guarded by the Lotusbirds, identified by their specially designed spreading toes and graceful movements. Their targets are the myriads of emerging aquatic insects, many of which have a winged stage, and the lily flowers attract them into striking range. Those insects that are missed by the Lotusbirds may be snapped up by stunningly coloured Rainbow Bee-eaters which are strategically perched around the swamps specifically for ambushing flying insects. The various species of dragonflies are at the top of their list.

Gudjewg represents the beginning of a 'time of plenty', not only for Rainbow Bee-eaters, but for all life forms in the paperbark swamp.

Beneath the surface, among the riot of aquatic vegetation, stalks the ever-hungry Northern Long-necked Turtle. With the Arafura File Snake, the Water Python and the Estuarine Crocodile, it forms a team of reptiles which exploits the flooded landscape of Kakadu.

The Northern Long-necked Turtle feeds voraciously during floods

The very last weeks of Gudjewg see another paperbark swamp plant flowering prolifically—Mardjakalang, the Giant Water Lily (*top right*), with its heavily scented white, blue or mauve flowers. The plants rejuvenate from a dormant bulb when woken by the penetrating rains of Gunumeleng and spend most of Gudjewg producing long-stemmed leaves that cover the water surface. Once their 'solar panels' are in place, the plants turn their energy to the production of large amounts of seed. When the rains ease off, the flowers begin appearing and reach a peak in Yegge. The broad

Estuarine Crocodiles move into the flooded grasslands to feed

Rain transforms the openness of the woodlands...

... into a dense, grassy understorey

TROPICAL WOODLANDS

The bulk of Kakadu's floodwater comes from the annual monsoon flow and particularly from occasional cyclonic depressions. The early storms saturate the ground and start the creeks flowing. This breathes new life into the ecosystem, but the major responses in the system occur when the heavy rain arrives.

Now the creeks and watercourses cannot cope with the vast run-off produced by endless days of heavy rain, and local flooding is common. This is a good time to glimpse those shy subterranean creatures which are temporarily forced to vacate their premises. The robust King Cricket (*right*), whose vertical tunnels and brightly coloured earth mounds are such a feature of the dry season woodlands, now seeks refuge on tree trunks or amongst piles of leaves. This makes it vulnerable to a range of insectivores that includes the Brown Antechinus, Brush-tailed Phascogales, Northern Quolls and Northern Brown Bandicoots, all of which enjoy the rich bounty that Gudjewg provides.

In the woodlands, branches break in the heavy rains and green leaves cover the ground, only to be swirled away as debris. Small creeks surge with chaos and power, directing muddy run-off into the swollen rivers. In most places, the water table is quite close to the ground surface. Trees appear to stop growing while their roots are waterlogged but the dense stands of Anbedjerr, native sorghum or spear grass, grow centimetres each day. So dense does this yearly crop become that it obscures the other native grasses and shrubs and even the larger trees. In places it reaches four metres in height. It has its own understorey and many tiny annuals live out their seasonal cycles completely obscured by this dominating forest of spear grass.

Perhaps one of the most characteristic sounds of Gudjewg is the periodic booming call from the grasses of Bukbuk, the Pheasant Coucal. For the rest of the year, Bukbuk is quiet. Its breeding season begins with a plumage change in Gunumeleng. It is the only member of the cuckoo family to involve itself in nest-building and brood-rearing. The resounding call is to announce the territory of each pair and no doubt also helps the pair to stay in contact in the dense undercover of wet season growth.

White Currants are a wet season fruit enjoyed both by people ...

... and wildlife such as this Northern Rosella

Often seen after a rain shower drying their waterlogged plumage on a dead tree, these birds prefer to walk rather than fly and spend most of their time hunting lizards, frogs and insects for their fast-growing chicks. Several broods can be raised each wet season.

Andjundjek, the Wild Grape, begins to flower at this time. The vines have been growing vigorously from their first appearance in Gunumeleng. The flowers tell Bininj that Gurrih, the Common Northern Bluetongue Lizard, is about to give birth to live young while the edible grapes, which follow in harvest time, Banggerreng, indicate that the lizards are fat and ready to catch and eat.

Patrolling the woodland by day are two large, ground-dwelling goannas or monitors which, until recently, were thought by taxonomists to be the one species. They look very similar but behave quite differently and do not tolerate each other. Djanay, the Sand Monitor, prefers to live in the tropical woodlands and occasionally venture out to the more open areas, whereas the slightly larger Galawan or Yellow Spotted Monitor prefers the open grasslands but does spend some time, mainly during Gudjewg, hunting in the woodlands.

Unlike the floodplains, the woodlands rarely become inundated, although the watertable is high and the soil is soft and easy to dig. The burrowing insects and other subterranean delicacies, which both types of monitors seek, are easily obtainable. The deep holes which they dig are a common feature of the woodlands and a blessing to the other wildlife. Later in the year, when fires sweep through and consume the dross of the previous wet season, many small mammals, reptiles and invertebrates dive down the numerous goanna holes and take refuge from the flames. They provide a haven that might not otherwise be available to them in times of danger or stress.

The highly social Yellow-throated Miner fiercely defends its territory

Male Gurndamen or Frilled Lizards, in their breeding colours of red frills and black chests, continue to spar and joust with each other on the ground for rights to the females in the vicinity. They are frequently encountered at this time because of the amount of time they spend on the ground, in contrast to the dry months when they spend most of their time up trees.

When monsoon rains set in, the Frilled Lizards (the male *below* is in threat display) continue to feed

voraciously on displaced invertebrates as the soil in which they live becomes increasingly waterlogged with rainwater. At this time, earthworms form a large part of the diet as they seek refuge on higher ground from the rising watertable.

Constantly alert, a Yellow Spotted Monitor surveys the woodlands

The Northern Bandy-bandy can be seen above the ground in the wet

Northern Spadefoot Toad calling

Other interesting ground-dwellers seen at this time include the beautifully marked Northern Bandy-bandy Snake and the related Half-girdled Snake. Both of these small and relatively harmless snakes may be encountered as they cross roads and tracks, particularly at night. The Northern Shovel-nosed Snake (*right*) is a burrower. Members of the Blind Snake family may also be found under similar circumstances. This is the most vulnerable period in the seasonal cycle for these subterranean inhabitants.

On the other hand, Gudjewg is the high point of the year for woodland frogs, such as the Northern Spadefoot Toad, which has been buried deep in the soil until the rains arrived. Now individuals group together at night by call and create an eerie chorus in the monsoon rain that carries far into the woodlands. Their squat little bodies puff up with air as they float between grass tussocks, periodically convulsing as they force the air out through their vocal sacs to produce the bizarre 'whooping' sound.

The females, of course, do not produce any sound but, paired with a suitable male, prepare to deposit as many eggs as possible in the surrounding water. The life cycle is quite fast as the floodwater may not last long.

Other woodland frogs active at this time include the Giant Frog, Roth's Tree-frog, the Red Tree-frog, the Green Tree-frog, Tornier's Frog, the Ornate Burrowing Frog and the Stonemason Toadlet. Woodland pools and waterholes can be very noisy places during Gudjewg.

Dahl's Aquatic Frog

Northern Spadefoot Toad

Green Tree-frogs spawning

Ornate Burrowing Frog

Red-eyed Tree-frog

Red Tree-frog calling at night

Tornier's Frog calling

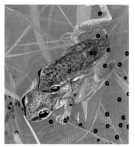

Red Tree-frogs spawning

Keelback or Freshwater Snake

Keelbacks are very active frog-eaters

Concentrated frog activity attracts predators such as egrets and Jabiru, as well as frog-eating specialists like the Common Tree Snake, the Slate-grey Snake and the Keelback. The abundance of frogs produced across the habitats each wet season provides a major food supply for a surprising range of animals throughout the following year. Nature's budget allows for this.

The dominant trees in this habitat are Anrebel, the Darwin Stringybark, and Andjalen, the Darwin Woollybutt. Other common species are Andubang, the Cooktown Ironwood, the Cocky Apple, the Green Plum, the Narrow-leafed Bloodwood, and the Northern Grevillea. These key trees provide shelter in the form of hollows or fallen timber, and food in the form of shoots, nectar, blossoms, fruit and seeds on a strongly seasonal basis.

Towards the watercourses and in the more fertile valleys grow Anbamberre, the beautiful Swamp Bloodwoods. In the middle of Gudjewg, these large-leafed gums burst into sprays of deep red blossom and become the focus of attention for honeyeaters, friarbirds, lorikeets, sugar gliders and flying-foxes. In the tropical woodland there always seems to be at least one species of eucalypt in flower at any one time of the year.

Swamp Bloodwood flowers provide copious nectar for wildlife

In a few locations where deep, sandy soils occur in open woodland, stands of the stately Kentia Palm occur. These palms have edible cabbage and produce strings of red fruit which drop during Gudjewg and Banggerdeng. A small percentage of the seeds which escape fire and predation by rodents will germinate in nine to 12 months.

Towards the end of Gudjewg, the rapidly developing sorghum seed matures and drops its seed straight into the soft earth beneath. The individual seeds have an ingenious spear-like design which enables them to wiggle their way deep into the ground, well below the scorch level of the coming dry season fires. The shaft on the spear straightens or coils in response to humidity, and the variation in humidity between night and day over a few days is enough to bury the seed to a suitable level. There the seed remains until triggered by the soaking rains of the next Gunumeleng.

Swamp Bloodwood blossoms

MANGROVE FORESTS

Gudjewg is the time of year when mangrove trees perform their greatest ecological role, that of stabilising the developing coastline and protecting the newly formed silt deposits from the pounding seas of the monsoon.

shallow sea floor beyond the mouths of the rivers to be gradually heaped up by tides, currents and gentle wave action along the shore.

Mangrove trees represent the front line of the terrestrial ecosystem, the advance guard. They soon colonise the mud deposits, species by species, until a forest develops.

Mud-stabilising roots of the mangrove exposed to the air at low tide

Geomorphologists have recently shown that the wetlands of Kakadu have only developed in the last 6000 to 7000 years and are superimposed over a marine environment. The same story is told in the Aboriginal historical records, like those displayed in the rock-art galleries today. They give a pictorial display of the transformation of the lowlands from a marine to a freshwater environment. The older art displays predominantly marine creatures while the more recent art concentrates on freshwater kinds.

These wetlands are still expanding seaward at a gradual rate and the mangroves form the front line of the advance. Massive amounts of silt and other eroded material from the Plateau region are being used to build the wetlands and Gudjewg is the season of transport. The silt load settles on the

Mangrove Monitor

Breeding Intermediate Egret in a mangrove rookery

Meanwhile, under favourable conditions, the front line continues to advance seaward at an estimated rate of about a centimetre per year. Over time, the silt is desalinated by the leaching of countless wet seasons until it is able to support other varieties and communities of terrestrial plants, and so the process continues. Today's wetlands are only a metre or so above the spring tide level and are still susceptible to breaches and occasional saltwater intrusion. The land-building process is still in progress.

During Gudjewg, the Barramundi, along with many other fish and crustaceans, are spawning in the protection of the mangrove roots. The sheltered but murky mangrove waters make an excellent nursery environment for an amazing range of marine and freshwater creatures.

SHORELINE

The Arafura Sea is now turning a yellow-brown colour, monsoon colour. The big rivers of Van Diemen Gulf are disgorging their massive silt loads and the sea is too restless to let it settle. This is a

White-bellied Sea-Eagle hunting

time of pounding and reshaping of the sand deposits, mudbars, channels and shoals. White-bellied Sea-Eagles, Brahminy Kites and Ospreys ride the incessant monsoon wind and comb the tidelines for the variety of dead or sick sea creatures washed in by the muddy waves. This can include dead seabirds, sea snakes, fish or crustaceans. Seabirds which normally operate far out to sea in the clearer waters are forced inshore by the stormy gales. Brown Boobies and Lesser Frigatebirds, driven in from distant fishing grounds, hang in the air in small flocks directly above the coastline, day after day, floating on the strong air currents and waiting for the winds to abate.

Despite the murky waters, fish are breeding around the coasts and estuaries, and of particular interest is Namarngol, the Barramundi. This is an important fish of the Kakadu wetlands. Mature fish move down from the freshwater reaches and billabongs when the water starts to run, and make their way to the estuaries and coastline to spawn in

Male fiddler crab

the protection of the mangroves.

With the appearance of large numbers of brown and gold butterflies, Andjirrwirr, one of the wattle trees, bursts into flower and Andjimdjim, the Aquatic Pandanus, produces its green, pineapple-like fruit. These natural events confirm to Bininj that Banggerreng has indeed commenced.

Kakadu coastline showing clear mangrove stratification

MARCH TO MAY

HARVEST TIME

BANGGERRENG

CHAPTER 2

CHAPTER 2

HARVEST TIME - BANGGERRENG

With the onset of Banggerreng the rain clouds disperse, and there is just the odd storm from the east. Sunny weather prevails, and the atmosphere changes markedly. For Bininj, this is a time of expectation and excitement—the long-awaited harvest is not far away.

Brown and gold dragonflies (*right*), which appear in great numbers over the floodplains and around all freshwater bodies, signal the end of Gudjewg and the beginning of Banggerreng. The annuals are all in bloom. Yamitj, the green katydid, is calling from the yellowing spear grass, announcing the ripening of the yams, many woodland and forest trees are preparing to drop the bulk of their heavy, wet season leaf growth and the air is heavy with the scent of curing grasses and flowering plants.

The last, violent southeast storms of the wet season perform an interesting task. They flatten the vast stands of spear grass which, by now, have dropped their specially designed seed and turned a golden yellow. These storms are locally known as 'knock-em-down' storms and they signify an exciting change in the seasons. As with the start of Gunumeleng and the arrival of much needed water, the spirits of both animals and humans are lifted at the onset of Banggerreng—but for another reason. The rains have allowed the development of abundant food resources.

The seed of the spear grass, shaken from the stems by the recent knock-em-down storms, is now working its way deep into the surface soil, assisted by the unique coil spring motion of its long tail shaft. This ensures that the next crop will be safe from the soil-sterilising effects of the coming fires. Surface water is extensive and, though humidity remains above average, it drops as Banggerreng progresses. Rivers begin returning to their normal levels and cumulus cloud formations at the end of the day produce stunning sunsets.

Banggerreng is a transitional period, but it announces clearly that the dry is on the way. One of the wattle trees called Andjirrwirr bursts into flower and announces to Bininj that Banggerreng is starting. Andjimdjim, the Aquatic Pandanus, also has ripening fruits which break up and fall into the water. The ripe fruits are eaten by larger fish and turtles, which in turn greatly aids seed dispersal and germination. In addition, the ripe fruit, which is another signal for the start of Banggerreng, also tells Bininj that the freshwater turtles are ready for eating.

Perfectly synchronised with the curing of the spear grass and the strong, resinous smell it produces is the appearance of Yamitj, a small, green cricket-like creature mentioned previously. It progresses through its life cycle in the short-lived spear grass, emerging as an adult with the curing of the crop.

Left: Beautiful evening skies follow the final storms of Banggerreng. Above: View from Nawulandja across to the main escarpment

Woollybutts growing in shallow, sandy soil on the Plateau

STONE COUNTRY

The sandstone is sparkling. This is 'stone country' at its best. Surface water lies everywhere on the rock shelves in the form of pools, streams and bogs. Giant mosses form thick, soggy carpets of pale green. Delicately flowered carnivorous plants are seen in these wet places in profusion. Bladderworts and Sundews grow in bright clusters in the damp spots. Mauve sprays of Trigger Plant flowers lean out from beneath the shady rock ledges.

In the pools, a delicate plant called the Water Pincushion has reached above the surface with a coronet of fine, white flowers. Like many other water plants, this one has both a delicate under-water and a robust above-water phase.

Piles of dried Sandstone Pandanus nuts have germinated and raise their spiky tentacles in competition and the air is full of the resinous smells of spinifex grass and the aromatic Pityrodia bush.

Sandstone Trigger Plant

Trigger Plant flower

Water Pincushion

The insectivorous Byblis plant

New leafy growth on the fleshy rhizome of a Basket Fern　　*A Cave Cricket reacts to intruders with its long feelers*

Basket Ferns, which have looked so lush and green on the rocks, are now beginning to yellow and dry out. In a few weeks they turn completely brown and look quite lifeless. Yet, hidden below the foliage, is a large, fleshy rhizome which stores a large amount of moisture and nutrients for production of new foliage in Gunumeleng, before the rains arrive.

Just as Yamitj dominates the spear grass of the lowlands, other long-legged katydid relatives abound in the sandstone vegetation, chewing away on the new growth. They themselves are the targets of dragons and other insectivores which lurk beneath the foliage.

Deep in the sandstone recesses lives another member of the cricket family, which spends its life in darkness, emerging only at night to forage on the rock surfaces. This Cave Cricket is also an important component in the sandstone food chain, for it is a primary food source for the carnivorous, and as yet undescribed, Arnhem Whip-scorpion and the secretive Giant Cave Gecko.

Long-legged katydid

The beautifully marked Noctuid Moth (*left*) also shares the same dark recesses as the Cave Cricket and is rarely seen. It emerges into the open at night to forage, as do so many cave-dwelling creatures but, as they spend their lives in perpetual darkness, their existence goes largely unnoticed by humans.

Tadpoles seem to abound in every pool, maximising their opportunities for survival and consuming the prolific algae growth that the wet has produced. The bulk of these amphibians will become food for other creatures, and so are a vital part of the sandstone food chain. Nevertheless, enough survive to ensure the species continues. Many of these shallow pools go through an amazing temperature range each day and the water can become extremely hot in direct sunlight. Despite this apparent peril, the tadpoles survive.

The sandstone frogs of Kakadu are highly specialised for a life of extremes. The Saxacoline Tree-frog, like other sandstone creatures, has turned from the trees to specialise in rock-dwelling. Its tadpoles develop extremely quickly in the shallow rock-pools and can tolerate water temperatures of more than 42º C. In the months to come, the young frogs must cope with an arid environment that has very limited surface water,

Pools evaporating after rain are ideal breeding-sites for sandstone frogs

Tadpoles of the Giant Frog in the grassy areas of the Plateau

usually carefully tucked away beneath a stone or under some flood debris, which increases the ventriloquial effect.

The Masked Rock-frog is another sandstone specialist found only in the escarpment country of Kakadu and Arnhem Land. It was described only in the late seventies and its trilling, canary-like call can be heard for a long distance over the sandstone at night. During Gudjewg and Banggerreng the calling males display bright yellow, brown and black colours. However, during the long dry, non-breeding periods, these vibrant colours are replaced

low humidity and lethal daytime surface temperatures, as well as an interesting range of predators. The cool, dark subterranean tunnels and passages in the sandstone provide the answer.

At night, the stone country echoes to the staccato calls of many frogs, but the most bizarre call is made by a robust and heavily mottled frog called the Carpenter Frog. It has earned this name because of the strange, acoustic knocking sound produced by the males. It carries down the gorges and can be very difficult to track down. The caller is

Copland's Rock Frogs are inactive during the day

Basket Ferns are a feature of the wet season in the sandstone

The characteristic 'three-leafed' configuration of the Anbinik Tree

A male Carpenter Frog calling at night beneath a rock overhang

Rockhole Frogs always rest in close proximity to water

by a pale cream with faded black markings as the frogs retreat to the cool, dark inner recesses of water-worn caves and passageways. In this dark environment, which they share with Rockhole Frogs, Saxacoline Tree-frogs and Carpenter Frogs, they sit quietly like prisoners, month after month, until a rise in outside humidity sets them free again.

The smallest of the sandstone frogs, and most numerous, is the very athletic Rockhole Frog, which prefers to congregate around small, water-worn potholes and pools amongst the sandstone boulders. Unlike the other sandstone frogs which become inactive in the dry season, this tiny frog remains active day and night throughout the dry period by sitting in moist patches around permanent springs and pools and preying on the insects which are attracted to the water. At the approach of danger, they confuse a would-be enemy by bouncing in all directions, some even skipping across the water surface as though it were ice. The skin colours and patterns vary greatly in this species and, like the other tree-frogs, this one can change colour rapidly. The danger in being active in the hot times is that, within centimetres of where they are sitting, the rocks may be at a lethal temperature. Escape routes therefore must be well planned and familiar. When disturbed, these tiny frogs disappear into safe places in seconds. Wet season choruses usually take place at night around a pool and involve a number of males calling in synchrony.

Monsoon forest growing beneath the protection of the escarpment edge is dominated by giant Anbinik Trees

Sandstone Pandanus growing at Nawulandja

Firetail Skinks may bask for short periods on very hot sandstone

Protected gorges shelter a wide variety of ferns in the wet

Chestnut-quilled Rock-pigeon

falling to the ground and forms the chief food source while the young birds are growing. A very soft and brief double coo is the only sound they utter as they wander in search of seed. This gentle call carries a surprising distance and serves to keep the birds in contact with each other, particularly if the party is surprised into flight by a would-be predator. The loud wingbeats alert other rock-pigeons to the danger.

At the end of Banggerreng, most of the wet places on the sandstone plateau will have dried up, leaving only dark algae stains on the rock surfaces where the run-off channels were. The lowland habitats take longer to dry out.

Colonies of skinks bask on rock ledges, enjoying the return of the sun. The rarely seen Arnhem Land Crevice-skink *Egernia arnhemensis* is the largest of the sandstone skinks and generally keeps well hidden in deep crevices and along high ledges when humans approach. This gives the mistaken impression that these lizards are rare.

Brightly coloured Firetail Skinks appear and disappear in the litter between the sandstone boulders, regulating their body temperatures to a fine degree in an extremely hot environment.

Most pairs of Chestnut-quilled Rock-pigeons now have partly fledged young following them along the rock ledges and among the spinifex tussocks. The prolific seed produced by the spinifex is now

Arnhem Land Crevice-skink

Spring-fed forest stream

Large dragonfly

Yellowing leaves of the River Almond

layer of litter is superimposed.

As the leaves of many trees, shrubs and ephemeral plants are now turning to yellow in the canopy and understorey, more light is able to penetrate through to the forest floor. Vines and other annuals have flowered and fruited as well as stored the necessary nutrients in their bulbous root systems. Some of the trees, like the Cluster Fig, are still fruiting, while some others are still developing their fruit. The variety of leaf-eating insects which have proliferated over the wet period has chewed patterns in the abundant foliage, giving it all a ragged appearance.

MONSOON FORESTS

Surprisingly, during this time of abundant nourishment, quite a number of plants drop their leaves immediately the rains finish. This highlights the strong seasonal nature of these tropical habitats. The leaf-drop helps to nourish the germinating seeds on the forest floor and to retain soil moisture after the rains cease. Constantly raked over and heaped up by Scrub Fowl, and to a lesser extent by other kinds of wildlife, this litter is the 'food' of the forest. The decomposition rate slows down considerably as the dry period sets in and the new

Makinlaya plant in flower

Fragrant Round Yam flowers

Black and White Tiger Butterfly

A resulting explosion of butterflies in the forest understorey is imminent. The Black and White Tiger and Crow Butterflies are the most common, and cluster in thousands in some forest areas towards the end of Banggerreng, particularly around natural springs and the resulting watercourses. Blue Tigers, Eggflies and Oak Blue Butterflies provide a splash of colour in forest clearings as they display their stunning patterns on the sunlit leaves.

Most of the ground-dwelling orchids have now produced large, green seed pods which will burst open as soon as the humidity falls sufficiently to dry them out. Masses of tiny seeds are then expelled into the air to float off to new locations in the forest. The new orchid plants will not manifest themselves until the following rains.

The Rainbow Pittas have raised their broods and have now become more elusive and less vocal than at the beginning of the breeding season. It is unclear whether the young birds remain in the vicinity of their parents' territory or are forced away, but the calls of migrating pittas can be heard high in the sky at night during the dry months.

The cheerful but raspy calls of the Spangled Drongo are a feature of the forests at this time of the year, and in the months to come, these birds will move out into the woodlands in search of nectar and insects. They become migratory in the dry season, although there always seem to be some drongos in the Kakadu area.

An atmosphere of torpor is settling into the forests.

Malaxis acuminata *orchid*

Rainbow Pitta

Spangled Drongo

Flooded billabong in the Magela system

Floodwater spills over the levee bank on the East Alligator River

RIVERS & BILLABONGS

Tangled debris in the Paperbark Trees high above the river banks bears testimony to the flood levels of the previous weeks. Now things are returning to normal.

It is not uncommon for floods to occur at the beginning of Banggerreng as a result of passing cyclones but, whatever the case, this season generally sees the river levels steadily fall as the last of the floodwater gushes down muddy gutters from the floodplains and mixes with the clear run-off from the sandstone country. The surface run-off will take many more weeks to slow down, but the tidal influence can again be seen in the upstream estuaries. Estuarine Crocodile numbers will increase again in the main river channels as they begin moving back from the draining floodplains

Around the lower sections of the rivers, as the floodwaters begin to fall back towards normal levels, the smell of rotting vegetation pervades. A layer of fine silt covers the previously flooded areas, speeding up the process of decay. New mudbars appear in the river channels as the water falls, highlighting the change of course the floodwater has taken. The course changes from year to year.

Water Pythons are a common sight in the treetops during a flood

Schools of Popeyed Mullet, a curious estuarine fish which swims along the surface of shallow, muddy water with its bright yellow eyes protruding above the water level, become a common sight at this time of year as they make their way upstream with the rising tide. When disturbed, the entire school breaks into a chaos of leaping and splashing. A major species in the estuarine food chain, they form an important food item in the diets of both the hatchling Estuarine Crocodiles and the young Barramundi, which themselves are migrating upstream. When a school is disturbed by a predator, they all leap along the surface of the river in a noisy commotion until well clear of the danger.

Popeyed Mullet swimming with its eyes above the water level

Estuarine Crocodiles are in their element during a flood

Three parents and a brood of young Magpie Geese battle against floodwater

FLOODPLAINS

The wetlands are at their busiest, and schools of young fish abound. The floodplains have been rich feeding grounds for most aquatic life throughout Gudjewg but, once the rains cease, the water levels quickly drop and this forces most aquatic life to return to the billabongs and river channels. This exodus from the floodplains in Banggerreng is fraught with dangers because predatory species such as Estuarine Crocodiles, large Salmon Catfish and Barramundi are set up in ambush at all points where the waters gush back into the main channels. No doubt this accounts for a considerable percentage of the season's bounty of fish and aquatic invertebrates.

Magpie Geese at this time of year are usually well into nesting mode amongst the wild rice and spike rush and many adults are already caring for groups of yellowish, fluffy chicks. Aquatic leeches abound in the warm floodplain waters in the vicinity of the goose colonies and no doubt these blood-thirsty creatures are both a blessing and a curse to the geese in that, while they do cause some discomfort to the birds and their chicks, they act as a powerful deterrent to many would-be predators.

The geese like to nest as the water level is falling, but a late cyclone can cause havoc with goose-nesting, drowning the maturing crops of rice and releasing the nests from their reedy moorings. Chicks become scattered by strong currents and exposed to predators as the plains return again to the high flood levels. This also means that the geese cannot breed again until the following year. High goose numbers can sustain these occasional heavy losses but, if numbers are low, populations can be decimated.

Male Magpie Goose defending the nest

Typical goose nest

East Alligator Floodplain from Gudjewg to Banggerreng

An Intermediate Egret stalks frogs and fish on waterweeds

Brolgas feeding on floodplains

The young geese grow rapidly and not only feed on the maturing seed-heads of the wild rice but also on the myriads of emerging insects which are so characteristic of Banggerreng. They have been born into the beginning of 'the time of plenty'.

Brolgas too are raising chicks born on bulky reed-nests in the shallower parts of the floodplains. The parents choose a nest-site with a commanding view. Like the Magpie Geese, the Brolga chicks hatch late in Gudjewg or early in Banggerreng to take full advantage of the wet season's production. The one or two chicks then stick close to the lanky parents as they are shown the ins-and-outs of floodplain life. Until they can fly, the chicks are defended fiercely by the parents.

Newly hatched and brightly coloured Yellow Spotted Monitors can be seen wandering over the drier sections of the plains in search of insects and frogs. Just like their larger kinsfolk, these little chaps can be quite bold when approached, standing their ground and puffing out their brightly marked throats. Unfortunately, this approach is sometimes employed on passing traffic while crossing the highway—with very negative results.

Before the end of Banggerreng, the wetlands have begun to re-form into discrete habitats, separate from the river channels. Water lilies and other perennial waterplants reach their best over the next few weeks.

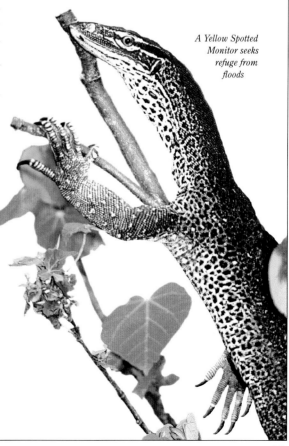

A Yellow Spotted Monitor seeks refuge from floods

PAPERBARK SWAMPS

This is a period of great beauty in the paperbark swamps. The Lotus Lily (*left*) and the Giant Water Lilies are maturing as the water level falls and the air is rich with the perfume of the lily flowers. Insects fill the air, keeping the Rainbow Bee-eaters busy, and green and yellow grasshoppers appear in large numbers to chew on the lily leaves and flowers. These grasshoppers are able to dive underwater if threatened, where they can remain for some minutes.

Among the branches of the flooded paperbark trees, waterbirds such as Darters, Cormorants and Night-herons are nesting in loose colonies. Towards

Paperbark Swamp during Banggerreng

Rufous Night-heron

the centres of the swamps, among the rushes and wild rice, the Magpie Geese are nesting, honking and arguing with the neighbours and maintaining a constant undercurrent of noise. Two (or often three) parents share in the incubation process, one sitting while the other flies off to feed.

Estuarine Crocodiles occasionally breed in heavy vegetation among the paperbark trees away from the main water body. The bulky nests, piled high with soil, grass and litter, are surprisingly well hidden. The female, who remains in shallow water nearby to keep an eye on things, has a well-beaten path back to the swamp. Her main fears are feral pigs, monitors and humans.

Anbangbang Billabong during Banggerreng

Paperbark Swamp at the end of Banggerreng

Bar-breasted Honeyeaters, which are one of only two Australian honeyeaters to construct fully enclosed nests, are strongly associated with paperbark swamps. At this time of year, they like to build their pendulous nests out of paperbark and cobwebs and suspend them from a drooping branch low over the water. During Gudjewg and Banggerreng they may construct as many as three of these nests within a few metres and their cheerful whistles are a feature of this time of year.

In the shallow reaches of some swamps, a delicate, blue-flowered Native Hyacinth appears during Banggerreng in quite large numbers. In places, the upright flower spikes are so dense that

Native Hyacinth in bloom in a shallow swamp

they appear to form a blue mist above the water.

At night, Rufous Owls hunt flying-foxes in the flowering paperbarks while the Arnhem Land Long-eared Bat and the Pygmy Long-eared Bat flitter between the paperbarks in pursuit of the abundant flying insects.

Aquatic activity reaches a peak in the paperbark swamps during Banggerreng as each species enjoys the lush conditions. In the days to come, this habitat will wind down as the water dries out and many of the animal species will move elsewhere. Like the floodplains, this habitat reflects the two extremes of a monsoon climate—total inundation and stark aridity.

Red Dragonfly on pandanus

Mature sorghum in open woodland

Violent knock-em-down storms signal the start of Banggerreng

A female Frilled Lizard excavates a nest chamber

Spear grass flattened by a knock-em-down storm

TROPICAL WOODLANDS

With the exhaustion of the monsoon system for another year, the easterly storms resume their afternoon deliveries and the final few outbursts in early Banggerreng are often the most dramatic. Their short-lived fury results in the demolition of the spear grass stands. The woodlands take on a new appearance with the spear grass suppressed and many smaller plants, previously hidden by this dominant annual, can now take a turn at flowering in the sunlight. Brightly coloured Gomphrena and Borreria flowers appear and cover large areas of the open ground surface and the competitive calls of Yamitj the katydid are heard day and night. Stringybarks are developing buds which burst open in Yegge. The cheerful piping voice of the Striated Pardalote is heard again amongst the eucalypts as they seek out partners and nesting sites in sandy banks.

In the early mornings and evenings, the woodland air is heavy with the scent of the Black Wattle flowers which now begin to coat the ground beneath the trees with yellow.

Woodland reptiles continue to be active and, by this time, most adult female Frilled Lizards have found a suitable location and deposited their eggs at the end of a short tunnel, which is then carefully back-filled and pounded down by the snout of the mother. She has no more to do with them from there. In a little over a month the beautifully camouflaged young dragons will emerge to take their chances with the ecosystem. Very few survive to adulthood from each clutch.

In a similar fashion, the woodland monitors have secreted their eggs in tunnels in sandy soils and left them to hatch in the warm moisture of Banggerreng. Like the young Estuarine Crocodiles and Magpie Geese, the young reptiles hatch during the most productive time of the year to maximise their chances of survival. By the time the dry period arrives, the surviving offspring have put on enough condition to carry them over.

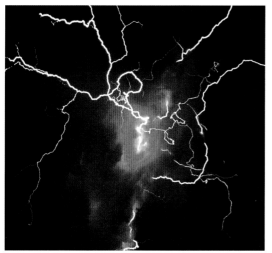

Yamitj, the green Katydid

Kentia Palm flowering

Blue-faced Honeyeater preening

The small palm tree seen growing throughout the Kakadu bush is a member of the Livistona genus, commonly called the Sand Palm. During Gudjewg and Banggerreng this dwarf palm produces a bright yellow flower spike which eventually produces bunches of shiny black fruit. Not palatable to humans, this fruit is eaten by Emus and bowerbirds which distribute the seeds throughout the area. If food became scarce, the cabbage in the central growing area of the Sand Palm could be cooked or eaten raw by Bininj.

Another much larger woodland palm that occurs from time to time, particularly in the sandy soils of the northwestern part of the Park, is the Kentia Palm. Stands can be seen on the Arnhem Highway at Flying Fox and West Alligator Creeks. These stately palms can withstand serious late season fires as adults, but the juvenile plants are easily killed in these circumstances.

With the new growth, Green Ants work feverishly to construct new leafy nests, using a special silk produced by their own larvae to stitch the leaves together. They may build more than a dozen nests in the foliage of the same tree and it appears that their presence may be beneficial to the tree as the ants repel most foliage browsing animals, one way or another. Anyone who has tried to climb a tree occupied by these ants will understand. The nests are abandoned after a period of time and fall to the ground when the tree sheds its leaves.

Gregarious Grey-crowned Babblers are feverishly building their bulky, dome-shaped stick nests in as many suitable places within their territory as possible. This is carried out by the group with an air of agitated co-operation. It is not easy to explain this compulsive nest-building but, after much commotion, the group finally settles on one particular nest in which to raise the brood. The other nests are useful for sleeping in from time to time and they have to be large enough to hold seven or eight birds because, with babblers, everything is a communal effort, even going to bed.

With a surplus of nests in their territory for the rest of the year, babblers inadvertently create openings for other opportunistic species such as the Blue-faced Honeyeater, which almost always uses babblers nests to raise its family in during Wurrgeng or Gurrung, when large amounts of nectar are available. During Banggerreng the honeyeaters are concentrating on the insect bounty found concealed in the dead pandanus foliage and similar locations. Their noisy searching in the dead leaves can often be heard in the quiet of a woodlands morning or evening.

Big Greasy Butterfly

Seed-eating birds such as finches, quails and pigeons now begin to nest with the dropping of a fresh crop of grass seed. After good seasons, these birds will raise several broods right through into Yegge.

On the rocky, sorghum-covered hillsides in the southern region of Kakadu, brilliantly coloured Gouldian Finches are preparing to nest in the hollows of one of the Salmon Gums, *Eucalyptus tintinans*.

Normally found in small flocks, the birds pair off to nest, though they still keep in loose contact with the group when feeding. Males become quite territorial in the nest-site area, chasing off any other inquisitive Gouldians or other types of finches which may attempt to steal nest-building materials. When the young birds leave the nest and join the main flock, their plumage is very drab-coloured in comparison with the adults. The seeds of the spear grass form a large part of their diet.

Nesting at the same time are the Long-tailed Finches and Masked Finches, which are often seen feeding with the Gouldians. Long-tails will compete with Gouldians for nest-sites and often become quite aggressive, but the quieter-natured Masked Finches prefer to nest low down, mainly in the dead sheafs of spear grass, just above ground level.

Forest Kingfisher

Partridge Pigeons too are incubating their one or two pure white eggs in a very simple nest in the leaf litter. It is no more than a shallow depression in the ground. These birds formerly had a broad range across the woodlands of the Top End of the Northern Territory but, in recent times, their distribution seems to have contracted to small centres, the main stronghold being in the woodlands of the Alligator Rivers Region. Altered fire patterns, grazing and feral cats all appear to have played a role in this disturbing decline.

Brown Quails are another seed-eating ground bird that breeds at this time. They are a common but rarely seen bird of the open woodlands and grassland fringes. Occasionally small parties are seen scurrying across roads and tracks or bursting into flight from the grass as you walk. Not only do they nest in Banggerreng when the seed supply is most suitable, but they also show a lot of interest in the freshly burned areas early in the dry months.

Male Black-headed Gouldian

Male Red-headed Gouldian

By night, the woodlands take on a totally different atmosphere when an amazing range of creatures emerge from their secret daytime retreats to take up their nocturnal roles. This is the time of greatest wildlife activity in the woodlands.

Invisible by day, the Tawny Frogmouth is a relatively common woodland bird, although the variety found here in the tropical north is much smaller than those of southern Australia. The gentle humming call often seems to over-ride the other night sounds and the birds are frequently seen pouncing on insects along roadsides at night. A counterpart of the Tawny Frogmouth, the Boobook Owl, also frequents the same areas at night, although its appearance and call are quite different. Even though they share much the same insect diet, there appears to be little competition between the two and the Boobook is capable of tackling larger prey items like Spiny-tailed Geckos and Delicate Mice.

A Delicate Mouse, smallest native rodent in Kakadu

Boobooks will often visit a campsite at night, watching for insects in the firelight from a high branch. The familiar double-noted call is a characteristic night sound in the Australian bush. The northern race tends to be slightly smaller and slightly redder than the southern Boobooks.

Tawny Frogmouths

Boobook Owl

A wide variety of insectivorous bats frequents the woodlands of Kakadu and this is probably the group of mammals that we know least about. They rarely come into contact with humans although they are flying all around us at night. It is difficult to gain information about these animals without interfering with them. We do know, however, that these tiny creatures consume large numbers of flying insects each night and that their night activities span all of the habitats.

Northern Mastiff Bat

One such diminutive creature is the Little Northern Broad-nosed Bat, one of Australia's tiniest bats, which is quite common in Kakadu and hunts below the tree canopy in both woodlands and monsoon forest, particularly near pools and creeks. By day it secretes itself in tree hollows in small social groups.

The Northern Mastiff Bat is another small but common species in the woodlands of Kakadu but it operates much higher above the woodlands canopy than the low-flying Broad-nosed Bat. The Little Northern Mastiff Bat also has the ability to move around rapidly on the ground. Its range extends into the islands north and east of Australia.

Management burning generally starts on the higher ridges during late Banggerreng where the grass is driest. These small, 'cool burns' act as a magnet to much of the wildlife, both by day and by night, and surveys have shown a sharp increase in species using the newly burnt patches. Regrowth begins immediately, but the risk of large, intense fires of a more destructive nature in late Gurrung or Gunumeleng is reduced considerably by these low-intensity burns. As the dry weather progresses, more and more patches are burned, creating a mosaic of differently aged regrowth. A good percentage of the woodlands does not require any burning.

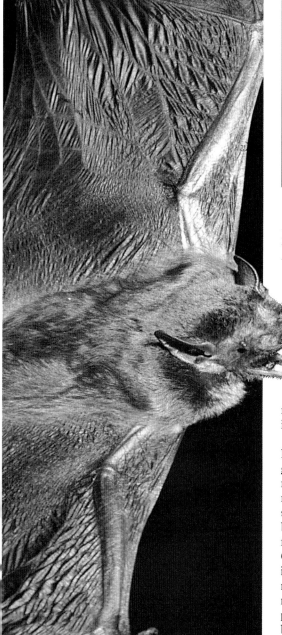

Little Northern Broad-nosed Bat

Solitary mangrove on the Kakadu coastline

MANGROVE FORESTS

The mangrove forests of Kakadu are a strange mixture of the old and the new. Protruding from the eroding mud at various points are ancient stumps, remnants of past forests which have been buried under new mud deposits, perhaps first destroyed by passing cyclones. As the rivers are constantly altering their courses and eating into the alluvial material, the past history of the wetlands is revealed.

Also preserved in time by the same process is a curious little crustacean called the Mud Lobster (*right*). Living Mud Lobsters are a common animal in the mangrove ecosystem, as they tunnel deep into the mud and pile mud walls high around the entrances to their burrows. They are rarely seen in the open.

At certain points around the tidal estuaries, large numbers of 'solidified' Mud Lobsters have been exposed like fossils from some ancient time. However, studies have shown that these solidified sea creatures are relatively recent creations of non-living matter. When a Mud Lobster dies deep in its burrow, the soft parts of its body quickly decompose, leaving the hard outer shell which soon fills with silt. Somehow this silt 'stuffing' hardens, much more so than the surrounding strata, which remains quite soft. The shell eventually falls away, leaving a rock-hard replica of the animal.

Mangrove worms, which are actually a relative of the oyster, occupy tunnels in dead mangrove wood. Driftwood in the intertidal zone is often well occupied with colonies of these molluscs, which filter their food from the seawater on the high tides. Mangrove worms are a nutritious food, highly prized by Bininj, and Banggerreng is one of the best times to harvest them. While the molluscs are being located and chopped out of the logs, many other types of shellfish and crustaceans are collected. Mangroves represent one of the richest of all habitats in terms of Bininj food resources and once added greatly to the quality of life of the coastal people.

Interestingly, many of the shellfish species that Bininj collect in the coastal mangroves today are also found in deposits up to one hundred kilometres inland from the present coastline. These are middens and remains of campsites from former times when the saltwater and mangroves were that much further inland. This was in the early development period of the present wetland system.

Developing mangrove forest on Barron Island

After each monsoon, driftwood is piled up along the coastline, much of it from South-East Asia

SHORELINE

The Shoreline is now decorated with a new range of flotsam and jetsam, including large logs, bamboo poles and even dugout canoes from South-East Asia. For many centuries before the arrival of Europeans, this process no doubt brought examples each year of cultural wares from faraway places to the Bininj of the Kakadu region.

The sea remains a murky colour with the excess silt still suspended in the coastal waters, but with the prevailing winds now from the southeast again, the waters of Van Diemen Gulf have quietened down considerably. Mangrove seeds of various species are establishing themselves on new mudbars and in piles of debris at the high tide mark. Having germinated on the parent trees even before they fell into the water, the seeds then float and are carried by the tide to other locations. Most will eventually die but, in suitable circumstances, extensions to the existing forests appear as a new wave of green.

Waterbirds above the rookery, East Alligator River

An extinct mangrove forest is exposed by eroding mud

Fresh water from the saturated watertable behind the mangroves and beaches seeps out at the shoreline and mingles with the saltwater. Some of these seepage points last well into the dry months and a few are permanent. These were very important to Bininj in times past and were widely known. References to these water points were often recorded in stories, legends and songs so that people who had never visited the site still knew of their existence.

As the waterbird rookeries in the mangroves are tailing off and the young birds are now flying with their parents, pairs of Jabiru begin the drawn-out process of nest construction or renovation in the top of a tree which provides a good vantage point for the surrounding area. Like the White-bellied Sea-Eagle, the Jabiru prefers to nest in the cooler part of the year.

Some pairs choose to nest right on the coastline and usually select a suitable tall mangrove on which to construct the bulky stick-nest. When the young ones hatch during Yegge, the parents draw the food supply both from the shoreline and the associated tidal flats, as well as from the freshwater swamps and sedgelands behind the mangrove line. The nest gives a commanding view of both areas.

In former times, when the Bininj people of the northern Kakadu region depended more on the coastal products for their livelihood, Banggerreng was the time when the men turned their attention to spearing and cooking young sharks and stingrays. This is the time when these creatures are in top condition and have large reserves of body fat—a highly prized item necessary in the cooking and preparation of the flesh. These conditions only last until Yegge when the sharks and rays are of no further interest to the hunters.

When the Turkey Bush bursts into its mauve flowers and the first Stringybark flowers appear, we know that Yegge has arrived. The onset of cold nights, early morning fogs and heavy dews signal that Banggerreng has come to an end and that Yegge is about to begin.

MAY TO JUNE

COOL WEATHER TIME

YEGGE

CHAPTER 3

CHAPTER 3

COOL WEATHER TIME - YEGGE

The oppressive conditions of the rainy season are giving way gradually—to cooler day and night temperatures and much lower humidity. Yegge leads into the main cool-weather period of Wurrgeng. Mists and fogs may develop overnight in the valleys and on the plains but, as the sun rises, they soon lift. A typical dry-season cloud pattern sets in consisting of a scattered middle layer of small, fluffy cumulus clouds drifting across from the east.

The atmosphere now takes on a constant smoke haze. The combined output from 'cool' woodland fires to the east in Arnhem Land drifts gently across the Kakadu landscape. The skies generally clear again at night as most fires go out by evening in Yegge. However, with the overnight temperature inversions that may occur in this cooler weather, the smoke layer can be trapped quite low until the morning sun causes it to rise again.

A small Turkey Bush called Anbaandarr bursts into flower at this time. It tells Bininj that Yegge is starting and that the Gumugen or Freshwater Crocodiles will soon be laying their eggs. The yam harvest which was announced in Banggerreng is now in full swing, together with numerous other sweet-tasting bulbs which are skilfully located from their cryptic seclusion in the woodland understorey. Bininj knowledge of plants and their seasonal responses is extremely detailed, way ahead of the scientific fraternity.

Visually, this is the most spectacular time of the year in the wetlands because the receding floodwaters have allowed the maturing and flowering of masses of water lilies. The powerful perfume from the flowers fills the early morning air which drifts across the plains and through the paperbark forests, giving the visitor a lasting memory of Yegge.

As the cool weather sets in, the most dominant woodland tree, Anrebel, the Stringybark, is preparing to flower. This is a sign for Bininj that Angung or Sugarbag will be ready for harvesting. A number of species of these stingless native bees produce a very edible honey that in times past was a prized source of sweetness and energy. Collecting Angung in Wurrgeng is still greatly enjoyed by young and old alike.

Left: Burrungguy escarpment from Anbangbang. Above: Monsoon forest growing in the mouth of a sandstone cave

STONE COUNTRY

Several types of Jewel Beetles are seen in the stone country of the Arnhem Plateau but, as yet, very little is known of their life histories. They are most often encountered at this time of year following the wet weather when many of the sandstone plants are in flower.

Around this time of the year, many of the smaller, more delicate animals, frogs in particular, disappear from sight and seek refuge from the coming heat and dryness. This habitat provides an interesting solution to these physical extremes.

The uncommon Diadem Bat

Large jewel beetle

The Arnhem Whip-scorpion

Throughout the rugged sandstone hills of Kakadu is a variety of water-worn caves, many of which are connected to a labyrinth of tunnels. These are the result of water action over thousands of years eroding the softer beds within the sandstone layering and today the process continues.

These caves are the homes of a variety of interesting animals, many of which never emerge into the outside world. These animals belong to a complex but little-known subterranean ecosystem and a good percentage of these still await collection.

A heavily dissected sandstone valley

Jewel beetle

Juvenile rock-wallaby

The Giant Cave Gecko lives in areas decorated with rock art

One such example is a recently discovered and rather sinister- looking spider-like invertebrate from deep in the caves of the East Alligator River catchment. Locally known as the Arnhem Whip-scorpion, it spends its entire life in total darkness on the walls of underground caverns where both temperature and humidity remain constantly high. To support its predatory lifestyle, it is equipped with an unusually long pair of feelers which slowly sweep around the rock surface in search of Cave Crickets and other insects. Once located, the prey is gently guided by the feelers towards a waiting pair of spiny, crab-like pincers which quickly despatch the meal. Perhaps well known by earlier generations, it still awaits scientific description.

Living alongside this set of animals is another group which seeks refuge there each day and returns to the outside world nightly. Moths, flies, dragonflies, geckos, snakes and bats are all regular cave users. Narbarlek and Short-eared Rock-wallabies, Euros and Black Wallaroos also enjoy the cool daytime conditions of the caves.

The Giant Cave Gecko lives a double life. It is at home in the sandstone caverns by day, and emerges at night to feed on insects in the foliage of adjoining monsoon forest trees. Its nearest relative, the Cape York Pad-tail Gecko, is also a specialist tree-dweller and both lizards are equipped with prehensile tails for feeding at the extremities of the foliage.

The Black Wallaroo is at home on the boulders of the escarpment slopes

On the narrow ledges and associated fissures and crevices lives the Common Rock-rat. These pale-coloured, fast-moving rodents are largely nocturnal, although occasionally they may be seen in the late afternoon darting about amongst the rocks. Their primary food is the seed of the spinifex grass, but they also gather many other seeds and fallen fruit and store them in caches in the safety of their ledges.

The Common Rock-rat

The tasty kernels of the Emu Apple are a favourite food of the Common Rock-rat. The Emu Apple is one of the hardest nuts in the stone country and may require many years of exposure to weather to break down and germinate. The Common Rock-rat laboriously gathers up the nuts, one at a time, for the larder. By systematically gnawing away these industrious rodents eventually are able to gain access to the inner chamber where the edible kernel is housed.

You may observe the elongated wax entrance tubes of Nabiwu, the small native bee, which builds its nests in sandstone crevices around the art-sites of Kakadu. At this time of year the honey production is at a maximum with the flowering of Northern Grevilleas, Stringybarks, Woollybutts and numerous smaller sandstone species.

Spiny Anteaters (also known as Echidna) are most active at this time, particularly in the cool evenings. They prefer to live around rocky hillsides in caves and overhangs where they sleep in the cool during the day. Their main food is the spinifex-harvesting termite which constructs the grey, spire-like mounds seen on top of sandstone outcrops. They build waxy tunnels which radiate from the mound across the sandstone in all directions for the collection of dead spinifex shafts. The resin from the spinifex blades is not eaten but used as a cementing agent in the tunnels. The strong, aromatic smell of the spinifex is retained in this resin. Spiny Anteaters break into these tunnels at night and, with the aid of their long, sticky tongues, they mop up the agitated termites together with a great deal of gritty material. This ultimately aids the digestion process, before it is excreted.

In the permanent shady pools of the deeper

One of several varieties of Eel-tailed Catfish found in Kakadu

sandstone creeks, large schools of young Eel-tailed Catfish swim lazily in the clear water. Here they spend the dry months, filter-feeding on the stream bed with a number of other freshwater fish, including Sooty Grunters, Purple-spotted Gudgeons, Saratoga, Archerfish and Chequered and Black-striped Rainbowfish. All of these fish species are known to swim far and wide throughout the lowlands in the Gudjewg inundation, but seem to find their way back into these protected escarpment pools for the remainder of the year. It highlights the importance of these small places to the wildlife.

A Spiny Anteater forages in a rock shelter

Twin Falls Gorge is fed throughout the dry period by water seeping out of the aquifer in the plateau above

Green Ants construct a nest in a Black Wattle tree

Minnie Alderson extracts Long Yams from beneath a Banyan

MONSOON FORESTS

Green Ants are always associated with monsoon forests. Though they are found in almost all other habitats where trees occur, they reach their highest densities in monsoon forest. Their large, leafy nests are woven together with silk produced by their own larvae and they range through the neighbouring trees, along vines or across the open ground in search of invertebrate prey.

Green Ants are not particularly tolerant of humans and will respond to a disturbance in their territory by swarming over the intruder. Their multiple bites are mostly nuisance value and do little damage, but their habit of directing a fine jet of acid up to eight centimetres from their abdomen can cause extreme discomfort if it hits a person in the eye. The relationship that Green Ants have with trees in which they live is unclear, but it is thought to be a beneficial one.

Monsoon forests produce a wide variety of foods which are harvested throughout the year by Bininj, particularly in Banggerreng and Yegge. Two of the most popular yams for eating are the Round Yam and the Long Yam. To the untrained eye, both vines appear almost identical. However, the Round Yam is quite poisonous to eat without careful preparation, while the Long Yam may be eaten raw or cooked and is by far the most popular. Distinguishing between the two is not a problem for Bininj, even though the differences are subtle. The best time to dig the yams is when the vines are dying off and the root has finished developing.

Indiscriminate fire can destroy all traces of the yam vines which indicate the presence of this much favoured subterranean food. For this and other reasons, Bininj tend to manage entire forests as a resource and, in many instances, controlled fires are used around the boundaries of forests in Yegge and early Wurrgeng to prevent major fires damaging the delicate ecology later in the year. This traditional system of fire management has now been incorporated into the ongoing management policy of Kakadu and involves the input and guidance of the older Bininj.

Freshly dug Long Yams from sandy coastal soil

Leaves of Round Yam (L) and the much sought after Long Yam (R)

Fire is one of the major factors influencing the advance and retardation of monsoon forests and evidence shows that the forests of Kakadu have suffered badly over the the last century with the interruption of traditional burning patterns and the indiscriminate use of fire by non-Aboriginal people.

Under healthy ecological conditions, monsoon forest is not a particularly flammable community of plants, but the forest trees themselves have little defence from scorching, unlike the thick-barked woodland trees. They die very easily from exposure to heat or flames.

When a major fire sweeps through the woodlands and hits the margins of monsoon forest, it generally stops, having scorched the outer ring of forest trees. These trees and the seedlings around them invariably die, which effectively shrinks the forest. If this happens repeatedly, season after season, islands of monsoon forest can shrink alarmingly or even completely disappear, to be swallowed up by fire-tolerant woodland species. This is known to have happened in recent times in the Kakadu area. In places, long-extinct mounds of the Orange-footed Scrubfowl, which now stand in woodlands far from the nearest forest, bear testimony to a past forest. The Orange-footed Scrubfowl is exclusively a monsoon forest-dweller. The evidence does suggest that monsoon forests were once much more widespread than those we see today.

Damage to forests by feral animals, particularly by pigs and water buffalo, has also been a problem in recent times and is generally followed by weed invasion. Weeds are very volatile and carry fire right into the forest.

As monsoon forest is perhaps the most fragile and restricted of the Kakadu habitats, care is now being taken to manage what is left. Fire and feral animal control are high on the list. Evidence now indicates that when conditions are favourable and fires are controlled, monsoon forest can advance at quite a rapid rate.

Like the water-worn caves, monsoon forest becomes a dry season retreat for many smaller creatures which spend the wet period in the stone country. The coolness, low light and extra moisture are essential for their survival. A good example of this is the tiny Northern Territory Frog (*inset right*). It is our only representative of a family of true rainforest frogs found in the wet forests of New Guinea and Northern Queensland. Presumably, this is a relict population from times when a wetter climate allowed these

Monsoon forests are home to many endemic life forms

frogs to spread from Cape York across northern Australia.

Today the Northern Territory Frog depends heavily on the protection of monsoon forest for its survival. It lives amongst the leaf litter close to water, frequently around natural springs. Not much more than a centimetre in length, it can be very difficult to find, other than tracking it down by its rather ventriloquial call, which is a high-pitched, insect-like note repeated in rapid succession.

Males begin calling in the pre-wet, as the humidity rises. When the rains arrive, the frogs move out away from the forest, often into the high sandstone country among the spinifex clumps. It is not known if they breed away from the monsoon forests, but this family of frogs has managed to bypass the tadpole stage.

Numerous billabongs are a feature of the East Alligator River floodplain

RIVERS & BILLABONGS

Fish diversity has increased again in the upstream sections since the rains, with many species sharing the streams and pools. As the dry conditions increase and the pools shrink, so competition will increase amongst the fish species. External predator pressure also increases as the dry progresses, with hungry water goannas, egrets and herons, cormorants and water rats.

In the deeper reaches, larger predatory fish such as Saratoga, Barramundi, Sooty Grunters, Sleepy Cod, Salmon Catfish, Ox-eye Herring and Freshwater Long Toms feed heavily on the smaller species. These in turn are food for file snakes, Freshwater Crocodiles and White-bellied Sea-Eagles.

In the still, deep waters of the billabongs, amongst the thick aquatic weeds, lives the beautiful Carp Gudgeon. This fish, though common, is rarely seen because of its small size and its preference for living in deep, still billabongs among the weeds.

The Purple-spotted Gudgeon

One of several varieties of Reticulated Perchlet

Tailed Soles

The Sooty Grunter

The Red-claw Yabby

Chequered Sunfish or Rainbowfish

A Freshwater Prawn migrates upstream over rocks during Yegge

Male Carp Gudgeon in territorial colours

Unlike Ginga the Estuarine Crocodile, Gumugen the Freshwater Crocodile nests in the dry months in the upstream sections of the rivers where there are high, sandy banks beside the deeper stretches. In late Yegge the females begin wandering the sandy banks at night in search of a suitable nesting site. This wandering may go on nightly for some weeks before a site is chosen. Unlike the elaborate nest of Ginga, Gumugen simply excavates a deep chamber in the moist sand as the turtles do, allowing the sun's warmth to incubate the eggs. Egg-laying usually takes place during Wurrgeng.

Newly hatched Estuarine Crocodiles gather in the mother's wallow

The female Estuarine Crocodile remains in the vicinity of the nest

Soon they will alternate between the wallow and the river's edge

For the next three months the female lurks in the deep water nearby to defend the nest against minor predators like goannas. Major predators such as feral pigs and humans go unchallenged. The eggs take many weeks to develop, depending upon ground temperatures, and the bulk of hatchlings appear during late Gurrung and Gunumeleng.

The young Gumugen emerge with much squeaking and sometimes assistance from the mother, who continues to tend them for several more weeks until their natural defences take over. Recent information indicates that other females may also assist the young at this time.

In the tidal regions, the creches of Estuarine Crocodile hatchlings continue to be guarded by the female while the young learn to stalk mud skippers and other small fish in the shallows. It will take two years before these young ones reach a metre and perhaps ten years before they reach three metres.

Competing with the young crocodiles for the mud skippers is a very large, river-dwelling ray which hunts along the muddy waters of the river's edge as the tide rises. It has the rather disconcerting habit of suddenly throwing itself half out of the water on the mud in the hope of trapping mud skippers and any other small creatures under its flaps.

Mud skippers are the main food of hatchling crocodiles

Estuarine Crocodile nest beside the East Alligator River

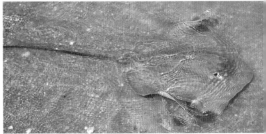

The Freshwater Whip-ray preys on the abundant mud skippers

The first scientific record of Warradjan's presence in Kakadu

Pig-nosed Turtle

Another creature of these deep, shady sections of the rivers is the very secretive Pig-nosed Turtle, known in Kakadu as Warradjan. Until relatively recently, this large turtle was known only in northern Australia from old bone fragments in ancient human occupation sites, as well as from several unmistakable rock paintings. Bininj, of course, were well aware of its presence and relied on it as a major food source. The irony was that, unknown to western science, these unique creatures were living peacefully in the billabong several hundred metres from the best known Warradjan painting!

To date, six species of freshwater turtle are known from Kakadu and the main river-dwelling species are the Northern Snapping Turtle and the less widespread Saw-shelled Turtle. These can

The Saw-shelled Turtle lives in the upstream sections of the rivers

often be seen surfacing for air in the deeper pools in the sandstone country, or in the shady sections on the lowlands. In the billabong systems they are replaced by the Northern Short-necked Turtle.

The Northern Snapping Turtle is the most frequently seen freshwater turtle in the river systems. In the middle sections of the rivers above the tidal zone, they often occur together with the Northern Short-necked and Pig-nosed Turtles.

While all these species overlap, each kind of turtle occupies its own niche and so competition is reduced to a minimum. This holds true for most animal species in Kakadu and is a balance developed over a long period of time.

Northern Snapping Turtle

Lily flowers reach their peak after the wet

These small, yellow lilies are a feature of Yegge

FLOODPLAINS

The floodplains are still drying out and on the outskirts appear beautiful carpets of tiny yellow lilies. Each morning the flower buds point towards the rising sun and open as the warmth of the sunlight strikes them. They follow the sun across the sky and close in unison during mid-afternoon.

It is only in recent years that such displays of these yellow lilies have been seen, which coincides with the government initiative to remove the feral buffalo. Prior to this, these animals were in such large numbers that they trampled and overgrazed the wetland areas, preventing most of the delicate plant species from appearing. To the surprise of local residents, many species quickly re-established themselves and the floodplains have been transformed.

Adult Pied Heron

It may take many more years for an ecological balance to re-establish itself on the wetlands, for we have very little understanding of the situation that existed prior to European arrival. For the same reason, it is also very difficult to determine if we have lost any species as a result of the buffalo intrusion.

The well-organised diary of Ludwig Leichhardt provides our earliest account of the nature of the wetlands as he and his party passed briefly across the plains on their way to Victoria Settlement in November, 1845. Little did he know that his careful observations would one day form the basis for the management of what are now classified as 'world class wetlands'.

Pink-eared Duck

Water lilies are at their best during Yegge

Surface water plants help reduce evaporation

Little Corella

PAPERBARK SWAMPS

One of the major features of this time of the year is the magnificent flowering of the water lilies in the wetlands. During the early 1980s, a control program for feral buffalo was initiated which has since removed all the uncontrolled herds which previously roamed the wetland areas. For over a period of about sixty to eighty years, these animals had caused severe ecological alterations to the wetland ecology and throughout the last decade it has been greatly encouraging to watch the wetland systems recover after the removal of the buffalo. Vast beds of lilies flourish once again, just as the very oldest Bininj remember them from their childhood.

In the swamps themselves, the abundance of aquatic life is reflected in the busyness of the place. The early morning air is filled with birdsong, especially that of Lemon-bellied Flycatchers, Yellow Orioles, White-throated Honeyeaters, Little Corellas and Bar-shouldered Doves. The honking duet from pairs of White-bellied Sea-Eagles is heard periodically from the topmost branches of the paperbark trees and the trilling of Rainbow Bee-eaters is heard constantly over the water as they swoop from their vantage points on passing dragonflies (*left*). Their

Lotusbird

torpedo-like flight is too much for the newly emerged dragonflies which are snapped up and carried back to the perch and pulverised, before being swallowed.

Long-necked turtles are feeding voraciously on all forms of aquatic organisms, particularly fish, tadpoles and frogs. The female turtles are producing eggs ready for laying in the soft mud during Wurrgeng, and so require lots of protein, but the main reason for this heavy feeding is fat storage. The swamps eventually dry out completely and the turtles bury in the soft mud beforehand. The mud then dries like concrete, locking the reptiles in until the rains return. They survive by absorbing the built-up fat reserve within their bodies.

Black-fronted Dotterel

Jabiru seeking eels in a Ludwigia bed

Long-necked turtle prior to burying in the soft mud

Some turtles die from exposure if they cannot bury in the mud

Little Red Flying-foxes roosting in the paperbarks

The yellow flowers of the Kapok Bush

Turkey Bush

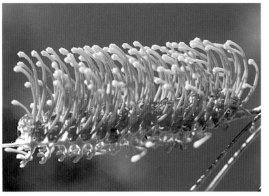

Northern Grevillea

Sorghum is the main fuel for wildfire

TROPICAL WOODLANDS

The dry season colours are now appearing in the woodlands—the yellow flowers of the Kapok Bush, the orange of the Northern Grevilleas and Woollybutt Trees and the mauve of the Turkey Bush (Anbaandarr).

By the start of Yegge, fires have been lit to begin 'cleansing the bush', as Bininj put it. These fires are generally of low intensity and burn only over a limited area before going out in the early evening. Different parts of the woodlands dry out at different rates and some areas will not carry fire till well into Wurrgeng. Each clan group knew their territory intimately, and knowing just when to burn is crucial to good ecology. Today it is more difficult for the people to do this properly because many clans have passed on since the time of Leichhardt's journey. The remaining clans are significantly smaller yet have a much greater area to manage. The story of social change in Kakadu since the time of

Leichhardt is a heartbreaking story, but Bininj are positive in their outlook and, hopefully, the creation of Kakadu has reversed a cultural decline.

This is a burnable landscape and covers more than seventy per cent of the surface of Kakadu. Fire is an annual feature and the woodland ecology revolves around it. Excluding fire is not an option. If humans don't introduce fire, nature will. Both the plants and animals of this habitat have developed strategies for coping with fire and, early in the dry period, many woodland animals actively seek out these freshly burnt areas.

Fire management in the Park is now a joint operation. Guided by the accumulated knowledge of the old people and carried out largely by younger rangers from both cultures, using traditional philosophies combined with modern technology, we are beginning to see ecological recovery in many areas. Fire monitoring is now an important process in the management of Kakadu and this technology is now being employed in other places.

Double-barred Finch

Partridge Pigeon

Juvenile Whistling Kite

Adult Whistling Kite

The first creatures to react to a fresh fire are the kites. Black Kites drift in at the first puff of smoke and their numbers increase as the fire spreads until they are too numerous to count. They are joined by the similar-looking Whistling Kites, swooping through the smoke and flames to snatch at fleeing grasshoppers, mice, skinks and dragons. Black and Brown Falcons also join the banquet as the fire exposes the generous wet season bounty of microfauna. Dingos also keep an eye on fire zones for anything they may chance upon. After nightfall, Northern Brown Bandicoots, Northern Quolls, Fawn Antechinuses and Bush Stone-curlews take over while Boobook Owls and Tawny Frogmouths observe from the canopy above.

Continued fire at this time of year produces a mosaic effect of burnt and unburnt patches in the woodlands and the burnt areas soon turn green again with the lingering moisture in the soil.

Under normal conditions, many burnable areas remain unburned each year and this has a desirable effect for the wildlife. Species like the Partridge Pigeon, the Brown Quail and the Masked Finch nest in the dead spear grass stands during Banggerreng and Yegge. If fire disrupts this process, they are known to move to an adjacent unburnt area and begin nesting once more. These birds are swift breeders and will raise multiple broods when conditions allow.

Wedge-tailed Eagle

The woodland animals take a keen interest in these freshly burned areas, mainly for the available food resources, but they still rely on the unburned areas for cover. By day, Sand and Yellow Spotted Monitors roam the charred ground, excavating the holes of smaller animals for any edible morsels that

The Sand Monitor chiefly inhabits the woodlands

they may uncover. These holes are usually about a metre deep and go in at an angle. Their burrowing activity is a common feature of the woodland and, inadvertently, they are creating underground homes for a host of other animals. They are particularly useful refuges during bushfires.

As soon as the early fires make it possible, the Red-tailed Black Cockatoos, with their very short legs, can land on the ground to forage for the seeds of the spear grass as well as the hard seeds of assorted fruit trees. Large flocks of these impressive birds can be seen feeding beside the main roads and tracks, which is where many of the first fires of the season are lit.

Australian Bustards will quickly respond to the smoke of grass fires by flying in over quite long distances to feed on the abundant insect life disturbed by the fire. Bininj capitalise on this response by carefully planning these fires so that the highly prized Bustards may be ambushed on arrival. Many other animals are also captured at this

The Yellow Spotted Monitor

time as they take shelter from the flames in the numerous monitor burrows. Skilful hands can determine just which type of animal is hiding at the end of the burrow. In times past, venomous snakes, which were occasionally encountered during this process, were fearlessly allowed to slide away.

Although they have never occurred in large numbers in the tropical woodlands, Emus, according to old time residents, are less common in recent times than they were in days gone by. The reason for this apparent decline is unclear. Nevertheless, from time to time they are observed crossing roads and tracks, either as individuals or family groups.

The new green grass which shoots soon after a fire is much sought after by both the Agile Wallaby and the much larger Antilopine Wallaroo. Agile

Agile Wallaby

Wallabies are generally seen in loose colonies and prefer low-lying woodland areas adjacent to paperbark, mangrove or monsoon forests, whereas Antilopine Wallaroos usually occur in family groups and prefer the gently wooded hill country more common in southern parts of the Park. Early morning and late evening are the best times to observe these macropods as they tend to avoid any activity during the heat of the day.

Ecologists and others constantly debate the amount and extent of change that fire has effected to the tropical landscape.

Woodland communities can cope with hotter, dry-season fires, unlike monsoon or paperbark forest. The cooler, early fires, however, are generally lit by humans to remove the dry fuel left over from the wet season and reduce the risk of a serious fire later in the year. Such fires do not pose a serious threat to the vegetation or wildlife. Regular hot fires appear to cause an increase in the amount of native sorghum or spear grass, the primary fuel in woodland fires, thus encouraging a cycle of more frequent hot fires. Regular early burning appears to reverse this trend, thus leading to a less flammable landscape.

A gradual climate shift from moist to dry in monsoonal Australia has also greatly favoured the dominating effect of eucalypt woodland and a

Wedge-tailed Eagle

decrease in monsoon forest.

During late Gurrung and Gunumeleng, lightning strikes frequently cause woodland and grassland fires, some quite extensive and severe. Traditional Bininj dry season burning practices over a long period of time have certainly manipulated the effects of these late natural fires, probably greatly lessening their ecological impact.

During Yegge, the large eagles are breeding. Pairs of Wedge-tails are well spaced across the woodlands of Kakadu and are most frequently seen

along the highways, feeding on the carcasses of road-killed wildlife.

Towards the end of Yegge, Spotted Nightjars arrive in quite large numbers, presumably from colder regions of southern Australia. They are gentle birds, related to the frogmouth and just as

Olive Python

well camouflaged, as they lie motionless in the leaf litter during the day. At night they hawk insects from an open vantage point on the ground and, unfortunately, they often choose a road or a track. Many are killed by vehicles as they rise into the bright headlights dazzled and confused.

Some nocturnal woodland reptiles have gradually become inactive as the days and nights

Children's Python

have become noticeably cooler. The Olive and Children's Pythons, Northern Brown Tree Snake and the delicate Orange-naped Snake are normally the only snakes encountered at night during the cool weather.

Partridge Pigeons are now leading their newly fledged and rather drab-coloured chicks through the woodlands. They regroup as a loose flock after the breeding season and occasionally up to a dozen birds may be seen at once. In the coming months the young birds will moult into their adult colours.

A forest of Prop-rooted Mangroves

MANGROVE FORESTS

There are over thirty species of mangrove trees known to be growing in these tropical waters and each has an individual role to play in the stabilisation of the developing shoreline.

Some tough species face the onslaught of the sea while other larger ones prefer the centre of the forest where they may reach a great height and form a dense canopy, similar to their closely related rainforest cousins. Still others prefer the more arid landward side of the forest where they may only come into contact with the saltwater on the very high tides.

When viewed from the air, the stratification of these forests is much clearer as each species is a slightly different shade of green. This is revealed as a longitudinal band.

As a result of this 'organisation' of the trees, the animals arrange themselves in a similar fashion according to the trees which they relate to. This is perhaps most obvious with the smaller climbing crabs, many of which identify with particular tree species.

The other crab species, such as the Fiddler Crabs (a male is pictured *left*) and the well known Mud Crab, align themselves with the mangrove drainage systems rather than with the advantages a particular tree may provide. While Fiddler Crabs are sedentary and rather territorial, the much larger Mud Crabs frequently move with the tides over long distances.

The landward side of a mangrove forest

Mud Crab

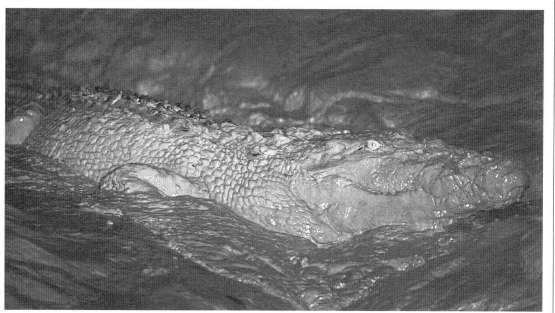

Estuarine Crocodile resting in a tidal gutter at night. Despite their bulk, these crocodiles are very agile in soft mud

Crabs have many enemies and the stately Jabiru rates high among them. Just as much at home in saltwater as in freshwater, they are constantly seen walking the gutters at low tide and probing the burrows and muddy pools with their long, sharp bills. Inside the mangrove forest, the White-bellied Mangrove Snake moves in and out of the larger crab holes, hunting the owners of the burrows and devouring them with slow, python-like muscular contractions.

Mangrove snakes come in a variety of colour patterns, each one with its own unique design. They, in turn, frequently become food for Jabirus in the never-ending mangrove food chain.

Estuarine Crocodiles are more frequently seen using the mangroves from now on as the wetlands gradually dry out. In the cooler weather their metabolic rate slows and they spend much more time basking on the banks and mudbars and less time in the water during the day.

White-bellied Mangrove Snake

Jabiru frequently hunt in the mangroves

The tiny beach at Field Island is of great ecological importance

SHORELINE

As the weather and tides settle into a dry season routine, migratory bird species have all but departed and the inshore waters regain some clarity as the wet season silt settles.

Though few, Kakadu's beaches are typical of the far more extensive beaches of the Arnhem coast away to the north and northeast.

Ghost crabs rule the beaches by night and, in Kakadu, the family is represented by the Smooth-handed Ghost Crab. They are both scavenger and predator to most other creatures their own size or smaller. By day, their presence is indicated only by fresh tracks around their burrow entrances, which have usually been blocked off from the inside by a plug of sand.

Above: Brahminy Kite

Ghost crabs normally keep clear of the water, but will retreat into the sea if cornered. They are a favoured food item of a wide variety of fish, as well as being sought after by foraging Water-rats.

Much smaller Hermit Crabs also share the beaches with the ghost crabs at night. They are often in vast numbers and are very efficient at keeping the beaches clean of all dead material, both plant and animal.

The opposite number to the beach-patrolling crabs is the Shovel-nosed Ray or Skate, which performs a similar task in the shallow water along the beaches. They are particularly noticeable on a rising tide when they eagerly move up the sand with each fresh wave, frequently with their tail and dorsal fins protruding from the water. Their flattened body shape allows them to operate in very shallow water.

Smooth-handed Ghost Crab

Shovel-nosed Ray

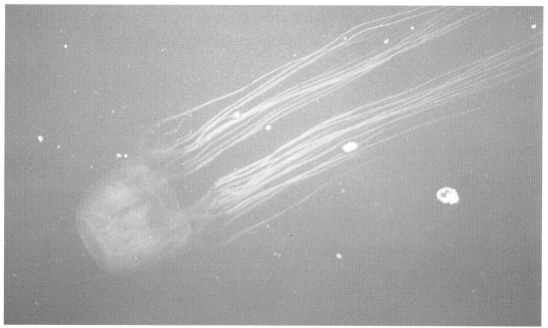

Box Jellyfish or 'Sea Wasp'

A range of predatory fish patrols the inshore waters by day and night, especially around the mangrove nursery areas. They include Mangrove Jack, Queenfish, Trevalley, Barracuda and Black-tipped Sharks. The presence of these fish tends to cause the schools of young fish to hug the shoreline.

In the tropical waters of the Arafura Sea, particularly in the monsoon season, is found a member of the jellyfish family which is known to have a lethal sting when it comes into contact with human skin. It is locally known as a 'Sea Wasp' or, more correctly, Box Jellyfish, and Yegge is traditionally the start of the 'safe' period for humans to be in the water. Box Jellyfish reappear in numbers during Gunumeleng, but have been recorded in all seasons.

The biggest problem with Box Jellyfish is that they are so difficult to see. They inhabit coastal waters, particularly in the vicinity of estuaries and sheltered bays where they pulse slowly along with the tide. The long, sticky tentacles can reach a length of three metres.

Towards the end of Yegge, overnight temperatures become pleasantly cooler as the result of an atmospheric inversion effect. Flowering plants such as paperbarks, wattles and water lilies produce fragrances which are trapped nightly at ground level in this cool air layer, adding to the human experience of Wurrgeng.

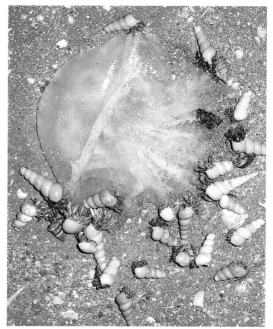

The predatory Barracuda

Hermit Crabs devour a stranded jellyfish

JUNE TO AUGUST

EARLY DRY SEASON

WURRGENG

CHAPTER 4

CHAPTER 4
EARLY DRY SEASON - WURRGENG

This is the main cool weather season. The cool nights of Yegge become cooler still while the days are very pleasant with low temperatures and clear skies. In some low-lying parts of Kakadu during Wurrgeng, overnight temperatures have been recorded as low as 5° C, although temperatures this low are unusual.

Cooler weather makes this a favourable time to visit Kakadu, although there is one major disadvantage. Mosquitoes, which have come through their larval stage in the quietly receding wet season overflow, reach the peak of their adult life in early Wurrgeng. It is essential that visitors to the wetlands take suitable precautions against mosquitoes at this time of year.

The riotous wet-season plant growth has now slowed down and most annuals have turned yellow or brown. The weather remains cool and dry with an occasional passing shower. Both overcast and windy days are not uncommon during Wurrgeng.

Many mammals breed during Wurrgeng. The cool period is the time of greatest activity for all of the carnivorous marsupials, including Djabu the Northern Quoll. These animals have a distinct breeding season during late Yegge and throughout Wurrgeng. This is also the breeding period of Wirk the Northern Brushtail Possum and Lambalk the Sugar Glider. Gowarrang, the Spiny Anteater, is rarely seen by visitors to the Park, although it can be seen in good numbers if you know where to look. It too is breeding at this time.

Left: View from the top of Gunlom during Wurrgeng. Above: The main escarpment face and clear skies

The escarpment's ledges and crevices are home to many endemic species

STONE COUNTRY

The bright orange blossoms of Anmadba, the Scarlet Gum, are now a feature of the rocky sandstone slopes of the escarpment. This is an extremely important tree at this time of year in the sandstone. The nectar-loving friarbirds adopt individual flowering trees and attempt to keep all other birds away from the blossoms, which seems to work sometimes. Other birds arrive in such numbers however that the friarbirds eventually give up in frustration.

In the early mornings, the bird chorus is dominated by the rather raucous but cheerful discussions of the three species of friarbirds which are claiming ownership of the various flowering trees. These are the Silver-crowned Friarbird, a large honeyeater found throughout the woodlands of Kakadu, the Little Friarbird, which is equally common and just as noisy, and the Sandstone or Helmeted Friarbird. The latter, in keeping with its name, is the dominant friarbird in the stone country and its characteristic voice, like that of the White-lined Honeyeater, is part of the spirit of this habitat. This interesting bird also has a strong association with the mangroves and is found throughout the islands north of Australia.

Native bees frequently nest in Scarlet Gums, which also provides them with an ideal source of honey. The rough, orange-coloured fibrous bark gives the tree good protection against hot fires which occur from time to time, and the hollows which form in the mature trees are ideal living sites for many birds and animals.

The entrance to the nest of tiny native bees called Nabiwuh

Northern Grevilleas, which grow in the deeper, sandy soils, are also coming into flower and the rich nectar which drips from the orange blossoms has a very powerful fragrance that permeates the air of the rocky valleys. Lorikeets, honeyeaters and many other birds come and go throughout the day, as do the tiny native bees. For the bees, this is their busiest time and the copious nectar must be gathered and stored. The flavour of this grevillea strongly permeates the Sugarbag at this time of year.

Anmadba, the Scarlet Gum, is now in full flower

Helmeted Friarbird

A Short-eared Rock-wallaby forages beneath a Rock Fig for fallen fruit and flowers

Two species of rock-wallaby are known from Kakadu and both live in colonies at suitable locations throughout the stone country and the associated outliers. These are the Short-eared Rock-wallaby, or Badbong, and the much smaller Nabarlek. Both are very shy animals, well camouflaged in their natural habitat, and they usually only allow a quick glimpse before silently disappearing into the rocks. Lots of small, compact droppings on the sandstone indicate the presence of the elusive rock-wallabies.

Badbong (pronounced bud-bong) are by far the most common and widespread. They are usually found living close to permanent water, with access to the softer grasses at the base of the escarpment. They are most active at night and feed on a variety of sandstone plants, shrubs and fruit. One of their favourites is the fruit and leaves of the Rock Fig, which is a common tree in the stone country. They even enjoy eating the dry, fallen leaves of this tree.

In the cool, early mornings of Wurrgeng, rock-wallabies can be seen basking in the first sunlight, their bodies hunched up and their backs turned towards the sun. This can be the best time to observe them because they are reluctant to move from their warm positions.

The distribution of the Nabarlek is less clear. Its dainty appearance is very similar to a half-grown Short-eared Rock-wallaby and the two species are known to share the same habitat. This makes it very difficult for an untrained person to distinguish between the two species.

Nabarleks are unique in the kangaroo world because they have molar teeth which are constantly replaced. This is probably due to the amount of grit they chew while feeding. They show a preference for inhabiting the sandstone outliers close to the coastal plains. In the dry times, they like to move from the rocks down to the low, grassy valleys to graze at night, but they never move more than a few hundred metres from the safety of the rocks.

Rock-wallabies bask in the morning sun

105

The rock-wallabies share their habitat with two larger kangaroos. The largest is the Euro, locally known as Galkberd (pronounced gulk-bed). This is one of Australia's most widespread kangaroos, although the type found in the Alligator Rivers region is classified as a unique sub-species. The other is a smaller relative of the Euro called the Black Wallaroo or Barrk.

Barrk is a unique animal. It is found only in the rugged northwestern part of the Arnhem Plateau, giving it one of the smallest distributions of any Australian kangaroo. However, within that area they are relatively common, but rarely encountered by humans. They are dark coloured, very shy and come out at night. Widespread in Kakadu, they are beginning to become accustomed to human intrusion into their habitat and there are more and

The energetic Sandstone Antechinus

Male Rock Possums actively defend their mate and young ones

more sightings around art sites and lookouts.

Djorrgurn, the Rock Possum, is a specially modified member of the ringtail possum family. Its tail is much shorter and thicker and its hands much broader than the other ringtails, and this has

come about through a long association with the rugged sandstone cliffs and ledges.

Rock Possums are usually found in the same places as rock-wallabies and this is partly because they have similar diets. They are largely leaf-eaters and expert tree-climbers, and they too are very fond of the products of the Rock Fig. By day, they sleep in cool, breezy crevices with several escape routes in case of predators and they always seem to be in pairs. They are strongly territorial and have quite small home ranges. Some pairs live on very small islands of sandstone.

The smallest marsupial in the stone country is the Sandstone Antechinus, which is in the same group of carnivores as the Northern Quoll, the Brush-tailed Phascogale and the Fawn Antechinus. Like most of the sandstone mammals, it is nocturnal, but can often be seen in the late afternoon as it frenetically searches between the boulders for grasshoppers, skinks, geckos and other small prey. These small carnivores have a very high metabolic rate and the urge to satisfy their hunger often drives them from their hiding places quite early in the day. It pays to move quietly about in the sandstone during the late afternoon and you may well be rewarded with a good view of some of these unique animals.

Euro at dawn

Nawaran, the Oenpelli Python, relaxes in a dark sandstone recess

One of the major predators in this rugged country, in addition to the Dingo, is Nawaran the Oenpelli Rock Python, and the old Bininj are quick to point out that this large snake is one of the greatest predators of rock-wallabies.

Many of the mammals in this habitat are breeding at this time of year. Female Black Wallaroos are carrying young in the pouch, as are the other sandstone-dwelling members of the kangaroo family. Rock Possums too are carrying their single baby on the back and it is carefully guarded by the adults of the group. At night, males will challenge an intruder larger than themselves (including humans) if the female is threatened. This involves much grunting and tail-slapping until the intruder moves off. Behaviour of this kind is not known in other members of the possum family.

Ghost Bat females congregate in certain caves to give birth to their young which are born in late Wurrgeng. These maternity colonies may have many thousands of females or simply a few dozen. When the young are born, they cling to the mother's stomach and feed from the nipple under her armpit. When she flies, they hook their legs backwards over her shoulders and face the opposite direction, creating less drag as well as keeping their heads out of the wind.

The tiny but highly animated Sandstone Antechinus, which has relatives in the Kimberley and Central Australia, also has a specific breeding season synchronised with the cool weather. The young are born about the middle of Wurrgeng and cling tenaciously to their hyperactive mother for some weeks while she pursues insects around the rugged sandstone rock faces. Although nocturnal, they can frequently be seen late in the afternoon foraging amongst boulders and along ledges, or even basking in the late afternoon sunlight. If the observer is quiet, these little marsupials can be quite bold.

Ghost Bats remain wary throughout the day

Sharing the same sandstone ledges as the Sandstone Antechinus is the Arnhem Land Crevice-skink, a powerfully built but extremely shy lizard which lives in colonies amongst the rocks. It is active mostly in the late afternoon and early evening and quickly disappears deep into the sandstone recesses at the first hint of danger.

Arnhem Land Crevice-skink

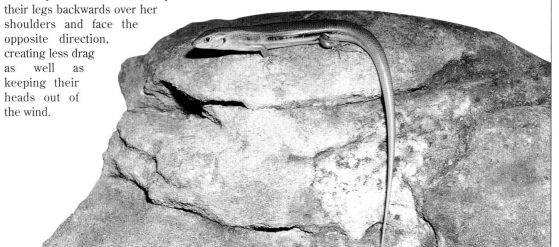

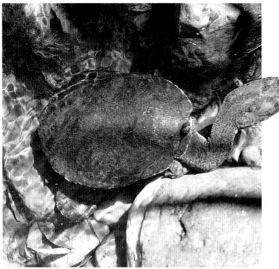

Burrungandji, the rare long-necked turtle from the sandstone

many of the sandstone plants, such as spinifex, are quite volatile. However, in earlier days, Bininj reduced this problem with their cool, patchwork burning beginning early in Yegge, which prevented bigger fires from spreading too far.

There have been some major social changes since the days when Ludwig Leichhardt passed this way. Today, with far fewer Bininj to cover these vast areas, the Australian Nature Conservation Agency is addressing the problem with technology to achieve the same effect.

Fire has been a constant component in the sandstone ecology for a long time and it appears that most plants and animals have developed ways to survive or avoid the potentially lethal effects of intense fires. Regeneration on the whole is rapid. Some species, however, like Aldjurr the beautiful

Since the declaration of Kakadu, another interesting reptile has come to light. It is a large long-necked turtle with an elliptical shell and a very large neck and head. It is yet to receive a scientific name. Unlike Almangiyi, its relative from the floodplains, this one emits a strong defensive odour when handled. It lives in the fast-flowing freshwater streams of the escarpment country where it ambushes fish and other aquatic animals from beneath logs and branches at the bottom of rapids. Another interesting feature is strong brown freckling on the creamy undersurface.

Gracing the sides of the pools where this turtle lives is a tiny, orchid-like flower with no common name. It is one of a number of aquatic plants in the bladderwort family which grow in very wet, sunny situations. The attractive, orange-coloured flowers often appear in dense swathes in the rocky creek beds, enduring the dry months by defying the sun's heat.

At this time of the year, fire can sweep through the sandstone community. On occasions, fires burn across the Arnhem Plateau from the east, southeast or the south, fanned by the dry season trade winds and these can be quite extensive as

Tiny orange Bladderworts grow in a creekbed

Leichhardt's Grasshopper, or Anlarr the Northern Cypress Pine, appear to suffer serious setbacks to their populations with intense fires. Some of the most intense fires in Kakadu are triggered by lightning in Gunumeleng and this subject is discussed in that chapter.

Most of the sandstone frogs have already found their way into the cool recesses of the water-worn tunnels and caves by the beginning of Wurrgeng, before the hot weather arrives. There they remain, preserved in cool, moist air and wearing their drab, non-breeding colours until that day in Gunumeleng when the humidity begins to rise.

Distinctive speckled underside of the long-necked turtle from the sandstone streams

Volatile spinifex clumps flare in a sandstone fire

The dense canopy of a lowland monsoon forest

Eel-tailed Catfish seek refuge in spring-fed monsoon forest streams

MONSOON FORESTS

Much of the surface water left over from the previous rains has dried up and the remainder will soon be gone. Many of the pockets of monsoon forest in the escarpment valleys and under the cliffs have established themselves on permanent springs and moisture seeps. Often the chain of clear pools resulting from these springs only goes a short distance and is absorbed by the porous, sandy soils of the lowlands, even though they may be connected to the river systems in the wet months. In the dry months, these places are like oases to the animal life.

Schools of young Eel-tailed Catfish, Sooty Grunters, Purple-spotted Gudgeons, Saratoga and Primitive Archerfish are often seen together in these forest-clad pools. The food supply is relatively rich and energy expenditure is low. When the rains come and the streams begin to flow, the fish move downstream to fulfil their life cycles, but their offspring seem to find their way back each year.

Invertebrate life in the forest is quite diverse at this time of year, but many of the interesting ones are small and unobtrusive. You need to take time and look closely.

Brilliantly coloured Harlequin Bugs (*inset left*) cling to the undersides of fig leaves during their periods of inactivity and, at night, the large and wide-ranging Fruit-piercing Moth can be found drinking the juices from the fruit of the Cluster Fig. This productive tree provides food for many forest animals including native rodents, possums, flying-foxes, bandicoots and wallabies. It is also enjoyed by a variety of birds, but for the tree, this popularity has the great advantage of spreading the tiny seeds far and wide.

Fruit-piercing Moth on Cluster Figs

Northern Brushtail feeds among Cluster Figs

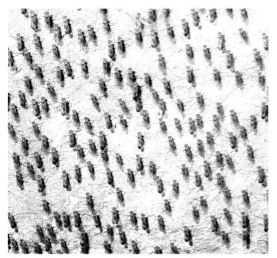

A mass of tiny, moisture-loving flies on wet sandstone

The acrobatic Northern Fantail feeds on the tiny flies (left)

An innocuous little fruit-fly inhabits the escarpment forests and it suddenly draws attention to itself by assembling in thousands on the cool rock surfaces surrounding springs and soaks. Each fly faces exactly the same direction with uniform spacing. When disturbed, they all rise in a buzzing cloud, but soon resettle in the same position. The reason for this aggregation and peculiar behaviour, like so much of the tropical world of nature, is not yet understood.

A jewel in the forest invertebrate life is the tiny Spiny Spider, sometimes called the 'Hang Glider Spider'. It can easily go unnoticed because of its size and, if disturbed, it invariably turns its colourful back away from the disturbance. Close examination of its carapace reveals a work of art unrivalled among the spider fraternity of Kakadu.

The other notable spider of these forests is the giant black and yellow Golden Orb Spider, which is found throughout the tropical world from Australia to Africa. The female spins her remarkably strong and sticky web in the understorey of the forest, often near or over water in areas of low light. A number of tiny, orange-coloured males can usually be found within the perimeter of her web.

Life for them is tenuous. Her main prey items are larger insects, such as butterflies (*above*) and beetles, but lizards, frogs, bats and small birds have also been recorded as victims of this amazing web. Fortunately, the spider is no threat to humans, although bites are reputed to be painful.

The Common Rock-rat has a close relative called the Arnhem Land Rock-rat, but this rodent is nowhere near as common as its smaller cousin. Arnhem Land Rock-rats prefer the heavier vegetation of monsoon forest-clad valleys or where sandstone adjoins well-vegetated billabongs. They generally keep a very low profile.

The cheerful Northern Fantail is one of the more frequent and noticeable users of the forests and the fringing woodlands as it pursues the myriads of small flying insects seeking refuge in the forest canopy.

Living quietly in the overlap zone between the forest and the woodlands is the beautiful Marbled Velvet Gecko. This large gecko is a tree-dweller. It spends the day beneath exfoliating bark on the tree trunks or inside hollow limbs and emerges in the evening to hunt both on the tree trunks and on the ground. Its very close relative, the Dotted Velvet Gecko, has specialised on the sandstone rock faces rather than the trees.

Marbled Velvet Gecko

RIVERS & BILLABONGS

The river systems have all returned to their normal dry-season levels. In the upstream pools, water plants are flourishing now that the current has slowed down. Myriads of hatchling fish hug the shallow weed beds as large numbers of dragonflies in a variety of colours hover and dart over the water surface. Primitive Archerfish and schools of young Eel-tailed Catfish have returned to the shady escarpment springwater streams for the duration of the dry months. Together with Saratoga, Sooty Grunters, various rainbowfish and the beautiful little Black-blotched Analfin Grunter,

There are at least four kinds of rainbowfish in Kakadu's streams

The beautiful Spotted Scat loses its colours as it grows

they make the crystal clear pools of the escarpment forests a most captivating sight.

Further downstream amongst the pandanus and paperbarks, the time has come for the Freshwater Crocodiles to begin nesting. In this time of plenty, the Freshwater Crocodiles spend a lot more time out of water basking, as the overnight temperatures can remain quite low for the first weeks of Wurrgeng. Basking is an important activity for the crocodiles as it helps bring their body temperatures to a suitable

operational level. They also eat very little at this time while their metabolic rate is so low. They can be quite reluctant to move from a sunny spot when they are cold. Downstream, the Estuarine Crocodiles are doing the same thing and this is perhaps the best time of year to view them. Night is their main feeding and activity period and, at this time of year, the Freshwater species appears much more active.

Females have laid their eggs in the warm, sandy banks and keep a watchful eye on the nest-site from the water. Monitors and feral pigs are the major threats to the eggs but, once they hatch, there are

Pig-nosed Turtles leave the water only to lay their eggs

many more dangers. High on the list of threats to hatchlings are other crocodiles, pythons, sea-eagles and most of the larger fish. There are so many dangers that it is surprising that any young ones survive to adulthood.

Pig-nosed Turtles too are preparing to lay eggs in the moist sandbanks beside the deep billabongs. Like the marine turtle, this is a totally aquatic species and only the female leaves the water briefly at night to lay her eggs. The eggs develop during Wurrgeng and Gurrung and hatch in late Gunumeleng as the first floodwaters begin to cover the sandbanks. When the water makes contact with the eggshell, the young turtles break out and feverishly dash for deeper water.

The fine-toothed Freshwater Crocodile

Distinctive skies and deciduous trees signify Wurrgeng on the rivers

Only metres from the habitat of the Pig-nosed Turtle, among the paperbark trunks and fallen fronds of pandanus, lives a very colourful but shy little marsupial called a Red-cheeked Dunnart. Active by night, this little carnivore is mainly associated with the heavier vegetation of the river corridors and adjacent swampy grassland areas. It is at this time of year that the female Red-cheeked Dunnart produces her six or so young ones, which she then carries with her for many weeks.

Further downstream in the tidal section of the rivers, some of the larger trees are beginning to drop their leaves. The majestic Kapok Trees, with their solid but thorny trunks, are the first to shed their wet season foliage. The symmetrical crowns of these large trees are a favourite nesting site for Jabiru and the young birds are growing fast during Wurrgeng.

The giant stick nest gives the young birds a commanding view of the surrounding wetlands. The parent birds glide from the nest across the wetlands to the feeding areas, only to return with morsels like One-gilled Eels, Arafura File Snakes, Eel-tailed Catfish or young Barramundi. By Gunumeleng, the young birds themselves are down on the feeding grounds with the parents. Their drab colouration is in stark contrast to the brilliant plumage of the adults. It will be at least 12 months before they moult into their adult colours.

The silt-laden estuarine waters are suitable only to specialised river-dwellers such as Barramundi and Estuarine Crocodiles but, from time to time, fauna from the clearer waters of Van Diemen Gulf find their way into the rivers of Kakadu. Dugong, Green Turtles, various sea-snakes and dolphins are all sighted occasionally in the rivers. One dolphin, however, is accustomed to life in these murky estuarine waters. It is known as the Irrawaddy River Dolphin and small schools of these now rare marine mammals are regularly seen in the tidal sections of the Kakadu rivers. They are quite a small dolphin, pale in colour and with no pronounced beak.

Red-cheeked Dunnart

Surface water is contracting to the channels and gutters of the plains

FLOODPLAINS

Wurrgeng is an interesting time on the floodplains of Kakadu. The surface water is disappearing fast and the ephemeral vegetation is dying off. In many places, the black soil is already cracked and dried. Animals like the Dusky Rat and the Common Planigale have moved back on to the plains from the adjacent woodlands and the Dusky Rats are in rapid breeding mode.

The abundance of the Dusky Rats attracts an interesting range of predators, from local inhabitants like the Dingo, Yellow Spotted Monitor, King Brown Snake, Barn Owl and Water Python, to itinerant predators such as the Grass Owl and Letter-winged Kite. Despite this impressive range of enemies, the Dusky Rats keep multiplying till the rains arrive.

Letter-winged Kites and Grass Owls can suddenly

A Grass Owl rises from its daytime roost at the approach of danger

appear in large numbers on the plains at the peak of the Dusky Rat's breeding cycle and exploit the abundance. They can then disappear as quickly as they came and may not be sighted again in the area for several seasons. Letter-winged Kites have the advantage of being able to hunt at night as well as by day.

Grass Owls, which are uncommon over most of their range, can occasionally be seen in loose groups of between 60 and 80 birds on the floodplains of the Alligator Rivers, camped in the tall swathes of blady grass by day. They take to the air and patrol the plains by night and may be seen in vehicle headlights standing on roads in the vicinity of floodplains. They are easily distinguished from the more plentiful Barn Owl by their greater size and extremely long legs.

Water Python eating a Dusky Rat

Garrkanj, the ever-watchful Brown Falcon

One of the most common and easily recognised birds on the floodplains during the dry periods is Garrkanj, the Brown Falcon. Featuring strongly in Bininj mythology, this bird is the sentinel of the plains, perching on regular vantage points and launching itself down on skinks, dragons and grasshoppers, or occasionally a young Dusky Rat or Common Planigale. During floodplain fires, this bird becomes particularly active, darting in and out of the flames to capture fleeing creatures and often displaying some fancy footwork while on the ground.

The similar-looking but slightly larger Black Falcon is also seen on the floodplains, but not as regularly as its Brown cousin.

Kakadu has many migratory birds, most of which arrive in the 'build-up' period of late Gurrung and early Gunumeleng and stay over the wet months. However, a few species do the opposite. The Australian Pratincole and the Spotted Nightjar are two such examples.

The delicate Pratincoles are a common, dry

season occurrence on the floodplains, particularly during Wurrgeng to Gunumeleng and they appear to be able to withstand the shimmering heat better than any other bird.

The rapid drying effect of Wurrgeng means that animals which depend upon surface water need to find an alternative solution quickly—or perish. Needless to say, each plant or animal in this habitat has a way of coping. Waterbirds simply move away to permanent water. Estuarine Crocodiles often undertake a cross-country walk, once the food

Letter-winged Kite

supply has run out or the water body is too limited. The walk, which may involve many kilometres through a variety of habitats, is usually the shortest possible route back to permanent water and is often undertaken at night. While the accuracy of the crocodile is surprising, there are many dangers involved. The big reptiles are cumbersome and vulnerable away from water. In several recorded instances, they are known to have been caught in bushfires in transit and killed.

Geese begin to mass together on the drying plains after the breeding season

Other less adventurous crocodiles may opt to remain in the area of the dry waterhole and retreat into a tunnel beneath the root system of a paperbark tree, or to dense ferns and other heavy fringing vegetation around tributary lowland springs, or simply bury in the mud on the exposed plains. In the latter case, some crocodiles sustain severe sunburn when all the moisture evaporates and the rains of Gunumeleng are late arriving. This can also result in the death of the animal. The bulk of the Estuarine Crocodile population, however, has contracted back to the tidal sections of the larger rivers till the rains come.

The disturbed turtle peers into the sunlight

the energy reserve which the turtles depend upon when the water eventually dries up. They simply select a suitable spot in the soft mud and burrow in, creating a small chamber with a tiny airhole to the outside world. As the blacksoil dries completely, it sets like concrete, locking the turtles in to their earthen prisons until the following rains release them.

Turtle with lots of body fat is a favourite food of Bininj, who know how to locate the cunning reptiles by the telltale airhole and slight disturbance marks in the setting mud. Many of the rock-art paintings of this turtle show quite clearly the prized yellow fat deposits.

Northern Long-necked Turtle

Another floodplains reptile which specialises in burying in the mud is Almangiyi, the Northern Long-necked Turtle. This truly remarkable reptile can survive the wettest and the dryest times on the floodplains and associated paperbark swamps.

During the wet times the turtles are feeding heavily on a wide variety of aquatic animal life, especially frogs, tadpoles and fish. By the end of Yegge, this excess living has provided the turtles with a large build-up of body fat. This then becomes

Trained eyes spot the telltale signs of a buried turtle

The turtle sits in its moist compartment 10-15 cm under the surface

The lilies have reached their peak and now begin to die off

PAPERBARK SWAMPS

The water is now contracting to the deeper central parts of the swamp where the lilies continue to flower profusely. The seeds of the Giant Water Lily are now developing on the muddy bottom, as the flower stems curve downwards into the water once the lily flowers have been pollinated. These seed-heads are collected in large numbers by Bininj women at this time of year as the oily seeds are a rich, sweet-tasting food which can either be eaten raw or baked into little cakes. The stems, flowers and bulbs of this useful plant are also edible, being particularly popular with children.

As the mud is gradually exposed by the drying swamps, the long-necked turtles are burrowing into the mud beneath the swamp grasses and lilies in anticipation of the long dry period ahead. Their fat reserves have been building up since the last rains and by Wurrgeng they are ready for a long sleep.

The Northern Long-necked Turtles are a very important food item to Bininj and from now until Gunumeleng the 'turtle sticks' will be probing the likely places for fat Almangiyi.

Estuarine Crocodiles too will be retreating from the food-rich drying swamps. The bulk of them will make their way back to the river channels, but some, like the turtles, will prefer to aestivate in the mud or beneath tree roots.

Both the Little Red and the Black Flying-foxes are regular visitors to the paperbark trees when they are flowering. Their noisy squabbling in the blossoms can be easily heard at night and the following morning there is the telltale evidence on the ground

A Black Flying-fox peers from the foliage

beneath the trees in the form of fallen blossoms and broken branchlets. These clumsy-looking megabats are actually quite efficient pollinators of the paperbark trees and are a vital link in the paperbark swamp ecosystem.

Flying-foxes themselves have many enemies and under the dark canopy of the paperbark forests lurks one of their major predators. The elusive and rarely seen Rufous Owl sleeps by day high in the taller thickets of the paperbarks. By approaching quietly, it is possible to catch one sleeping with a partly devoured flying-fox in one talon. These impressive owls, the largest in Kakadu, specialise in preying upon larger mammals such as possums, bandicoots and, most frequently, flying-foxes.

An inquisitive Northern Quoll

TROPICAL WOODLANDS

Female quolls are now carrying three to five young ones around on their backs while hunting at night. This only lasts for a week or so until the young are able to run and keep up with the mother as she feverishly searches for insects, reptiles or nesting birds. The young ones soon become independent and generally

The phascogale is the second largest marsupial carnivore in Kakadu

live a solitary life until Wurrgeng comes around again.

Brush-tailed Phascogales are doing much the same thing, although they are generally more secretive and wary of approach than their larger, spotted cousins. They are more squirrel-like in their movements and spend more of their time foraging in and out of hollows and up and down tree trunks. They also have a specific breeding season in Wurrgeng, allowing the young ones to grow up on the benefits of the wet season energy flow-on.

Fawn Antechinus

Further still down the woodland carnivore scale is the Fawn Antechinus. This small animal, like the Brush-tailed Phascogale, is an excellent climber and divides its nocturnal energy between scouring the tree trunks and foraging on the ground amongst the leaf litter. It seems to prefer taller eucalypt forest, although populations of this animal, one of Australia's largest antechinuses, do not occur everywhere in Kakadu where there is suitable habitat. Populations are patchy,

The streamlined Orange-sided Bar-lipped Skink

occurring mainly in forests of the South Alligator catchment.

Many areas of woodland have now been burned and circling flocks of Black Kites attracted by the fires are a common sight. They compete with each other to swoop and dive through the flames to grab fleeing insects and reptiles, many of which seem to make it to the safety of abandoned monitor burrows ahead of the flames and kites.

Pale Field Rat

One such reptile seen scuttling through the leaves on such occasions is the beautifully streamlined Orange-sided Bar-lipped Skink. Normally active from sunset and on into the evening, they aggressively hunt invertebrates in the deep litter of woodland and monsoon forest.

Fire also discloses the presence in the woodlands of the Pale Field Rat, which lives in colonies where sandy soils occur. Numerous burrow entrances and excavated mounds of sandy soil, usually concealed by

Fires are now more intense

The result of a 'hot' fire

Pandanus, though highly flammable, are resistant to fire

The nectar-bearing Woollybutt flowers

Varied Lorikeet feeding on Woollybutt blossom

the tangled woodland grasses, betray the presence of this handsome native rodent. Both the Varied and the Red-collared Lorikeets are feverishly exploiting the prolific blossoms of Wurrgeng and excited flocks of these brightly coloured birds can be seen noisily flying between the feeding sites.

Varied Lorikeets travel in small, fast-flying flocks over large distances and do not remain long in any particular place. Their movement is dictated by the blossoms of particular trees, particularly the bloodwood group. Red-collared Lorikeets remain all year in a much smaller home range, exploiting a much wider range of blossoms and a variety of seeds.

Stringybark flowers are a feature of Yegge and Wurrgeng

Red-winged Parrot about to open a Kapok Bush pod for the seeds

Red-tailed Black Cockatoo in a Bridal Tree

At this time, the Red-tailed Black Cockatoos may choose to remain feeding in the trees on the various fruit and seeds or to feed on the build-up of seeds on the ground. Immediately following a fire, large flocks of these can be seen cracking seed on the exposed ground. The red tails of the males make a spectacular show when the flock rises.

Meanwhile, the yellow flowers of the Kapok Bush have set seed and the large green pods are now appearing in the place of the flowers. The pods will turn brown by Gurrung and split open to reveal a puffy, white, cotton-like filling in which the seeds are borne. The seeds are a favoured food of the Red-winged Parrot and these beautiful birds usually don't wait until the pods turn brown before they chew holes in them.

Closer to ground level, Striated Pardalotes (*inset right*) are nesting in small tunnels dug into sandy banks. They commonly choose roadside embankments for the nest-site and it is not unusual during Yegge and Wurrgeng to see these tiny birds rising bullet-like from their tunnels as your vehicle passes.

Most eucalypts, and many other tree species, are piped by termites when they are only saplings.

This immediately gives the impression that they have been weakened and thus do not have much of a future. However, the reverse is true. The termites are actually opening up a whole range of possibilities.

Recent ecological studies into the role of termites in the woodlands have brought to light some interesting facts. For instance, many eucalypts grow in very poor soils; in fact, the soils can be so deficient in nutrients that they are incapable of sustaining normal tree growth. Yet, trees grow there. Further investigation showed that colonies of termites, nature's recyclers, living within the trees were importing nutrients, in the form of harvested litter and grasses, from the surrounding area for their own use. Indirectly, the trees were extracting a percentage of this food. Thus, the quality of life for the tree was greatly improved by the presence of the termites.

The termites gain access to the young saplings through cracks in the roots caused by dry season soil stresses when the natural chemical defences of the trees outer layers are temporarily breached.

Pandanus trees showing that fire has not occurred here for some time

Later in the life of the mature tree, the termite colony will move to a younger tree, leaving behind a system of hollows which then become homes for many woodland creatures. The continued use of the tree hollows by pythons, monitors, quolls, possums, parrots, owls, kookaburras and many other creatures ensures a continued supply of additional food for the tree.

Bininj also find termites nesting material extremely useful for burning as a mosquito repellent, as a heating agent and for flavouring meats during underground cooking of large animals, such as kangaroos and Emus. The smoke from smouldering termite nest material is used as a purifying agent with childbirth, for both mother and child.

Termites harvesting grass

The inner 'carton' of the termite nest repels mosquitoes when burned

Mangrove forests protect the shores of Barron Island

MANGROVE FORESTS

Mangrove forests may be used by several sets of fauna, particularly at this time of the year and on into the dry. Primary use is by those species that are unique to the mangrove habitat, such as Chestnut Rails, Red-headed Honeyeaters, Yellow White-eyes and Mangrove Monitors. There are also those species which exploit the mangroves from adjoining habitats, particularly open woodland and monsoon forest.

A Chestnut Rail forages along the tideline of Field Island at night

A Northern Brushtail forages through the mangroves

Mangroves and monsoon forest have much in common. The tree species are largely related, mangroves being highly specialised forms of rainforest trees, and the wildlife therefore has little difficulty in moving between the two. In areas where monsoon forest grows alongside mangrove forest, birds appear to treat the two as one unit, exploiting nectar, fruit or insects according to season. Chestnut Rails visit monsoon forest patches and Orange-footed Scrubfowl frequently venture into the mangroves. Carpet Pythons and Northern Brown Tree Snakes also move between the two habitats as well as the Northern Brushtail Possum.

The Deciduous Mangrove stands out in Wurrgeng

There is some evidence to support the opinion that populations of Northern Brushtails live permanently in mangroves. Their tracks may be found in the mangrove mud in the early morning at any time of the year and individuals have been observed foraging along the high-tide mark at night in search of mangrove fruit and other morsels brought in by the tide. Bininj elders talk of hunting possum in the mangroves in earlier times by searching the hollows of larger mangrove species, such as *Bruguiera*.

The tiny and little-known False Water Rat has been observed at night at low tide foraging among the tree roots in the mangroves of the Kakadu coast, but as yet, no further biological information has been brought to light on the species. As with much of our more obscure wildlife, this little rodent is probably more plentiful than we think.

The various shades of mangrove green are broken at this time of year by the beautiful yellows and oranges of the Deciduous Mangrove as they shed their leaves. These colourful leaves soon end up piled on the high tide mark to be broken down over the next few months by marine creatures and the elements. In places, large amounts of mangrove detritus are dumped by the tide, then buried under layers of silt and mud—an ideal base for a future forest.

At the rear of the forest the stabilisation process is more advanced

Mangroves line the mouth of the East Alligator River at Point Farewell

SHORELINE

The sediment from the previous rains is now settling and, with the improvement in water visibility, it is sometimes possible to see various marine mammals, particularly from the air. Pilot Whales, dolphins and Dugong are commonly found in these waters. In the murky inshore waters, it is mainly the Irrawaddi River Dolphin and the Dugong that are regularly seen but, unlike the dolphins, the Dugong is quite cautious about disclosing its presence.

Of the five common species of marine or sea turtles that frequent the Van Diemen Gulf, only one regularly nests on the limited beaches of the Kakadu coast. This is the Alabika or Flatback Turtle, which is also the only endemic species of sea turtle in Australian waters.

Flatbacks appear to be the only species which enjoys the cloudy waters of the Kakadu estuaries and coastline. The other species prefer to keep to the clearer reef waters well away from the estuaries, although both the Green and the Hawksbill Turtles turn up from time to time in the rivers, where they are sometimes eaten by crocodiles.

In Kakadu, Flatback Turtles appear to have two distinct nesting times. The major one is in Wurrgeng and a second but smaller one is in Gunumeleng. The female Flatbacks select beaches on Field Island and between the Wildman and West Alligator Rivers.

Dugong on the beach

A female Flatback Turtle lumbers up the beach

Dry surface sand is flung away

A Yellow Spotted Monitor patrols the beach

Up to fifty eggs are deposited in the egg chamber

They come ashore at night, normally on a rising tide, to lay an average clutch of around forty soft-shelled eggs. After filling in the egg chamber, the females will often lumber off some distance, throwing loose sand behind them in an effort to disguise the location of the eggs. Unfortunately, this does not deter the excellent sensory powers of their major predators, the Yellow Spotted Monitor and the Dingo. On the mainland beaches, Dingos account for most clutches of turtle eggs and the present survival rate is alarmingly low. On Field Island, where Dingos are absent, goannas account for many eggs, but hatching rates appear to be

Flatback hatchlings

much healthier. It is difficult to know just what happens to the young turtles once they scurry down the beaches and disappear into the water, but good numbers of adults in Van Diemen Gulf attest to a reasonable survival rate.

Anrebel flowers which heralded the start of Wurrgeng are now carpeting the ground. Another seasonal change is about to take place. Once the pleasant days of Wurrgeng are past, the hot, dry weather returns and the natural systems prepare for the other annual extreme.

Monitor tracks over turtle tracks

AUGUST TO OCTOBER

HOT DRY SEASON

GURRUNG

CHAPTER 5

CHAPTER 5

HOT DRY SEASON - GURRUNG

This season begins as the last blossoms of Anrebel, the Darwin Stringybark, fall from the trees. Smoke haze fills the skies from numerous woodland fires further to the east. The gentle easterly winds are accompanied by light, scattered cloud. Each day is much the same.

Conditions have now moved to the other extreme of the seasonal spectrum. This is the 'tough' season, the time of greatest pressure on all life forms. The days soon become intensely hot and surface water is extremely scarce. The light, easterly breezes which drift across the Top End tend to be deflected by the Arnhem Plateau, leaving the Alligator Rivers catchments hotter than most other coastal areas.

Entire plant communities may go into 'stress mode' by shedding or drooping their leaves to conserve moisture. The remaining leaves often yellow and curl, giving the trees a gaunt appearance. This is merely a strategy which is easily reversed with the next shower of rain. The tree itself remains quite healthy and can continue in this condition for much longer.

The animals too experience this seasonal pressure. Herbivores such as Agile Wallabies are forced further and further away from cover in search of green pick; hunger drives them out earlier in the day and keeps them out later in the morning than at other times of the year. This makes them more vulnerable to Dingo attack and subsequently they display a much greater degree of nervousness. Very few young ones are produced at this time of the year.

Reptiles which are normally diurnal, such as the King and Western Brown Snakes and the Common Northern Blue-tongue, revert to night hunting in order to avoid the excessive daytime heat.

Frogs are now very difficult to find as all but a few species are tucked away in safe places until conditions improve. Some, however, like the Dwarf Green Tree-frog, can still be seen during the day sitting quietly in the thorny leaf-shafts of pandanus thickets. These delicate little frogs display a great deal of tenacity in hot, dry weather, which is characteristic perhaps of all life forms living in the wet-dry tropics.

Left: A view of the northern outliers from Ubirr Lookout. Above: Tilted sandstone bed of Nawulandja outlier. Inset: Inactive Masked Rock-frog

STONE COUNTRY

This habitat more than any other in Kakadu exhibits the extremes of a monsoon climate. In Gudjewg it is awash with swamps, pools and streams, but most of these are activated seasonally by rainwater and run-off. This surface water soon dries up and by Gurrung, the habitat becomes intensely arid.

Nevertheless, dotted throughout this arid landscape are waterholes, springs and soaks which are well known both to Bininj and to the other life forms with which they share the landscape. This vital knowledge of the whereabouts of drinking water is woven into the language and lives of Bininj in the form of stories, legends and songs. If language is allowed to die, thousands of years of accumulated environmental information dies with it. Thus the various Bininj languages of Kakadu are extremely important to the future management of the land.

All of the sensitive animals in this habitat are now tucked away from the extremes of light, heat and dryness. Many of them can be found by exploring the underground drainage systems in the sandstone. Pools of water in caves create micro-environments which are cooler, more moist and have better air circulation than elsewhere. The complex tracks in the fine sands on the floor of these caves attest to the amount of use these places receive from wildlife.

Some of these animals are emerging from a state

Little Brown Bats in aestivation in a sandstone cave

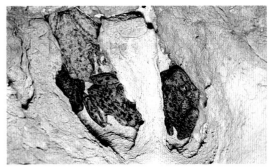

Copland's Rock Frogs tucked away in a cave for the dry months

of semi-torpor in Gurrung, after the cool weather of Yegge and Wurrgeng, although they will not become active until well into Gunumeleng. This particularly applies to the frogs and bats.

The greens turn to yellows on the plateau during Gurrung

The escarpment edge is not always distinct and may be shrouded in foliage of Anbinik trees

Ghost Bats, however, remain active throughout the dry months and the females are now flying with their large young ones clinging to their chests. By day the females tend to gather in isolated maternity groups in suitably humid caves and, once the young reach a certain size, they are left behind while the mother flies off to forage at night.

The beautiful and particularly shy Banded Fruit-dove, one of a number of endemic species in this sandstone country, can be more easily seen at this time of year as it comes down to drink at springs and seepage points at the base of cliffs. Sitting quietly and observing the wildlife drinking at these places in the late afternoon can be a very worthwhile exercise during the hot weather of Gurrung.

A most unusual member of the goanna family, the Black-palmed Rock Monitor, lives and hunts among the large boulders and slabs of the escarpment country. It is shy and difficult to approach and most often seen around sunset when it basks on the warm rocks warmed by the last rays of the sun. At this time monitors are

The elusive Black-palmed Rock Monitor

reluctant to move and can be quietly approached. They are easily identified by their creamy white tail-tips.

In the same habitat, a tiny tree-climbing gecko related to the Marbled Velvet Gecko can be seen at night stalking insects on the thin branches of the sandstone shrubs. Like so many of the small creatures which inhabit this rugged sandstone, it awaits scientific classification.

A tiny undescribed Velvet Gecko hunts on sandstone shrubs

Rock-wallabies move down to the foot of the escarpment at night...

...to graze on the green pick that remains

Kangaroos are now finding the going a little tough in the stone country. Green pick is very scarce and the best grazing is now in the vicinity of the foot of the escarpment. The grassy blacksoil valleys still manage to produce fresh growth from deep moisture reserves, particularly after fire. During Gurrung it is not uncommon to find all four species of sandstone kangaroos foraging in the same area at night. Limited water supplies also help to keep these marsupials in close proximity.

Just as native sorghum provides the main fuel in the open woodlands, so the versatile and life-giving spinifex is a volatile fuel in the stone country. From time to time, fire sweeps through the sandstone community and, if it occurs in Gurrung, it can reduce the landscape to a forest of blackened sticks. Leichhardt saw a similar landscape as he crossed the Arnhem Plateau on his epic journey. If this happens, it takes quite a few seasons before

A female Black Wallaroo with a large pouch-young

regeneration is complete.

In the stone country, just as in the woodlands, plants regenerating after a fire attract a lot of attention from the animals. The herbivorous rock-wallabies and wallaroos enjoy the succulent green pick which sprouts from the bases of the gnarled roots and blackened sticks.

In the morning and late afternoon, pure whistling notes ring out from the tops of the sandstone cliffs—a beautiful sound that blends well with the rugged scenery. The rusty coloured Sandstone Shrike-thrush announces its claim to the surrounding territory while hunting for insects and spiders along the ledges and in and out of the caves. It is yet another shy bird that is not easy to observe unless you are prepared to sit quietly for some time among the rocks and wait. If you have the time to do this you will see more than you bargained on.

Dominant male Short-eared Rock-wallaby

Towards the end of Gurrung there is a marked change in the cloud pattern

MONSOON FORESTS

Gurrung is a time when many monsoon forest trees produce flowers or fruit. On the bare branches of the thorny Kapok trees, striking, large, red flowers (*inset below*) are now appearing. Soon they will cover the tree. Once pollinated, large pods develop which are packed with a cotton-like material which is blown by the wind as a means of spreading the small, black seeds. These large, deciduous trees are often seen growing along the levee banks of the Alligator Rivers and, in late Gurrung, a fine layer of the kapok from the seed pods may cover the entire surface of the river.

In the spring-fed forests, endemic Carpentaria Palms produce bunches of attractive red fruit. The fruit, which is an important food for many of the forest birds and bats, is produced throughout the dry months and the seeds are distributed far and wide by the wildlife. In fact, many of the monsoon forest trees are transported as seeds over long distances by birds

Permanent springs support lush forest in dry times

Torres Strait Pigeons are one of the primary forest seed carriers ...

They are thus very important in spreading monsoon forest

and animals and when conditions are right, new forests may quickly establish.

One of the primary links in this forest-building process is the Torres Strait or Torresian Imperial Pigeon. This robust and common fruit-pigeon has migratory habits and many individuals spend the dry months in the lusher conditions of the islands to the north of Australia, returning during late Gurrung when the Carpentaria Palms are coming into full production. It is always possible to find some of these pigeons in Kakadu at any time, but they are in much greater numbers between Gurrung and Yegge. The distinctive deep cooing notes quickly alert one to their presence.

Carpentaria Palms protrude from the canopy of lowland forest

Fruit of the Maranthes tree

An Emerald Dove on the forest floor

The Orange-footed Scrubfowl

Two more important fruit trees are also coming into production. The Maranthes Tree is one of the largest of the local monsoon forest trees and often forms a major part of the forest canopy, particularly if it is growing on sandy soils. The prolific, white flower masses of Yegge become large clusters of grape-like fruit in Gurrung, often weighing the branches down with their bulk. This fruit is enjoyed by a wide range of animal life and makes a good focus for observation. The Torres Strait Pigeon, Banded Fruit-dove and the Rose-crowned Fruit-dove are never far from these fruiting trees. The Emerald Dove collects the ripe fruit knocked down by the fruit-doves above while the Orange-footed Scrubfowl rakes through the layers of rotting fruit to get at the invertebrates which are attracted to it.

Flowers are now appearing on the smaller Polyalthia Tree and soon the soft orange and black fruits will replace the Maranthes as a primary target of the forest animals. Polyalthia fruit, like so many other kinds of forest fruit, is timed to coincide with the arrival of wet weather. This gives the germinating seed the greatest possible chance of establishing itself before the rains stop.

Rose-crowned Fruit-dove

Banded Fruit-dove

Fruit of the Polyalthia Tree is an important fruit-pigeon food

Freshwater Crocodiles are largely inactive during the day

Estuarine Crocodiles are quite at home in freshwater

RIVERS & BILLABONGS

In the furthest sections upstream , a game of life and death is being played out. The variety of freshwater fish in the shrinking pools has been dwindling as the more voracious species prey on the less aggressive ones. Ultimately, a particularly pugnacious fish called Bort, the Spangled Grunter (*inset right*), is the only species left in the smaller pools. They can tolerate stagnation, high temperatures and low oxygen levels. They harass and worry the other fish, nipping off their fins and eventually immobilising and devouring them. The Spangled Grunters in turn become the targets for Freshwater Crocodiles, water monitors and cormorants. When the rains return, Spangled Grunters are always present and are usually the first to swim upstream into the new pools.

The nutritious Wurrumaning or Lotus rhizomes are dug up by Bininj and cooked at this time. The low water level gives easier access to these lengthy but brittle root systems.

Suddenly, life in a billabong may undergo a decline as many large dead fish float to the surface. Barramundi and Salmon Catfish are the most common. Their bloated bodies accumulate across the billabong. Masses of rotting waterweed can deplete the water of the necessary oxygen and the larger fish usually die first. Other species such as Saratoga, Bully Mullet and Ox-eye Herring follow. This is not an ecological catastrophe, as many fish survive and those that do not become food for crocodiles, monitors, water rats, file snakes, kites, sea-eagles and Dingos.

Lotus and Ludwigia weed on the East Alligator floodplain

Major fish-kill in the Nourlangie Creek system

Darter or Snake-bird

Yellow-faced Cormorants

Billabong fish life

Bininj enjoy eating Saratoga

A young Spotted Scat

Smaller species of fish and invertebrates in the billabongs such as Spotted Scats and Freshwater Prawns are normally unaffected during a fish-kill as their oxygen requirements are very low.

A young Freshwater Prawn

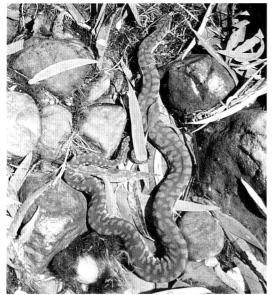

Above: Arafura File Snake. Right: Northern Short-necked Turtle

Arafura File Snakes are a harmless and very common reptile in the billabongs of Kakadu although they are rarely seen. They are completely aquatic and need to surface every twenty minutes or so for fresh air. Only their nostrils break the surface and they are usually entangled in

thick weed beds or among lilies. This gives them some protection from sea-eagles and Jabiru, which are their main enemies. They are more active by night and feed largely on fish, especially catfish. Catfish have long, poisonous dorsal and pectoral spines which are erected whenever the fish is disturbed or threatened and they are always erect when swallowed by a file snake. Frequently these spines perforate the body wall of the snake, protruding to the outside. This appears to be of little consequence to the snake as the fish is soon digested and the offending spine is pushed out from the inside. The poisonous substance on the barb, which causes so much agony in humans, appears to have no effect on the reptile and the small wound soon recovers without a trace.

The striking face markings of the Northern Short-necked Turtle

The Northern Short-necked Turtle lives in the same locality as the file snake but is seen more frequently as it surfaces for air or basks in the sun on logs or muddy banks. One of their favoured foods is Freshwater Mussels which live in the sand and mud at the bottom of the billabong. Adult turtles may develop very large jaw muscles from crushing the hard shells of these bivalves and this gives them a rather 'boof-headed' appearance.

Both file snakes and turtles are highly valued as food by Bininj but, like all other animal foods, they are exploited only in the right season when they are in the best condition. At the other times they are left alone. This is perhaps why the wetlands of Kakadu are so well stocked with wildlife today.

A ripening crop of Cluster Figs

Large Cluster Fig trees often grow on the banks of the rivers and billabongs and at this time of year they produce bunches of yellow and orange figs on their trunks and branches. These figs attract many animal species, from the handsome Fruit-piercing Moth, through to the Northern Brushtail Possum and the Black Flying-fox. Much of the fruit is knocked down in the scramble for the ripe ones and the figs frequently fall in the water. The plopping sound attracts the Northern Short-necked Turtle which often has great difficulty biting the large floating fruit. Several turtles may join in the game of water polo until one successfully manages to take a bite out of the prize.

Although not heard at this time, Dwarf Green Tree-frogs can be found in large numbers at the edges of billabongs throughout this period. They particularly favour pandanus clumps and beds of floating Hymenacne Grass where they are afforded good protection from their many enemies by thorns and cutting edges.

Freshwater Mangrove flowers, which like the Cocky Apple last only one night, carpet the surface of the water with deep red in the early morning. Pairs of Green Pygmy Geese feed on the fallen blossom.

A Black Flying-fox eating a Cluster Fig

Freshwater Mangrove flowers bloom for only one night

Northern Short-necked Turtle eating fallen Cluster Figs

Green Pygmy-geese feed on water plants

Typical Gurrung scene on the East Alligator River

A five-metre Estuarine Crocodile rushes for the safety of the river

Now is the time that the White-browed Robins begin breeding along the river corridors and their melodic whistling can be heard proclaiming their territories. This family of robins has its base in Papua New Guinea and this is the only member of the group represented in the Northern Territory.

Standing quietly in the shadows is the solitary Black Bittern, also a resident of the dense river corridors and billabong fringes. It likes to hunt fish and invertebrates in the shadows of overhanging branches and is very wary of human approach.

The estuarine section of the Kakadu rivers is one of the last stronghold areas of the Irrawaddy Dolphin, a rather unusual, blunt-nosed and light-skinned member of the dolphin family which was formerly found throughout New Guinea and South-East Asia up to India. They enjoy the murky, estuarine waters and are usually seen in small parties moving with the tide. They are known to tolerate fresh water. Identification is difficult as they are not easy to observe in the muddy water and they do not rise out of the water to breathe like the other dolphins. Subsequently, very little is known of the natural history of this unusual marine mammal. The small, rounded dorsal fin is the most distinguishing feature.

White-browed Robin

The shy Black Bittern is a bird of the shadowy river fringes

FLOODPLAINS

Fire can sweep across the plains at this time of year. It may originate either from fires in the adjoining woodlands or from fires purposely lit by Bininj while hunting on the plains. As mentioned earlier, the fire drives the small fauna into crevices in the dried blacksoil or into monitor holes where they can be captured if required. The floodplain vegetation is mostly dead by Gurrung and fires simply remove this dead material. The smoke from these fires attracts numbers of Kori Bustards as

Early morning on the floodplain

The plumage of the geese becomes 'grubby' during Gurrung

well as kites, falcons and Dingos.

The Magpie Geese now look lean and grubby, their feathers stained from the thick mud around the drying waterholes. They have been digging as deep as their necks will stretch, using the strong hook on the end of their beaks to lever the mud away from the edible roots, tubers and various invertebrates which they encounter.

The intense heat and lack of surface water now forces the geese off the plains during the day. This is the critical period in the year of the goose. Food is scarce and competition is high. They stand in flocks among the shady paperbarks on the fringes of the plains until the late afternoon. In this weakened condition, individuals make easy targets for Dingos and sea-eagles. Many lose the strength to fly and die of thirst, but the majority will make it into Gunumeleng and recommence the cycle of life.

The catchment of the South Alligator River has, in recent times, become the greatest refuge for Magpie Geese in northern Australia. The floodplains around the confluence of Jim Jim Creek and the South Alligator River provide a haven for these and other waterbirds during the driest

period each year.

In the drying depressions on the plains, a few Estuarine Crocodiles always seem to run the risk of staying put in the areas which were so good to them between Gudjewg and Yegge. Most years this pays off but, occasionally, particularly after poor rains, it is fatal. The bleached bones of large crocodiles are not uncommon on the plains—the unfortunate reptiles having died a slow and cruel death under the relentless Gurrung sun. Even the leathery plates on the back of a crocodile burn in the sun.

Geese are forced to dig deep for bulbs . . .

The long-necked turtle has good forward vision for striking prey

Both crocodiles and freshwater turtles may attempt to migrate from dry waterholes across the floodplains to the safety of the rivers at this time of year, with mixed success. They usually display an uncanny accuracy for taking the shortest route back to permanent water. Those that are able to reach the water under the cover of darkness dodge the main peril.

At night, Orange Horseshoe-bats flitter about the plains close to ground level. It is

Orange Horseshoe-bat

known that these tiny bats breed in sandstone caves which have particularly high humidity, but at this time of the year it is assumed that they are roosting in tree hollows in the woodlands close to the edge of the plains. They are also known to be a prey item of the much larger Ghost Bat.

King Brown Snakes are one of the largest venomous snakes in the Kakadu region and, though they may be found in all habitats, they are especially fond of hunting on the floodplains in the dry weather, particularly during Gurrung and Gunumeleng. Like the Water Pythons, they spend a

King Brown Snake

lot of time tracking Dusky Rats in and out of the blacksoil cracks, but King Browns have a much wider dietary range than the python. They eat a range of other lizards and snakes, including young Water Pythons, as well as mammals up to the size of bandicoots and a range of ground-dwelling birds.

These snakes, while often quite fearless, are not a significant threat to humans as they either move to avoid encounters or try to bluff their way past a threat, giving humans plenty of opportunity to move back a safe distance. Bites are rare, but if one should occur, seek medical help immediately.

Geese settling for the night on Kapok tree

Birds crowd around the available surface water on the plains

The beautiful Yellow Chat

Small birds are not particularly common on the floodplains, with the exception of flocks of Chestnut-breasted Mannikins and Crimson Finches which feed in the reed beds and pandanus fringes. Occasionally Yellow-rumped Mannikins may join in with the Chestnut-breasted variety. Towards the mangrove-lined gutters which drain back into the rivers are found colonies of colourful Yellow Chats. They are difficult to locate and appear to be somewhat seasonal in their movements after breeding in this location in Banggerreng.

These floodplains are still in the recovery phase from the upheaval of almost a hundred years of ecological abuse from large numbers of the introduced Asian Water Buffalo. Their numbers peaked in the 1950s and 1960s. One does not have to look very far to see the old wallows and swim-channels which crisscross the plains and which were active right up until the mid-1980s. The vegetation is now recovering well, making it possible for the wildlife to move back and reclaim what was theirs. In the years to come we can look foward to a much improved floodplain ecology.

Buffalo damage is now a thing of the past

Anbangbang Billabong may dry right out in Gurrung

Burdekin Ducks

P A P E R B A R K   S W A M P S

Many of the paperbark swamp areas are now dry and cracked. In contrast, the few that still hold water are teeming with waterbirds, if only for a short time.

The water plants have died back and the bulk of the wildlife has moved away. Things appear to be quite lifeless and the heat shimmers off the dried mud during the day. The prolific bird calls of the previous seasons have now ceased, all bar a few. The paperbark forest has become a ghost town, or so it seems.

Royal Spoonbills

Plumed Whistling Ducks

A Black-winged Stilt seeks invertebrates in a shallow billabong

The stately Jabiru

143

Paperbark swamps rapidly dry out during Gurrung

Wallabies spar in the early morning

Surface water is at a premium for waterbirds

Kakadu's largest owl, the Rufous Owl

In the evening, Agile Wallabies may move in to dig for morsels in the remaining moist areas with their long front claws, or to graze the fine grasses which grew as the water dried up. Rufous Owls continue to roost high in the paperbarks but hunt now in the adjacent woodlands. Barn Owls (*below*) move in at night to hunt rats in the centre of the swamp. The Dusky Rats and Common Planigales which occupy the blacksoil cracks also attract Water Pythons and King Brown Snakes. Dingos circulate through the area regularly in the hope of catching weakened wildlife. Lemon-bellied Flycatchers and White-throated Honeyeaters hunt insects in the paperbark canopy although they do not advertise their presence in song as they did back in Banggerreng and Yegge. Though subdued, life goes on in the paperbarks.

Bininj know that good drinking water can be found stored in the trunks of certain paperbark trees. These can be easily recognised from the abnormal bulges which develop in the lower trunks. By tearing off the outer bark and breaking through the thin, woody layer with a rock or an axe, the litre or more of water which is usually stored under pressure is allowed to squirt out. After this water has been obtained, it may take the tree a year or so to repair itself.

Fire is a real danger to this ecosystem in Gurrung and Gunumeleng. It is not a habitat which carries fire well and is generally protected by early burning. However, if fire does occur, the results can be ecologically disastrous. The thick papery bark burns well and the natural oils in the chemistry of the tree make it possible for live trees to burn right through the trunk. The flames move up the tree until the volatile foliage catches fire. For days, the sound of giant paperbarks may be heard crashing to the ground as the smouldering trunks burn through.

The hilly woodlands of the upper South Alligator valley

Cocky Apple flowers bloom at night

TROPICAL WOODLANDS

The beautiful, red, bell-shaped flowers of the Northern Kurrajong are now a feature of the dry woodlands. The flowers appear to be growing on dead sticks, as the large, trifoliate leaves were shed soon after the rains finished. The roots and seeds of this tree are edible after cooking to remove fine bristles, but the greatest value of this small tree is in the use of the bark. A very strong string or rope can be produced by stripping and rolling the fibrous

Red-flowered Kurrajong

A deciduous eucalypt in new leaf

bark on the bare thigh. Intricate string bags and mats are produced by weaving the dyed string of this plant.

Another unusual Gurrung flower comes from the very common Cocky Apple tree. It produces large numbers of white, filamentous flowers with pink to red centres and they unfold at night. Hawk Moths and Blossom Bats visit these flowers all night for the nectar and, by morning, the flowers slide off the stamen and fall to the ground. A large, green fruit develops at the base of the stamen, edible to both humans and wildlife and, as the name suggests, it is a popular food of Sulphur-crested Cockatoos.

There is a wide variety of eucalypts in Kakadu, but only one variety has the deciduous characteristic of dropping all its leaves in early Gurrung and bursting into a complete, new, maroon-coloured foliage. This is one of the Cabbage Gum group known to Bininj as Angombolok.

Not all individuals will completely drop their leaves but those that do, or those that become scorched by late fires, will put on a stunning display of new, maroon-coloured leaves, lasting a week or more before they change back to green.

This young Red Goshawk will grow into a major woodland predator

White phase of the Grey Goshawk with a freshly taken Brolga chick

Spotted Nightjar resting at night

Little Woodswallows cluster at night for safety in a tree hollow

With the open nature of the woodlands at this time of year, ground-dwelling birds are able to move around much more easily than at other times. Many of the diurnal predatory birds, such as falcons and goshawks, are rearing chicks high in the canopy. The Grey Goshawk is often seen in areas adjacent to well-wooded river corridors where it preys on small mammals and birds. A white phase individual of the Grey Goshawk was once observed to take a newly hatched Brolga chick as it ran along behind its parents in the vicinity of Maguk.

Spotted Nightjars are now present in large numbers in the woodlands, having migrated from other areas, and their bright eyeshine makes them quite easy to locate at night.

Five species of Woodswallows are found in Kakadu and these gregarious insect-hunters are often seen huddled together along outer branches of prominent trees. They also roost at night in clusters and the Little Woodswallow is well known for communal roosting inside fire-eroded tree hollows. They frequently nest in the rocky crags of the sandstone cliffs. Woodland marsupials are now having to work harder to find the variety of food that they require, although there always seem to be a few tree species either producing nectar or fruit.

The aerobatic Sugar Glider

The more versatile types such as the Brushtail Possum and the Sugar Glider can turn to an enormous variety of food sources rather than travelling long distances in search of specific foods. Agile Wallabies spend a lot more time digging roots, bulbs and shoots with their powerful front claws. They also collect a lot of fallen fruit under the Green Plum trees. This fruit has recently been shown to be extremely high in vitamin C.

Those areas of woodland that have not received an annual burn have developed a very dry understorey by this time of year. The annual grasses are dead and the perennial species have yellowed and are waiting for the stimulus of rain.

In areas which have been burned, the continued post-fire leaf drop from the eucalypt trees tends to carpet the scorched ground giving it a uniform, but lifeless appearance. This is the time of year when least wildlife is visible to the average observer in this habitat. In actual fact, the wildlife diversity remains quite high throughout the dry, but the animals restrict their activity to the cooler nights and remain well tucked away in hollows, burrows and nests during the day. Bininj have little trouble locating woodland species at any time, but it can be a problem for visitors to tropical Australia at this time of year.

Northern Brown Bandicoots continue to be active throughout the hot nights, digging feverishly for soil invertebrates with the aid of a highly tuned nose. At this time of year they often revert to living in fallen logs or abandoned monitor holes because fire can remove all the undergrowth in which they normally build their nests. This is only a temporary inconvenience, soon remedied with the arrival of the rains.

A bandicoot may travel over a wide area each night in order to get enough food to satisfy its rapid

Female Agile Wallaby and young one eating fallen fruit

metabolic rate. During this solitary ranging, they frequently encounter other bandicoots where there is a brief exchange of hissing or pouncing or chasing before each goes its separate way. This is because these bandicoots do not generally tolerate the close proximity of their fellows outside the breeding season.

Reptiles, however, remain active. Both the Yellow Spotted and Sand Monitors continue to patrol the forests daily, digging deep in the soil to reach moisture-seeking insects and their larvae.

Northern Brushtail Possum and young one

Northern Brown Bandicoot

Claw-snouted Blind Snake

Northern Brown Tree Snake

Below ground level, a strangely designed burrowing snake called the Claw-snouted Blind Snake preys upon the eggs and larvae of ants and termites. It is rarely seen above ground level except during wet weather. It is thought that these totally inoffensive reptiles live within the tunnels and galleries constructed by the ants and termites upon which they depend. This snake is in turn preyed upon by another burrowing snake, the Northern Bandy-bandy.

delivers the fatal bite with lightning speed.

If disturbed by a human, the adder will flatten its body, displaying a stunning colour pattern while making a few mock strikes. If the threat continues and the warning is ignored, the bluff is abandoned and a serious bite may be inflicted.

Another snake which relies on bluff is the relatively harmless Northern Brown Tree Snake. This is a common species in the woodland which hunts at night and has an uncanny ability to locate

Northern Death Adder in hunting mode

Northern Death Adder in defensive mode

Two types of death adder are found in Kakadu. A small but colourful variety is found in the woodlands and monsoon forests, while a much larger type is found on the floodplains. These are venomous snakes which rely on trickery to obtain their prey. The thick-set body tapers suddenly to a slender tail with cream-coloured flattened scales which terminate in a small spur. The snake positions itself in a horseshoe shape so that the tail- tip curls around in front of the head, while the beautifully camouflaged body is covered with leaves and grass so as to be almost invisible. When a potential meal appears in the vicinity, in the form of a skink, a dragon or a small mammal, the specially designed tail-tip turns into a very effective lure. It dances seductively, attracting the prey to within striking distance and the adder

and devour sleeping birds. These snakes are frequently encountered crossing roads or entering buildings at night in search of geckos or mice. In a confrontation they give the impression of being a highly venomous snake, and this usually has the desired effect, allowing the reptile to go on its way. Unfortunately many are killed in the mistaken belief that they are dangerous. It should be remembered that all wildlife is protected in Kakadu and snakes should be respected, not killed.

Recently, the smallest and least known member of the Whipsnake family was found to exist in Kakadu. It is the Grey Whipsnake (*inset below*), known initially from the Kimberley region of Western Australia.

Throughout the seasons in the woodland there are always several trees which are flowering and providing nectar to those animals which specialise in this high energy food. There always seems to be at least one eucalypt in flower at any one time. Sugar Gliders, flying-foxes, blossom bats and even quolls are following these trees as they come into flower.

By day, it is possible to hear from a distance which trees are in flower by the commotion made by the birds. Friarbirds, lorikeets, Blue-faced

Male Red-winged Parrot—a splash of colour in the woodlands

Harvester Termites at work

Honeyeaters, Brown Honeyeaters, White-throated Honeyeaters and Yellow-throated Miners all join in and share the bounty.

One of the big nectar-producing trees of the woodlands during the dry times is Anbulu, the Bridal Tree, which flowers several times each year.

Day and night, the dry understorey is being harvested and recycled by a number of species of the humble termite (*inset right*). Some construct mounds above ground level or live in hollow trees; others live completely subterranean lives and only come above ground at night to gather grass or leaves. This constant removal of literally tonnes of litter per acre per season is the major nutrient conversion process of tropical woodlands. These blind toilers are doing a recycling job equivalent to that of the vast herds of mammalian herbivores on the grasslands of Africa. However, it is not yet understood just what effect the seasonal woodland fires have on the termite colonies.

In woodland areas where a lot of wattle regeneration is under way, many of the small wattle trees have their limbs ring-barked by beetles. This is the work of the Twig-girdler Beetle, carrying out an egg-laying ritual. When the eggs hatch, the beetle larvae feed on the dead wood of the limb. Twig-girdler Beetles are members of the widespread Longicorn family.

Twig-girdler Beetles

A typical stand of Prop-rooted Mangroves

MANGROVE FORESTS

At a time when the other habitats are suffering from a shortage of water, the mangroves are basically unaffected as the tides continue to supply their food

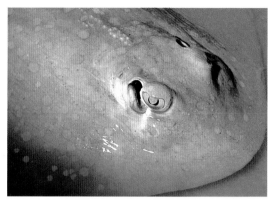

Blue-spotted Ray

and water requirements throughout the year.

The flowers of Andjuwit, the Narrow-leafed Bloodwood, tell Bininj that stingrays of several species have developed large reserves of body fat and are ready for hunting. In the same way, the appearance of mauve flowers on Anbaandarr, the Turkey Bush, indicate that shellfish, particularly oysters and mussels, are ready to be eaten. Mud Crabs too are now ready for harvesting, as indicated by the orange flowers of Andjalen, the Woollybutt.

Many of the creatures which live in the mangroves have adapted their lifestyles around the

A male Mud Crab raises its claws in defiance

tides rather than the day/night cycles. This applies not only to mangrove specialists like the False Water-rat, which normally constructs its burrow system on the high tide mark and does all its foraging below that point, but also to creatures like the beautifully marked Mangrove Monitor, the Northern Brushtail Possum and the rarely seen but often heard Chestnut Rail. Even the much larger true Water-rat will patrol

the littoral zone and those that adopt this lifestyle become tidal in their habits, regardless of whether it is day or night. The large, rear webbed feet of this rodent leave unmistakable tracks on the mud.

The tide often carries in interesting morsels and

Great Egret and catch

deposits them on the beaches at the back of the mangroves. These morsels include succulent mangrove fruit and flowers, dead fish and invertebrates and other marine creatures. As a result, the high tide mark becomes something of a highway for animal life, particularly after dark. The abundance of various animal tracks in the sand the following morning attests to this.

The bonding chorus of a pair of Chestnut Rails has to be heard to be believed. It is a loud, hoarse, booming sound in stereo which echoes from deep within the mangroves and is often mistakenly attributed to crocodiles. The presence of these shy birds in an area can quickly be established by looking for their peculiar, chicken-like tracks in the mud at low tide. The best time for viewing them is at night (with a torch) on a high tide when the birds are forced out of the mangroves and are patrolling the high tide mark. In the process you may encounter a Northern Brushtail or a Water-rat.

White-bellied Sea-Eagle

Hunting Osprey

SHORELINE

By now, the young White-bellied Sea-Eagles, Ospreys and Brahminy Kites are fledging while being fed a diet of fish, sea-snakes and the occasional flying-fox. Threadfin Salmon are a common fish of the murky inshore waters of Kakadu and were once commercially fished and marketed along with the better known Barramundi. Both of these species feature prominently in the diets of these birds. Other species which are targeted by these birds include Queenfish, Long Toms, Diamond-scaled Mullet and Salmon Catfish.

Brahminy Kite

Also found in these inshore waters is a second and more strikingly coloured species of file snake known as the Little File Snake. Its colouring and actions mimic the venomous sea-snakes with which it shares its habitat. No doubt it derives some protection from this similarity, but this harmless snake is a regular target of the marine eagles, a fate that it shares with the freshwater Arafura File Snake. The turtle nesting has ceased until the latter part of Gunumeleng, the pre-monsoon season, when a second but smaller breeding season takes place. The adult Flatback Turtles appear to concentrate on the clearer water further out from the coastline in the meantime. The other marine turtles from the clearer reef waters of this area are the Green Turtle, the Hawksbill, the Pacific Ridley, and the Loggerhead.

It has recently been demonstrated by an extensive tagging program on the Great Barrier Reef that species like the Green Turtle, which are common in the Van Diemen Gulf and regularly stray into the rivers of Kakadu, may have been born on Barrier Reef islands. More research is necessary here, but it is clear that these marine turtles are far more wide ranging than was first believed and this places a far greater value on marine conservation.

The predatory Long Tom

Salmon Catfish

Exposed tidal mudflats on the Kakadu coast

Adult Hawksbill Turtle

Portrait of a Hawksbill

We still do not understand what happens to the hatchling Flatback turtles once they leave the beach, what sort of survival rate they have or whether they even return to the area where they were born to nest as adults. Even though most of these turtles feed beyond the silt-laden waters of the Kakadu coastline, their lifestyles are greatly enhanced by the great flood of silt. The incredible range of nutrients each wet season produces directly or indirectly affects the entire system.

As Gurrung progresses into Gunumeleng, the extremes of heat and dryness increase until there comes a sudden and long-awaited rise in humidity. For visitors from colder climates, this rise in humidity can be quite debilitating. However, this is the time to observe the incredible changes that make Gunumeleng such a dynamic season.

A steady build-up of afternoon storms follows the humidity increase and triggers the biggest transformation of the seasonal year.

OCTOBER TO DECEMBER

PRE-MONSOON SEASON

GUNUMELENG

CHAPTER 6

CHAPTER 6

PRE-MONSOON SEASON - GUNUMELENG

This is the time of greatest visual change in the seasonal year of tropical monsoonal Australia. Cloudless dry season skies give way to a rapid increase in humidity and the development of some of the world's biggest storm cells. The towering cumulus columns form in the east over the rugged sandstone country of Arnhem Land, expanding upward and outward as they move rapidly west, passing over Kakadu to deliver bursts of much-needed rain. These storms are known to travel west at an average rate of 100 kilometres per hour, frequently gaining in intensity as they go. They deliver a lot of rain in a short time and are often preceded by violent blasts of cold air which can tear down branches and uproot trees over a wide area. In the process, lightning strikes demolish many eucalypts, particularly Stringybarks.

The fires which may start from these lightning strikes, on floodplains or in woodlands, can be quite devastating if the area has not had some early burning to reduce the fuel load. The hot, windy conditions make it possible for fire to travel long distances in a short time and it may burn for a week or more through a variety of habitats including paperbark and monsoon forest. Many large, living trees are destroyed in this type of fire. Fortunately, however, a return to good fire management practice is greatly reducing the risk of this kind of destruction.

The first storm or two of the season may be dark and threatening, accompanied by violent winds yet without producing rain—but heavy downpours are never far away. The fastest and most impressive visual change of the seasonal year is about to take place.

Humidity and rain trigger a myriad natural processes. The landscape rapidly and miraculously transforms from browns and yellows to greens. Carpets of bright green grass appear on bare areas and trees burst into new leaf. As a result of this, animals become far more active and change from a lean appearance to sleek breeding condition in a short time. Many species reproduce during or soon after the wet.

This pre-monsoon period is a time of rapid growth, energy production, and nutrient storage for all life forms. It is the precursor for Gudjewg, the main rainy season. The ripening of the little green plums called Anduwitjmi tells Bininj that the pre-monsoon season is starting. Gunumeleng may last only a few weeks or several months.

Left: A temporary waterfall cascades from the Burrungguy cliff after a storm. Above: The first storm of the season looms from the east

LEICHHARDT'S RECORD OF KAKADU IN EARLY GUNUMELENG

LEICHHARDT WAS THE FIRST RECORDED EUROPEAN VISITOR TO TAKE A CLOSE LOOK AT THE AREA NOW KNOWN AS KAKADU. THE FOLLOWING EXTRACTS FROM HIS DIARY ACCURATELY DESCRIBE THE SEASON:

Nov 14th, 1845

"...During the night, thunder clouds and lightning were seen in every direction; and the whole atmosphere appeared to be in a state of fermentation. Heavy showers poured down upon us; and our tarpaulins, which had been torn to pieces in travelling through the scrub, were scarcely sufficient to keep ourselves and our things dry. But in the morning of the 15th, all nature seemed refreshed; and my depressed spirits rose quickly, under the influence of that sweet breath of vegetation, which is so remarkably experienced in Australia, where the numerous Myrtle family, and even their dead leaves, contribute so largely to the general fragrance . . ."

Nov 28th, 1845

"...The weather has been very favourable since we left the South Alligator River. It was evident from the appearance of the creek and the swamps, that the rains had been less abundant here. Cumuli formed regularly in the afternoon, with the setting in of the north-west sea breeze, but dispersed at sunset, and during the first part of the night.

Thunder clouds were seen in the distance, but none reached us. The clear nights were generally dewy...We had a heavy thunder-storm from the north-east, which, however, soon passed off..."

Dec 1st, 1845

"...A fine north-west breeze set in at three o'clock in the afternoon, and refreshed us, as well as the cattle, which were suffering most severely from heat and fatigue."

Dec 3rd, 1845

"...Cumuli formed very early in the morning, and increased during the day, sending down showers of rain all around the horizon. The sea breeze set in at three o'clock; and the weather cleared up at sunset, and during the first part of the night; but after 1 o'clock a.m., became cloudy again, with inclination to rain; heavy dew fell during the clear part of the night."

Journal of an Overland Expedition in Australia
Dr Ludwig Leichhardt

STONE COUNTRY

Recesses and ledges provide shelter for wildlife

The hot, dry conditions of Gurrung carry through into Gunumeleng, but all living things seem to know that change is coming—and some are not prepared to wait.

The paper-dry Basket Ferns which cling to the rock faces and tree trunks are shooting new green fronds. Yams are sending up new tendrils from underground bulbs.

Another variety of Sand Palm exists in the rugged escarpment cliffs and lower hills. It is very thin and wispy and much taller than its woodland cousin. It flowers from now through to Banggerreng and then develops bunches of small, black, shiny fruit. Emus, bowerbirds and orioles are known to eat the fruit and disperse the seed.

The rich yellow flowers of the small Prickly Wattle bushes are now a common sight among the sandstone boulders. This is offset nicely by another common native shrub, the pink-flowering Sandstone Hibiscus.

Rambirambi, the beautifully marked Northern Brown Tree Snake, is a night predator which can be found in most habitats. Totally harmless to humans, it hunts for mammals, birds and reptiles at night and is at home in the rugged sandstone. It frequently appears in caves inhabited by bats where it plucks easy meals from the air as the bats move in and out of the narrow cave openings. By day they sleep on cool, sheltered ledges away from the heat of the sun.

Basket fern

The shy Rock Possum

Prickly Wattle

Sandstone Hibiscus

Northern Brown Tree Snake

Earlier in the dry weather, the eggs of Aldjurr the Leichhardt's Grasshopper hatched, after being dormant since the wet season. The young nymphs climbed on to their host plant, the aromatic Pityrodia Bush, progressing through their various colourful growth stages. Now, as Gunumeleng arrives, they are moulting into their adult contrasting colours of orange, blue and black. As the storms of Gunumeleng arrive, the adults begin mating and the process begins again.

Aldjurr (*inset below*) was first described by the explorer Ludwig Leichhardt and then not seen for almost a century. It is thought that these brightly coloured insects, which are so obvious from a distance, are toxic to would-be predators as they do not appear to have any enemies. They occur in low numbers and form sporadic colonies throughout the stone country. It is believed that fire may be the major factor limiting their occurrence.

Ludwig Leichhardt also made reference in his journal to a bird call which intrigued him. The

Leichhardt's Grasshoppers are said to be the children of Namarrgurn

day when most other birds are silent.

A variety of small, freshwater fish is found in the permanent pools and streams on top of the main escarpment. One of these is the widespread Purple-spotted Gudgeon and another is the less well-known Exquisite Rainbowfish. This small member of the rainbowfish family is similar to the Black-striped Rainbowfish of the lowlands but more delicately marked. It is restricted to the furthermost upstream section of the rivers which flow from the Arnhem Plateau.

White-lined Honeyeater

pleasing qualities of this little bird can still be heard today ringing in the sandstone valleys and echoing from the cliffs. Without knowing it, Leichhardt was describing the endemic White-lined Honeyeater, which also has an outlying population in the rugged sandstone of the Kimberley Plateau.

This cheerful little honeyeater is quite plainly coloured, but its call is synonymous with this country and it is given throughout the hottest part of the

Purple-spotted Gudgeon

Exquisite Rainbowfish

Ring-tailed Dragon

Black-spotted Ridge-tailed Monitor

Rough Knobtail Gecko

Animal species which are active during the day in the stone country usually have ways of avoiding excessive heat. The Ring-tailed Dragon is found living on the open areas on the sandstone, one of the hottest of all areas during the day. Its movements are rapid and, when resting on hot stone, its palms are raised and its tail touches only at one point. If temperatures are extreme, it dashes in and out of shady ledges, but it likes to have an exposed vantage point from which to locate and pursue insects.

At night, when most lizards are inactive, the geckos take over. Perhaps the most bizarre-looking of these night lizards is the Rough Knobtail Gecko, which stalks mechanically around the base of rock faces and the floor of caves in search of large-bodied insects and other invertebrates and even other geckos. This is one of the few geckos which is found in the stone country and cannot climb. It has claws instead of pads on its toes.

There are at least six types of goanna or monitor in the stone country. The large and robust Yellow Spotted Monitor ranges up into the stone country and is often seen prowling the caves and ledges. This may, however, turn out to be a separate variety. The Black-spotted Ridge-tailed Monitor is a specialised rock-dweller, shy of human approach and seeking shelter in cracks and crevices. The backward-facing spines on the tail very effectively wedge the lizard in to the tight rock crevices in the event of predator attack. The least encountered species is the beautifully marked Kimberley Rock Monitor which, in Kakadu, appears exclusively to inhabit hollow limbs high in the endemic Anbinik trees.

The small but striking Kimberley Rock Monitor

The floor of the forest comes alive with small annuals

MONSOON FORESTS

Like the other habitats, monsoon forests can be stressed by a delayed beginning to the wet season. Drooping yellow leaves on the trees, piles of dead leaves on the ground, wilting understorey plants and much more exposure to sunlight through the more open canopy are characteristics of the monsoon forest at this time. There may be up to several weeks delay between storms, which appears to stretch the tolerance of certain life forms in this and other habitats. The beginning of Gunumeleng can be a difficult time although, generally speaking, the rains arrive on time.

Perhaps as a result of this variable start to the rainy season, a variety of plants have their own food and moisture storage capacity. This gives them enough energy to develop new growth at this time of the year without assistance from rain. They build up this energy supply the previous rainy season, after they have flowered and fruited. It is then stored in modified roots. A good number of these storage roots are edible and Bininj are experts on this subject.

Flowers of the leafless Northern Hyacinth Orchids and delicate Nervillea Orchids rise out of the leaf litter at the beginning of Gunumeleng and make a beautiful display of pink. Following the pollination of the short-lived flower, the Nervillea Orchid produces a single green leaf which acts as a solar panel to produce the energy necessary for next season's flower, stored in a bulb underground. In case the flower is not pollinated, a second bulb is also produced.

The largest flower in Kakadu also appears from a huge underground bulb at this time. It is the Amorphophallus plant and the football-sized flower gives off a foul odour which attracts flies and beetles in large numbers. Pollination is achieved in one or two days by these creatures and then, as the impressive flower withers, a large green shaft appears out of the ground and quickly develops into an umbrella-like leaf structure which lasts the entire wet season.

Northern Hyacinth Orchid

Nervillea Orchid

Large Amorphophallus flower

Small Amorphophallus flowers

Colourful pink-flowered Curcuma Lilies may also emerge from hidden bulbs and carpet the floor of the forest in certain areas, their large green leaves sheltering the showy compound flowers. They occur on the rich, dark forest soils adjacent to creeks and springs.

The stately Leichhardt Trees are now producing their rather unusual spherical flowers, made up of many tiny white flowers clustered on a large sphere. After moth pollination, tiny seeds develop in the pulpy sphere which enlarges into a soft, brown fruit. They are edible but relatively tasteless. Flying-foxes and wallabies, however, relish them and this no doubt greatly aids in their distribution.

Canopus Butterfly

An unusual fly is found in the forests of the escarpment, particularly around springs and moisture soaks in the sandstone country. It has prominent black and white rings on its abdomen and large red eyes. These flies can be seen in large groups sitting quite motionless in cool, damp situations on ferns, vines, tree trunks and roots. They are quite fearless, often landing on humans. Their obvious colouring and behaviour indicates that they have few enemies. During Gunumeleng they seem quite dependent on the moisture and are reluctant to move. If disturbed, they quickly resettle in much the same spot.

The unusual flowers of the Leichhardt Tree

A range of butterflies is now appearing in the forest, particularly around the fringe, visiting the flowering shrubs and trees and making the sunny mornings much more cheerful. The majority of them are a combination of black and white. The large, tailed Canopus Butterfly, a member of the swallowtail family, appears in numbers in Gunumeleng after the caterpillars have grown up on Glycosmis and Micromelum plants in the forest understorey. Other forest butterflies emerging in Gunumeleng include the Blue Tiger, two varieties of Oak Blue, the Evening Brown, the Orange Lacewing and the Brown Soldier.

Monsoon Forest Fly

Carpentaria Palm fruit

Canopus Butterfly laying eggs

Blue Triangle Butterflies feeding

One of the most prominent birds in the monsoon forest is the Great Bowerbird. Harsh, scolding calls are given by the dominant male whenever a human intrudes into its display area but, once the coast is clear, an amazing repertoire of calls, including mimicry of other birds, issues forth. This all focuses on the bower, a large structure of sticks, carefully thatched into two opposing walls which almost meet at the top. At either end of the internal corridor, the male bird deposits bleached shells and bones and other shiny curios that he has picked up elsewhere in his territory. Along with these objects he places round, green fruits from forest plants. These are picked and replaced daily. Each of these fruits is carefully manoeuvred during the dancing sessions when the male bird is trying to impress the females in his vicinity, as well as the younger males. It is at this time that the beautiful mauve crest, hidden in the feathers of his neck, is briefly erected. When the

Male Great Bowerbird in his bower

dominant male is away, the younger males take their turn and dance in the bower. Gunumeleng is the period of greatest activity for the Great Bowerbird.

Bowerbirds commonly collect Native Land Snail shells after the occupant has died. These snails bury in loose soil beneath the litter during the dry period and emerge again when the humidity rises in Gunumeleng. There are a number of species of native snails in Kakadu and a very delicate variety with a pointed shell inhabits the monsoon forests exclusively.

Delicate Forest Snail

Silently observing this activity in the forest is the Crested Hawk or Pacific Bazza. This bird (*above*) spends a lot of time in the hot weather sitting quietly on a shady perch while its keen eyesight locates prey items. Amazingly camouflaged, large, green stick insects are one of the hawk's staple foods and it locates these by detecting movement. The fact that the movements of this giant insect are so slow as to be imperceptible only highlights the efficient eyesight of this small raptor.

Native Taro plants grow in poorly drained forest areas, particularly where there is year-round moisture. In other countries these plants are used as a staple food, but in Kakadu they are not considered useful as food.

Native Taro Lilies or Cunjevoi

The shady upper reaches of the South Alligator River

Little Red Flying-foxes hang in the foliage above the river

RIVERS & BILLABONGS

One of the more commonly depicted fish species in the rock art of Kakadu is the Bully Mullet. This is a large estuarine mullet which migrates upstream in considerable schools during Gunumeleng to spawn in the freshwater reaches above the tidal influence. Traditionally at this time the mullet were easily speared or hit with sticks as they negotiated the rock bars and other obstacles. Their necks were then broken and they were threaded on to a waist belt worn by the hunter. These fish can still be seen migrating upstream at this time, particularly at Galarabirr Djokeng or Cahill's Crossing on the East Alligator River.

Many of the fish that utilise these river systems can tolerate both saltwater and freshwater. During the monsoon season, such a volume of freshwater flows down from the Arnhem Plateau that the tides are ineffectual and almost the entire length of the river becomes temporarily fresh. One common fish at home in either situation is the Archerfish (*inset left*), which ranges from the mangroves to the uppermost reaches of the rivers. As they are surface dwellers, they are easily seen and it is not uncommon to observe them spitting jets of water at insects and other potential meals in the foliage above the water. At this time of year, their other relative, the Primitive Archerfish (*inset above*), is occupying the clear, forested, spring-fed streams and pools of the escarpment area.

The newly hatched offspring of both Freshwater Crocodiles and Pig-nosed Turtles are now appearing in the rivers. The little crocodiles remain in small creches for some weeks and are protected by the female until they gain their own cunning. They have many enemies in the first few weeks of their lives and the survival rate is quite low. Those in the upstream areas seem to have a better chance of survival than those lower down. In every river there is an overlap zone where both species of crocodile exist. Large Estuarine crocodiles prey on the young of both species.

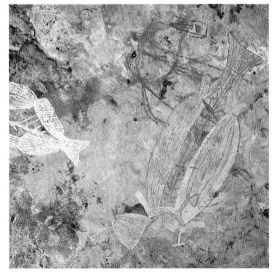

Mullet painting at Ubirr

The young Pig-nosed Turtles hatch after the first rains have caused the rivers to rise just enough for the water to cover the sandy nests. The eggs hatch as soon as the water makes contact with the eggs. This no doubt reduces the risk of exposure to predators faced by other turtles which have to scramble down to the water.

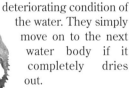

Freshwater Crocodile in drying pool

The greening of Gunumeleng is evident at Magela creek mouth

On the lowland creeks and smaller billabongs, the water level has dropped considerably and in some sections it becomes quite stagnant and discoloured from algae. Large numbers of fish and freshwater mussels suffer and eventually die from lack of oxygen. Great-billed Herons, Black Bitterns, Freshwater Crocodiles, Arafura File Snakes and Water-rats take advantage of this situation, feeding on the dying fish and crustaceans. As they are air breathers, they remain unaffected by the deteriorating condition of the water. They simply move on to the next water body if it completely dries out.

Geese working hard to obtain food

The normally pale-coloured Gilbert's Dragon, which dwells around the creek lines and riverside vegetation,

and regularly perform a variety of intricate, head-bobbing displays while females look on. Rival males are constantly challenged, threatened and chased away.

The first few storms transform the colour of the landscape, but do little to refill the creeks as most of the rain soaks into the dry ground. By the end of Gunumeleng, however, the watertable has been replenished and the creeks are well and truly flowing.

now takes on a strikingly different breeding pattern. Males turn a rusty red colour with a black throat and contrasting broad, white facial stripe. They vigorously guard the females in their vicinity

Gilbert's Dragon

The last remaining water

The rains of Gunumeleng put new life into the waterfalls—Jim Jim Falls is a magnificent example

FLOODPLAINS

More than any other habitat, floodplains are exposed to the heat of the sun and no more so than in the early days of Gunumeleng. Parched, cracked mud, baking in the searing, dry season heat characterises this time of year on the floodplain, along with shimmering heat-hazes under cloudless skies and the occasional dust-storm that sweeps across the plains, throwing up columns of grey ash from the hot fires of Gurrung. It is the harshest time for the wildlife and only the toughest forms remain visible. Black Kites keep a watchful eye on the plains from their much cooler elevations and Pratincoles sprint from one high point to another across the scorching mud. Most other ground-dwellers prefer to wait for a cooler time of the day or evening before becoming mobile. These include the King Brown Snake, the Yellow Spotted Monitor and the Agile Wallaby. They rely on fat reserves from the previous seasons to cover this period, but eventually hunger and thirst

Reptiles are more active when the rains arrive

Any delays in the first rains create conditions for hot fires

Delays in first rains also mean strong competition for birds

may force them out at a hotter time.

Deep down in the cracks of the mud, many animals are waiting. Dusky Rats (*inset below*) in their thousands tunnel sideways into the mud from the cracks and enjoy the cool, moist air circulation which is operating several metres below the surface. Planigales, Water-rats, Slate-grey Snakes, King Brown Snakes, Water Pythons, Northern Long-necked Turtles and many other life forms are housed below the surface. Some venture out at night while others just wait for rain.

From deep down in the blacksoil cracks, Marbled Frogs

begin to emerge. Hungry and ready to breed, they nestle into the growing grass tussocks from where they ambush insects and other frogs. By the time sufficient rain has fallen for these little amphibians to breed, they will have restored their lost condition. Marbled Frogs make a very distinctive, short, sharp 'bunk' sound, but even so are difficult to locate.

Marbled Frogs emerge from their blacksoil refuges

on the wing. They are frequently accompanied by flocks of Spine-tailed Swifts and these 'bird storms' just seem to materialise as the storms begin and the flying insects hit the skies.

From the regenerating grass beds on the fringes of the plains, Pheasant Coucals break their dry season silence with a series of deep booming calls. This denotes the start of their breeding season and nest construction begins soon after the rains arrive.

Pheasant Coucals are the only member of the cuckoo family to construct their own nest. It is a bulky, enclosed structure, often placed in a pandanus clump or similar situation, hidden from view but giving the parents a good view of the surrounding area. These ungainly looking birds walk rather than fly and much of their food is captured on the ground.

The Pheasant Coucal

The deciduous Kapok Tree turns green again in Gunumeleng

Changes in bird behaviour are taking place at all levels. Flocks of several hundred Oriental Pratincoles are not an uncommon sight in the skies over the floodplains. Unlike the solitary, ground-dwelling Australian Pratincole, these gregarious birds are more swallow-like, capturing emerging flying insects, such as termite alates,

The White-browed Crake and the less common Spotless Crake, while always difficult to observe, make quite a bit of noise in the dense vegetation beside the water. Soon they will be able to move out across the plains again under cover of a new wave of vegetation. By the end of Gunumeleng they too will be nesting.

White-browed Crake

Australian Pratincole

Late fires in the paperbark forests always have devastating effects . . .

PAPERBARK SWAMPS

In the exposed areas, the last of the small fish are dying, providing food for a variety of larger animals. In a very short time, no trace of the fish or their aquatic environment will be found, the waterplants dry out and dead paperbark leaves cover the surface. This is how the centre of the swamp will remain until the rains arrive. In the wooded fringe around the swamp, dead leaves and shed branches make a deep ground litter.

As in Gurrung, fire can be a hazard in the paperbarks at this time. Many stands of these magnificent trees are destroyed by fire and they are often still smouldering when the rains arrive. Regeneration from the burnt trees is minimal, if at all, but the exposure to the sun does seem to trigger a new wave of seedlings when the rains arrive, which will eventually form another forest on the same site. These paperbark trees are essentially a fast-growing pioneer species, but a new forest may take between ten and twenty years to develop.

Forest Kingfisher

Small fish dying in the last drying puddle of a paperbark swamp

and the female, heard at regular intervals throughout the day in Gunumeleng.

With the first rains, the powerful smell of the paperbark oils, released by the moisture, envelops the entire swamp. A carpet of green grass appears in the open areas and puddles form. Fish will recolonise the area when the floodwaters are sufficient to reconnect the creeks, billabongs and the floodplains with the main rivers.

Rain loosens the mud that has encased the Long-necked Turtles, setting them free for another year. Like the frogs, they emerge with voracious appetites.

Another hard-shelled creature is now emerging from its burrow deep in the mud. Freshwater Crabs, some brooding eggs or a cluster of newly hatched young, move from the burrow entrance to water carrying their young curled under their abdomens. Young ones are released immediately into the aquatic environment to begin the cycle for another year.

As the fire management strategies for the Park improve and stabilise, this problem should be minimised.

Forest Kingfishers have a close association with paperbark forests. They are generally seen in pairs and their territories frequently include woodland areas adjacent to the paperbarks. They construct their nests by tunnelling into the dark-coloured arboreal termite mounds seen in paperbark trees, Ghost Gums, Northern Box and others. The kingfisher's staccato call is a duet between the male

Freshwater Crab with eggs

TROPICAL WOODLANDS

Many woodland plants and trees scale back their production during the dry season to conserve water. Sometimes this means disappearing completely from view, as is the case with many small-bulbed plants, or the shedding of most of the leaves, as do many woodland shrubs and trees. This gives the bush a very drab and open appearance in the late dry. However, as Gunumeleng approaches, the majority of trees and plants suddenly burst into new leaf, usually ahead of the first rains. Some trees go even further and produce flowers and fruit in this, the driest of times. When the rains arrive, trees

In Gunumeleng in 1980, fire destroyed much of Kakadu's woodlands

White Apples

Green Plums

such as Anduwitjmi the Green Plum, Andag the Northern Geebung, and Andjarduk the Bush Apple and the White Apple are dropping ripe fruits which are much prized by people and wildlife alike. The trees are able to do this at such a stressful time because of special energy storage techniques.

Perhaps the most impressive example of this energy storage is Andingu the ancient cycad, which is restricted to several known colonies in Kakadu.

The two species known from this area are new to botanical science. Cycad species are otherwise widespread in the Top End and it is not clearly understood why they are so limited in the Kakadu region.

Below the ground, at the base of the trunk, a huge bowl develops which becomes a repository for water and nutrients. This allows the plant to put out a luxuriant new display of leaves several times each year, or whenever the leaves are eaten by caterpillars or scorched by fire. Immediately after a hot fire has swept through the area, the cycads are the first plants to respond by producing attractive, bright green heads of foliage. The poisonous fruits, produced on the female plants during the dry months, were a tediously prepared staple food for the Aboriginal residents of Kakadu, used especially to carry them over the times when long ceremonies were held. The importance of cycad bread in the past can be seen in the rock art records of Kakadu.

An undescribed cycad in the East Alligator River valley

Cycad painting in the East Alligator catchment

As the first rains hit, a carpet of green grass appears almost overnight. This is the new crop of native sorghum or spear grass. It is particularly successful in areas which experienced intense fires later in the dry months. After germinating, its growth rate is slow at first, then accelerates at the end of Gudjewg. In its early growth stage it is edible to a range of herbivores, but soon becomes rank and unpalatable. Its food value is very low.

The response of the woodland animals to the arrival of the rains is quite striking.

Cicadas (*inset above*) emerge from the ground at night and climb the trees to create a resonant chorus that heralds the beginning of the rains. Reaching a peak between storms, this throbbing cicada chorus personifies the excitement of Gunumeleng. Cicadas also represent a valuable food source to many other forms of wildlife, particularly the migratory Dollarbirds, which swoop on the unsuspecting insects as they fly between the trees.

Termites too are evident in amazing numbers, and this is what many animals have been waiting for. Underground, a special caste of termite has been prepared for the time in Gunumeleng when the humidity increases to a sufficient level to allow them to swarm up into the atmosphere, pair up and return

Winged alates of the Giant Termite

Male Frilled Lizard feeding voraciously on emerging termites

to the ground, shed their wings, mate and begin a new colony. This usually happens just before, during or after a storm, when the outside conditions are similar to those inside the nest. In some species the workers construct special vertical exit towers which save the alates (the high-caste winged termites) from attack from skinks, ants and other ground predators.

This is a time when the industrious termites give back to the ecosystem a good proportion of their nutrient bank. Most of the alates which swarm up into the sky with such enthusiasm quickly fall victim to waiting predators. Like krill in the Antarctic, the termites are high in protein and give the other animals a quick energy boost at the end of a long, lean period.

Northern Double Drummer cicadas emerging

Red-collared Lorikeet

Frogs have started calling again in the woodlands. From the humidity build-up onwards, Green Tree-frogs, Red Tree-frogs and Giant Frogs dominate the evening air waves. By the time the first storm unloads its rain, the other species have joined in. Northern Spadefoot Toads are traditionally last to surface.

In the southern parts of the Park among the rocky hills and valleys, Hooded Parrots

Green Tree-frog

Red Tree-frog

Giant Frog

are preparing to nest. These beautiful birds are virtually a geographical continuation of the Golden-shouldered Parrot of Cape York Peninsula. Because of their similar diet of seeds, they are frequently seen in the same places as Gouldian Finches, often feeding in mixed groups on the ground. At other times of the year it is not uncommon to see flocks of Hooded Parrots, but in late Gurrung and Gunumeleng they pair up and move into the lower areas to nest.

Hooded Parrots are very quiet birds and not always easy to locate. Like the Golden-shouldered

Male Hooded Parrot

Female Hooded Parrot

Parrot, the nest is a tunnel in a termite mound, normally about two metres off the ground. In the past, the accessible nest-site has made these beautiful birds extremely vulnerable to poachers and there was a marked decline in the population. Today, however, in a period of greater environmental enlightenment, these birds appear to be more secure and a good part of their range is now protected within national parks and the Arnhem Land Aboriginal Reserve.

Reptiles are one class of animals which become noticeably more active as the humidity rises. A combination of feeding and breeding activity begins.

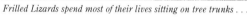

Frilled Lizards spend most of their lives sitting on tree trunks . . .

Frilled Lizards, which have been out of sight for almost the entire dry season, suddenly appear on the ground after the first shower and begin feverishly feeding on invertebrates. The males begin displaying and fighting on sight over rights to the females of the area. Soon after the rain sets in, the females are heavy with eggs and, following mating, they dig a short burrow in the moist soil in which they deposit the ten or twelve long white eggs. It will be several weeks before the ornately marked baby dragons emerge from the soil and climb the nearest saplings. They begin a life of

stealth and camouflage as their enemies are many. Very few of these young hatchlings make it through to adulthood.

A much smaller group of reptiles is also becoming active in the leaf litter. This is the family of rainbow skinks. There are a number of varieties of these engaging little skinks in the Kakadu area, noticeable because they have the curious habit of waving their tails in the air as a territorial display. The males assume striking breeding colours in Gunumeleng. The Orange-sided Rainbow-skink and the Desert Rainbow-skink are the two common species of the woodland litter.

As the storms give way to the saturating northwest monsoon rains, subterranean invertebrates are forced to the surface by the rising watertable. By day, these become the primary wet season diet of the ever-watchful Frilled Lizards which shimmy backwards down the tree trunks and pounce, once they have spotted their quarry. Earthworms form a large part of the lizard's monsoon food list as they crawl across the wet ground in search of drier turf.

By night, these same invertebrates fall prey to Northern Brown Bandicoots, Northern Quolls, Fawn Antechinuses, Red-cheeked Dunnarts and Common Planigales. The entire energy cycle seems to speed up at this time of the year.

Green Plums are now ripe   *Three-spined Rainbow-skink*

Spotted Tree Monitor

One of the smallest monitors in the woodlands of Kakadu is the Spotted Tree Monitor. This very active little lizard investigates the hollows and tree trunks as well as the litter, snaking its way along in search of small creatures. Grasshoppers and spiders are pursued with lightning speed, but larger items are also on the diet, such as Gilbert's Dragons, bird's eggs and nestlings and even small mice.

Bluetongue lizards also become more active with

the arrival of Gunumeleng, wandering the forest floor by day or by night in search of more stationary food items, such as fallen fruit, certain fungi, land snails or even the eggs of ground-nesting birds. Mating takes places now for this normally solitary skink.

The Lesser Wanderer (*inset above*) is one of the more frequently seen butterflies of the woodlands once Gunumeleng arrives. They appear to arrive from more northerly regions about this time. Some years, large numbers of these butterflies arrive on the coastline from across the waters of Van Diemen Gulf in an exhausted state. They cluster on driftwood and shrubs for some hours until they regain their energy. Then they move off over the wetlands and into the woodlands and forests where they are a common sight for some months.

In woodland areas with sandier soils, such as near the foot of the escarpment,

The Burrowing Scorpion

a large Burrowing Scorpion makes its home. The spiral tunnel may lead down more than a metre below the surface of the soil. At night, the scorpion sits in the entrance to the burrow ready to dart out and latch on to other invertebrates passing by. These are quickly immobilised by its sting and dragged into the burrow and devoured. This fearsome-looking creature is not a danger to humans. It quickly retreats backwards down the burrow when large animals approach. According to Bininj, a sting from this variety is not as painful as that of some smaller varieties.

Common Northern Bluetongue

A large male Antilopine Wallaroo

A juvenile male Antilopine Wallaroo

The emerging green carpet of annual grasses entices the Agile Wallabies to graze heavily after months of scratching and digging in hard, dry ground for roots and tubers. Some open grassy areas adjacent to woodland become so modified by wallabies digging for roots that it resembles pig damage. If the rains are delayed even longer, the wallabies begin chewing the bark of some woodland and forest trees, causing a ringbarking effect.

The first storm has almost an instant effect. Along with the Antilopine Wallaroos, the Agiles quickly put on condition and the breeding cycle resumes. This causes a major shift in the behaviour of the animals. No longer do they have to concentrate their energies to finding enough food and they now have a much greater mobility.

Although both these kinds of kangaroo only give birth to one young one at a time, effectively they can nurture three young ones at once—one young-at-foot still drinking from one side of the pouch, a new-born young in the pouch drinking from the other teat and a dormant embryo awaiting the weaning of the young-at-foot before being born. The ability of some marsupials to delay the birth of an offspring is thought to be an adaptation to uncertain seasonal conditions and perhaps predator harassment. On an average year, Agile Wallabies continue breeding through all seasons.

The Brush-tailed Rabbit-rat

The Brush-tailed Rabbit-rat is a large native rodent which lives in woodland areas and is a very skillful climber. Like the even larger Black-footed Tree-rat with which it shares the same habitat, its diet consists largely of seeds with some fruit and other plant material. A big bulky grass nest constructed mainly at ground level may be home for a number of these rodents. At night, they climb trees like Northern Grevillea to nip off the seed pods and carry them back to a safe location for dismantling and eating.

A forest of Stilt-rooted Mangroves

Seedlings replace the old trees in a healthy forest

MANGROVE FORESTS

With the quiet ebb and flow of the dry season tides, many floating mangrove seeds have been washed up and allowed to put down roots among the mature, senile and dead trees. This is the continuing process of coast-building. In the weeks to come, wave action will increase as storms sweep in from the east. Exposed mud will be eroded by driving rain and later by surging floodwaters. The serenity of the mangrove forest will be put to the test again.

Of all of the habitats, mangroves are the most ambitious and mobile, capturing and stabilising tonnes of mud each year and converting it back into fertile land. They are constantly trying to throw a protective mantle around tidal creeks and estuaries as they send out seeds to colonise virgin areas, creating buffer zones between land and sea. Moving foward as a unit with the new alluvial deposits, they allow the successive monsoons to cleanse the salt away behind them and create the ever-expanding wetlands.

The tangled root-mass in the larger Rhizophora (Stilt-rooted Mangrove) forests traps a different kind of nutrient. These forests collect driftwood which becomes entangled among the stilt roots and is then colonised by molluscs and crustaceans. Gradually the larger logs become wedged in by silt and are eventually honeycombed by Mangrove Worms. These worm-like molluscs were once a popular food among the Bininj clans in coastal Kakadu.

A mangrove worm is extracted from its shell-lined tunnel

The melodious Black Butcherbird

Great Egret fishing

Nest and eggs of the Black Butcherbird

In areas where mangroves come up against monsoon forest, many species move between the two. This is because the vegetation in both places is of a similar nature. Orange-footed Scrubfowl will happily wander deep into the mangroves and Chestnut Rails do the reverse. Varied Trillers, Yellow Orioles, Green-backed Warblers, Red-headed Honeyeaters, Rufous-banded Honeyeaters and Yellow White-eyes constantly work between both habitats in coastal areas. So too does the melodious Black Butcherbird. Like the Chestnut Rail, the deep, pure calls of this specialised butcherbird are heard far more than the bird is seen. Bininj say that it calls to notify people of the turn of the tide and in Gunumeleng these birds are nesting.

The storms of Gunumeleng create quite a bit of disturbance in the mangroves, particularly amongst the mud-dwelling creatures. After a storm there always seems to be a lot of activity on the mud flats, with holes being re-excavated, territories being re-established, and modified mudscapes being explored. This attracts the birds and one bird frequently seen on the mangrove flats in Gunumeleng is the Eastern Bush-curlew.

This is one of the many wading birds in the Kakadu area which migrates to the northern hemisphere between wet seasons. Eastern Curlews are ideally suited to life on the mud and their large, curved beaks give them access to the marine worms and molluscs that hide deep down. Fears are now held that the numbers of this interesting bird are mysteriously declining.

An Intermediate Egret displays its breeding plumes

A delicate shoreline protected by mature mangrove forest

SHORELINE

The clouds are now piling up in the afternoons and at the same time the afternoon humidity is increasing considerably. As the clouds roll in from the east and the sky darkens, a cold rush of wind precedes the storm and lashes the shoreline. It may only rain a few spots or there may be a heavy deluge and, as these storm cells travel west at an average of 100 kilometres per hour, the rain is generally brief. It freshens up the foliage and washes the dust and salt crust off the leaves.

At this time of year it is not uncommon to see a row of these towering storm cells in the afternoon stretching along the shoreline. They are known locally as 'line storms'. Initially, more rain does appear to fall in the coastal areas.

The Reef Heron is a common bird of the Northern Territory coast. In the Kakadu area it is predominantly of the grey colour phase, whereas further east along the Arnhem Land coastline there are many more birds of the white phase. The two colour phases intermix and grey and a white offspring are often raised in the same nest.

These birds are very tidal, stalking the exposed pools and gutters while the tide is out, then following the incoming tide to snatch tiny fish and prawns as the waters carry them fowards. During the height of the tide they roost and preen or fly off low over the water to exploit another area as the tide falls again.

The second breeding season of the Flatback Turtles is now drawing to a close. The small beach at Field Island, opposite the mouth of the South Alligator River, is an important nesting beach for the endemic Flatback Turtle. They are known to have a much greater rate of nesting success there than on the mainland beaches, due to the absence of Dingos and lower numbers of Yellow Spotted Monitors.

The tiny beach at Field Island

A Reef Heron on the mudflat

The Guettarda Tree

Flowers of the Stilt-rooted Mangrove

One of the coastal trees which grows very close to the high-tide mark and provides valuable shade for wildlife and people alike is the Guettarda Tree. It is a wind and salt-resistant monsoon forest tree which has very large, soft green leaves and Bininj readily use these leaves for plates when cooking fish or other meats.

The other very practical tree on the coastline is the Alabandja or Beach Hibiscus, which is often found growing on the high-tide mark among mangrove species. The long, thin branches of this tree are used to make multi-pronged fish spears. Once the shaft has been cut and the thin bark removed, the smooth, white wood is then painstakingly straightened over the fire to produce a remarkably straight

White-bellied Sea-Eagle

weapon. The three or four metal prongs are heated and burnt into the thick end of the shaft and bound into place with wire.

A very weather-resistant variety of Morning Glory creeper grows prolifically on sand above the high-tide mark. The leaves of this vine are well known to have a coagulating effect on bleeding wounds when heated over a fire and applied.

Ghost Crabs and Hermit Crabs continue to patrol the beaches at night, keeping them free of detritus and flotsam brought in by the storms and big seas. As the rain periods of Gunumeleng increase and fresh water is seen again on the ground surface, indicating that the watertable is rising, the salt smell of the sea drifts inland to the woodlands and forests and people sense that Gudjewg, the monsoon, is not far away.

Beach Hibiscus flower

Beach Morning Glory

ENDEMICS

THE SPECIAL CREATURES

CHAPTER 7

CHAPTER 7

ENDEMICS

Kakadu's endemics are mostly associated with sandstone

Every region in Australia features a distinctive flora and fauna. Because of its unique set of natural circumstances, Kakadu too has its share. Quite a number of newly revealed plant and animal species have yet to be sorted out by scientific taxonomists and, the more people explore this remarkable environment, the more they are likely to discover. To Bininj, however, these remarkable natural life forms have always been present and their role in the ecosystem is well understood

Extensive fauna and flora surveys have been undertaken in the Park in recent times and an interesting variety of new species has come to light. The Brown-backed *Ctenotus* and the *Magela ctenotus* are two small, endemic skinks which have been given scientific descriptions in the last few years. The new scientific name of the *Magela ctenotus* is *Ctenotus gagudju* after the Bininj language spoken in the area.

Although they now exist in geographical isolation, both the plants and animals of Kakadu show strong affinities with species in northeast Queensland, New Guinea and South-East Asia, suggesting closer bio-geographical connections in past times.

In addition to this, the Arnhem Plateau has a sister community in the Kimberley region of Western Australia, the Mitchell Plateau, which shares much the same geological history. These two sandstone regions also share many specialised plant and animal species, or have closely related species, most of which do not occur anywhere else. The species common to both areas include the Giant Cave Gecko, the Chestnut and White-quilled Rock-pigeons, the White-lined Honeyeater, the Carpenter Frog and the White-throated and Black Grasswrens. It is interesting that these 'prisoners of a changed climate' are all sandstone specialists.

It all indicates that these two regions, as well as other islands of sandstone, once had a common connection to Cape York, probably at a time when there was a much wetter climate. Such times existed in the past.

The list of these plants and animals is considerable and some of the more outstanding species are outlined here.

The distinctive character of an Anbinik forest

ANBINIK TREE

Allosyncarpia ternata

Perhaps the most impressive of all the Kakadu plants is the Anbinik tree, an ancient member of the Myrtaceae family which is now found only around the northern and western edges of the Arnhem Plateau. It grows to become the largest tree in the Arnhem Land region, reaching a trunk diameter of over three metres. In suitable locations over deep, sandy soils it forms complete forests which develop their own unique ecosystems.

The Anbinik is believed to have Gondwanan origins and its nearest living relative, currently known as 'Vic Stockwell's Puzzle', is only found as a small population of giant trees on the western slopes of Mt Bartle Frere in the Wet Tropics of Queensland. These trees are thought to represent ancestral stock of our present day eucalypts.

There are several puzzling aspects of this tree. Firstly, it is not known why today its distribution is limited to this very specific location. Secondly, it is not clear why it does not spread further afield when it appears to be quite hardy and apparently tolerant to most factors which limit plant distribution.

Anbinik flowers late in Gunumeleng and the small seed capsules open in Gudjewg, dropping masses of seeds which germinate immediately. Mature trees do not appear to flower every year and some individuals have been observed to wait three years between flowering.

Among the unusual wildlife associated with Anbinik is the small and beautifully marked Kimberley Rock Monitor which lives high in the hollows, the Cave Prickly Gecko, which lives lower down in the hollow trunks, and a type of Angung or Sugarbag. This bee is normally found in mangroves and, according to Bininj,

produces a 'cold' variety of honey. A type of antiseptic from a preparation of the crushed bark of the Anbinik is also made by Bininj.

WHERE: Some of the easiest places to observe Anbinik trees include Jim Jim Falls walk, Gubara Springs walk, along Barramundie Creek near Maguk and above Gunlom Falls.

ANWOLBON TREE

Lophopetalum arnhemicum

This is a less spectacular tree than the Anbinik but, like the Anbinik, it is confined to the western side of the Arnhem Plateau. It is restricted to the creek banks and billabong edges of the plateau drainage lines, where it is common.

It is easily recognised as it usually grows with its roots in freshwater, and it has smooth, light grey but deeply fissured bark. It can be found at regular intervals on almost any escarpment stream, freshwater river or billabong. It flowers in Gunumeleng and drops long, flat seeds from large, woody pods during Gudjewg. These are carried by water and deposited in sandy places where they germinate. As the root goes down into the sand, the seed stands up vertically before a green shoot appears.

According to Bininj, when Anwolbon is fruiting, it makes a good fishing shade because, as they fall into the water, the fleshy seeds are eaten by freshwater turtles and fish.

WHERE: These trees are a common sight along most freshwater creeks and billabongs. Easily accessible examples occur at Majela Crossing, Muirella Park Billabong, Mardugal Billabong walk, Maguk and above and below Gunlom Falls.

Anwolbon trunks have a somewhat battered appearance

Barrk eating Grevillea foliage

BARRK & DJUGERRE – BLACK WALLAROOS

Macropus bernardus

This beautiful marsupial has a natural distribution smaller than that of the Anbinik tree. However, within that area it is quite common. Until recently, virtually nothing was known about the status or biology of this animal, mainly because non-Bininj people rarely ventured into the rugged sandstone country of the Arnhem Plateau in the pre-Kakadu era. The few who did would not have seen much of them as these shy, black animals come out at night. If disturbed during the day, they quietly vacate their rocky lairs long before the intruder arrives and disappear quickly and quietly over the hill. The smaller females, which are called Djugerre, can be even more difficult to see because

they are a pale grey and merge into the sombre sandstone colours perfectly.

Barrk are never seen in large numbers but, at night, it is not uncommon to find a male and several females and young grazing in the grassy valleys. After lowland fires, they will often descend to the foot of the escarpment to graze. Their territories appear to be rather small as other mature males are usually never very far away. They are more solitary by day, preferring to rest alone in a cave or overhang with a good view of the surrounding area. Not only does this give the animal an early warning of danger approaching, but it provides much cooler air circulation during the heat of the day. During Gurrung and Gunumeleng they are never very far from sandstone springs or some other source of permanent water. They frequently share their territories with other sandstone macropods, such as Badbong, Nabarlek and Galkberd, although Barrk is not easily confused with any of these.

WHERE: Nowhere are these kangaroos seen regularly although they are becoming used to human presence in the vicinity of art sites, particularly Burrungguy and Nanguluwurr and also around Nawurlandja Lookout. The Barrk Walking trail is an ideal place to observe them. In Gurrung and Gunumeleng they take an interest in freshly burnt areas at the foot of the escarpment. Moving quietly around the escarpment edge between sunset and dark can be rewarding, as they are more relaxed towards nightfall.

The behaviour of these kangaroos is quite different from that of other family members

Grasswrens are curious about intruders in their territory

YILDING—WHITE-THROATED GRASSWREN

Amytornis woodwardi

One of the special experiences for ornithologists visiting Kakadu is to observe the antics and listen to the beautiful song of the White-throated Grasswren.

Similar in many respects to the other two northern members of the grasswren family, this bird is usually seen in family groups of three to seven individuals, on top or near the edge of the escarpment and its outliers. They associate with open areas of scattered boulders and spinifex clumps. Each group has a dominant male and a set territory.

Male birds begin singing from vantage points around their territories as early as Yegge. This vocal advertising heralds the breeding season which starts in early Gunumeleng. Nests are normally placed in the centre of a spinifex clump and all members of the group seem to take an active role in raising the brood during Gudjewg.

The most difficult part is locating the birds in the first place. When visiting their likely habitat, it is best to stop and listen periodically for the metallic buzzing and chirping alarm calls that the birds make. If you are not familiar with grasswren calls, you may be very close to them without realising it. However, they are masters at not being seen, sprinting mouse-like between the spinifex bushes, only to reappear momentarily some distance away. It is best not to attempt to pursue them but to sit quietly and allow their curiosity to bring them closer to you. Once you have seen and heard these birds, it is much easier to locate and observe them next time.

WHERE: Family groups of grasswrens are not uncommon on the sandstone plateau and they may be encountered on any of the longer Park escarpment walks. One of the more reliable observation areas is on both sides of the valley above Gunlom Falls.

ADJMU – BANDED FRUIT-DOVE

Ptilinopus cinctus

The Banded Fruit-dove, like the smaller Rose-crowned Fruit-dove, is a relatively shy bird but, like all the Kakadu endemic species, it is relatively common where it occurs, despite its limited distribution.

The presence of this bird relies upon two interdependent factors—escarpment gorges and monsoon forest. It is a bird of gorges, valleys and escarpment edges. Most of the fruit trees that it depends upon are monsoon forest species although, on occasions, these birds are known to fly out some kilometres from the sandstone to feed on woodland fruit such as Green Plum *Buchanania obovata*.

The Banded Fruit-dove is usually seen in pairs or small flocks and, when disturbed, will depart rapidly with a noisy clap of the wings. The wings also make a characteristic whistling sound in flight, which can help you locate the species if the forest canopy is dense. It has one characteristic which is unusual for the pigeon family, that of landing on vertical branches with the aid of its strong feet. The call is a very deep and quiet single "coo" repeated slowly many times. It may be heard on still days in shady gorges.

When searching in known locations for these birds, it is advisable to look for fruiting trees, as they feed on most suitable sized forest fruit. Popular food trees include the endemic Carpentaria Palm, the Banyan, Maranthes Trees, the Rock Figs (several types) and the River Almond.

WHERE: Banded Fruit-doves are frequently sighted in the vicinity of the major rock-art sites of Kakadu. You are likely to encounter these birds in any season, almost anywhere there is sandstone and native fruit trees. The sound of falling fruit or fallen fruit on walkways and tracks can be an indicator of their presence. They may also be seen feeding in the company of the more conspicuous Torres Strait Pigeons.

Banded Fruit-doves are much slimmer than Torres Strait Pigeons

Watering points are the best places to observe these foliage birds

BINDJANOK – WHITE-LINED HONEYEATER

Meliphaga albilineata

Although a small population of these birds is also found in the Mitchell Plateau area of Western Australia, the White-lined Honeyeater is treated here as a Kakadu endemic.

The haunting call of this bird is synonymous with the mysterious broken sandstone country that is so unique to Kakadu. It is almost as though the bird purposefully projects its voice from the high crags to obtain the best acoustic effects. The unusual descending half-tones can carry over a great distance in the sandstone stillness. The old Bininj say that this bird communicates with the Mimi, or sandstone spirit people, and warns them of human approach.

Some feel that it is unfortunate that such a beautiful call comes from such a plain-looking bird, but the drab colouration fits well with the sandstone country in which it lives. A very active bird, it spends its time visiting flowering trees and shrubs right down to ground level and it appears to have a large home range. It regularly visits springs and rockholes to drink and is often seen in aerobatic displays pursuing flying insects. It ranges throughout the open sandstone country but is never away from pockets of monsoon forest for very long. The diary entries of the explorer Leichhardt indicate that he was obviously listening to White-lined Honeyeaters when he and his party passed through the rugged sandstone escarpment country.

It nests mainly during Gudjewg and Banggerreng, often making the tight, cup-shaped nest in a small pendulous shrub under the protection of an overhanging ledge.

The White-lined Honeyeater is a curious bird and will often come in quite close to a person walking in remote country while sounding its raspy alarm call.

WHERE: The call of this bird will be heard anywhere in the vicinity of sandstone, particularly around shady cliffs, monsoon forest valleys, gorges and overhangs. They are active throughout the year. The birds themselves are a little more difficult to see. Waiting quietly near flowering trees or sandstone springs usually brings a result within half an hour or so. One such place is at the Nanguluwurr art site where water seeps out at the base of the cliff to form tiny pools.

KAKADU DUNNART

Sminthopsis bindi

The Kakadu Dunnart is a pale fawn above with white underparts and no other distinctive markings. It is a relative of the better known and far more common Red-cheeked Dunnart. So far it is known only from a handful of specimens. However, it appears to be more closely related to the Chestnut Dunnart of Cape York and the Carpentarian Dunnart of the Kimberley region. More recently, several specimens were collected on some rocky hills close to Darwin, and this has extended its known range beyond the Park.

The name Kakadu Dunnart is temporary, pending the collection of more specimens and full scientific examination. It may yet turn out to be a variety of a known species.

Having come to the notice of zoologists in the 1980s, the few specimens to hand so far have been collected in dry eucalypt woodland with a sparse understorey and heavy leaf-litter.

WHERE: Much more needs to be learned. So far the few known woodland locations for this little marsupial are remote and inaccessible to the average visitor with the exception of Gungurul (South Alligator Crossing) on the Kakadu Highway. Specimens have been found in the woodland in this area. Its status remains unclear at this stage. They are probably active throughout the year, as are the other tropical dunnarts.

This tiny marsupial has not revealed much about its private life

This tiny rodent shuffles rocks around with its strong teeth

CALABY'S PEBBLE-MOUND MOUSE

Pseudomys calabyi

Another newly revealed species from the southern sector of the Park is Calaby's Pebble-mound Mouse. It was given this name when it was discovered that it spends a great deal of its time arranging pebbles around the entrances to its burrow systems, just as its better known Central and Western relatives do. This is to ensure safety from burrow penetrating predators such as Yirrbardbard the Western Brown Snake. The pebbles block the entrance and form a well-ventilated door. The mice take a lot of trouble to interlock the pebbles for strength. At night, when the coast is clear, the pebbles are removed and the mice collect grass seeds and other vegetable material which are then stockpiled in the burrows.

Some confusion existed as to the status of this tiny rodent and it was first thought to be a variety of the Kimberley Mouse *Pseudomys laborifex*. However it is now confirmed as a species in its own right, and is named after eminent zoologist, John H. Calaby who discovered it in 1973.

WHERE: To date, these rodents are only known from the alluvial slopes and valley sides of the South Alligator River catchment. While they appear to be reasonably plentiful in the area, colonies are scattered and difficult to locate. Individuals may be seen crossing roads in the area between Kambolgie Creek, Guratpa and Gunlom, although they may be easily confused with other small rodents like the Delicate Mouse and the Long-tailed Mouse.

NAWARAN – OENPELLI ROCK PYTHON

Morelia oenpelliensis

This is one of Australia's largest and most intriguing snakes—intriguing because since its discovery by western biologists in the early 1970s, very little has been learned about its life history. It is a shy snake which is rarely encountered by humans, mostly because of the rugged nature of its sandstone habitat, but also because it is nocturnal and when digesting food it has long periods of inactivity.

Sadly, much of the traditional Bininj information about this snake has been lost with the passing of key custodians. It is said that its totemic place of origin or 'djang' is a pool at the top of a sandstone outlier in the rugged catchment of Cooper's Creek in Arnhem Land. It is a friend of the Mimi spirits which are thin spirit people of the rocky recesses in the stone country. It is also said that this snake grows much longer than the four metre specimens which are seen from time to time in the Park.

Harmless to humans, Nawaran is known to feed on various birds and small mammals such as flying-foxes, which are often captured in flowering trees such as Anboiberre. Large specimens of this rather slender python are said by Bininj to regularly capture and swallow the rock-wallabies Nabarlek and Badbong .

Sadly, the restricted range of this unusual python makes it a lucrative target for the international black market in wildlife. Specimens are known to have turned up on these overseas markets and the cooperation of the public in this matter will make managing this and other species more successful.

WHERE: Nawaran is a shy creature of the sandstone and is generally not active by day. It may occasionally be seen sleeping in a tight coil in a sandstone cave, under a ledge or in a tree. They can be encountered at any time of the year. They are not creatures of habit and thus are not seen in the same places regularly, as other animals are. They are sometimes seen crossing roads at night and motorists are asked to take care as they are a very slow-moving snake. Although virtually harmless and inoffensive to humans, they can bite if annoyed or disturbed and are best left alone.

Nawaran in a defensive pose

GURRBELAK

Chestnut-quilled Rock-pigeon
Petrophassa rufipennis

This distinctive bird is well designed for life in the rugged sandstone country. The dull brown plumage is freckled with fine white dots, allowing the birds to blend in with the rocks and tussocks while they search for seed. Its legs are so short that it sometimes appears to be on wheels when moving over the rock ledges and clearings. The tail feathers are stiff and strong and are fanned out as a support when landing on rock. The large, rounded wings can produce an explosive burst of flight when necessary, usually back to the protection of the sandstone ledges after being flushed while feeding. The shining bronze windows in the wings are easily seen while the bird is in flight, if one gets over the

In cool weather, these birds bask on rocks in the early morning

shock of suddenly having the birds take off like mortars from almost beneath one's feet.

Rock-pigeons are usually found in small parties which appear to have distinct territories. In the early mornings, particularly in Yegge and Wurrgeng, the parties can be seen basking in the early morning sunlight on the ledges in the areas where they roost. One by one they will glide down to more open feeding areas at the foot of the

sandstone slopes. Their chief food is the seeds of a wide variety of grasses, shrubs and trees. Spinifex

The nest is a flimsy platform of sticks placed on a ledge

seed forms a large part of their diet.

The hot part of the day is spent in the cool of the high caves and tunnels of the escarpment and another feeding session takes place in the afternoon. The group also visits the nearest spring at least once a day to drink.

Rock-pigeons are generally trusting birds, and, provided that you are slow and quiet, will allow a close approach. They are now becoming quite bold in some public areas, particularly art-sites.

While feeding, the birds keep in contact with a soft double coo, and this gentle sound is sometimes your first indication that a Rock-pigeon is close at hand.

WHERE: Rock-pigeons always live on sandstone, even though they may walk out into the nearby woodlands when feeding. They are found throughout the Park and their presence is always advertised by their explosive flight, which is a series of loud wingbeats followed by a glide, then more wingbeats, and so on. Active morning and evening in all seasons, they are also present on sandstone outliers, such as Ubirr, Burrungguy and Nawulandja.

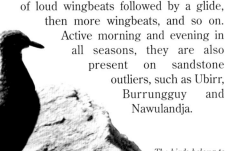

The birds belong to small social groups

MASKED ROCK-FROG

Litoria personata

Dry season colours fade with inactivity

This small sandstone-dwelling frog is actually a member of the tree-frog family. It lives a very unobtrusive life and it was not known to science till the late 1970s when wildlife ranger Greg Miles noticed its distinctive lifestyle and strikingly coloured tadpoles. The tadpoles were kept in captivity until they metamorphosed and this confirmed to which frog they belonged. The scientific name of *personata* refers to the black mask that the frogs wear.

Like all the sandstone-dwelling frogs, this one spends the dry months down inside the cool caverns and water-worn tunnels, well away from the hot stone surface. During this time of aestivation, the skin colour fades to a dull creamy brown. When the humidity and rain arrives, the frogs undergo a rapid transformation into the bright breeding colours of the monsoon. The call of the male, usually issued on rainy nights, is a series of high, canary-like trilling bursts given beside a running sandstone stream. At the height of the monsoon, when all species of frogs are feverishly calling, the rather delicate calls of this frog can be heard above the commotion and the sound carries for quite a long distance. Unlike other species which breed in the larger water bodies, male Masked Rock-frogs space themselves well apart and no doubt this gives their progeny a greater chance of survival if there is a break in the weather and the run-off water in which the eggs are deposited ceases.

The eggs are laid in small flowing rock-pools and

Wet season colours reach their peak during breeding

the distinctive tadpoles, black with gold longitudinal body stripes, are at home feeding in the fast-flowing run-off water. They are known to move upstream or downstream to more suitable pools.

Masked Rock-frogs are usually found in the company of Carpenter Frogs, Copland's Rock Frogs and Rockhole Frogs. Frequently they are all calling in close proximity.

WHERE: They are active only during the wet season (Gunumeleng to Banggerreng) in the vicinity of sandstone streams and pools, such as Gubara Springs, Burrungguy, Nawulandja, Maguk and Gunlom Falls area. Where suitable, a walk at night with a torch can help to locate the frogs by call. They may be discovered in the dry months tucked away in the dark recesses of caves near pools, waterfalls or permanent water.

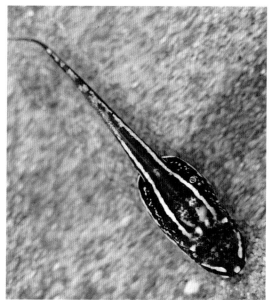

The brightly marked tadpole

USING THE PARK

A PRACTICAL GUIDE TO KAKADU'S REGIONS

CHAPTER 8

CHAPTER 8

USING THE PARK

Time always poses a problem for the visitor to Kakadu. No matter how much time you have, it never seems to be enough! It takes time to become familiar with the extreme climate, the great distances and lack of shade, the new world of natural species, and how everything interrelates as an ecosystem. Nevertheless, it is possible, with planning and preparation, to squeeze the maximum experience into the time you have available, even if it is just a day or two.

access to places like Jim Jim Falls, Twin Falls, Maguk, Gunlom and the East Alligator area is likely to be closed for varying lengths of time due to floodwater and the risk of personal or environmental damage. Park Headquarters provides a daily report on these conditions until the roads are open again.

Although weather conditions may limit where you can travel, there is still much to see in Kakadu during these wet months, for this is an especially

Kakadu National Park

An entry fee of $15.00 per adult (valid for 14 days) is required as you enter the Park. Children under 16 years are free of charge. There are campsites in each of the Park's five regions, with caravan sites at Mardugal, Muirella Park, Merl and Malabanjbanjdju. Camping fees of $5.00 per adult per night apply at the four major ANCA campgrounds (Merl, Muirella Park, Mardugal and Gunlom). The other Park camping areas with limited facilities are free of charge.

Hotel accommodation is available at Cooinda, Jabiru and Kakadu Holiday Villages. Not having your own vehicle need not be a disadvantage when travelling through the Park as there is a range of interesting tours available.

'Come, look and feel our culture' – Nipper Gabirriki

SOME SEASONAL VARIATIONS

Your experience in Kakadu may vary significantly, according to the season of your visit. While many visitors prefer to visit Kakadu during the dry season months from Yegge to Gurrung, people are becoming increasingly aware of the year-round attractions Kakadu can offer. Some of the Park's most spectacular attractions can be experienced only during the summer months.

From Gunumeleng through to Banggerreng (between the months of November and April), road

dynamic time of the year. Scenic flights in light aircraft are an ideal way to gain a quick overview of the Park. These are available from Jabiru or Cooinda Airstrips throughout the year.

Wurrgeng through to Gunumeleng (between August and December) is hot and dry with limited surface water available on tracks and walks. Outdoor trips need to be planned carefully. For extended overnight walks, Australian Nature Conservation Agency requires one week advanced notice to process camping permits and this gives the benefit of ranger backup in event of mishap.

A gentle approach is rewarded with a good photograph

TIPS FOR YOUR COMFORT & SAFETY

Remember that the average daily temperature in Kakadu ranges from 25°C to 35°C. It is sensible practice to wear a hat, use sunscreen and carry water. Avoid strenuous exercise. An ideal time for walking is in the morning and evening when it is relatively cool.

When walking any distance, it is wise to wear loose clothing which protects you against both sunburn and insect bites. When using sunscreen or insect repellent, do not swim as these chemicals pollute the water and threaten aquatic life. For the same reason, keep soap, detergent and shampoo well away from the water's edge.

PHOTOGRAPHING WILDLIFE

Most wildlife tends to avoid the heat and brightness of the day. A quiet walk with a good torch along a track at night, where permitted, is always rewarding. Australian Nature Conservation Agency advises against the feeding of any wildlife.

Remember, national parks have rules and some restrictions, but for the keen wildlife observer or photographer, often the best place to be is where the people are. In national parks, animals gradually become desensitised to the intense and noisy habits of people in their vicinity, safe in the realisation that they are not going to be attacked or harassed. Slow and quiet movements will usually be rewarded with an interesting observation or a good photograph, without breaking any rules.

For example, in the early years of the Park, endemic animals such as the Black Wallaroo and Chestnut-quilled Rock-pigeon were extremely shy and difficult to approach. Today, they are a regular sight at some of the popular lookouts and rock art sites as they have become accustomed to the large numbers of visitors to these areas.

It is of utmost importance that visitors 'fit in' with the wildlife, by causing as little disturbance or intrusion as possible. The future of our national parks relies on this observance. Most animals, no matter how approachable, appreciate their personal space. Using suitable camera equipment such as a long lens or carrying binoculars can help you achieve this.

It is always useful to remember that most successful wildlife photographers work on their own. Animals are less likely to flee at the sight of one person moving quietly. Wild animals can generally tolerate the presence of a person, but sharp sounds and rapid movements soon frighten them away. It is wise to seek the advice of rangers as to where and when particular wildlife may be best approached at any given time.

ROCK ART OF KAKADU

In the sandstone galleries of Kakadu is a rock art heritage of universal importance—one of the oldest known and best preserved records of human history. It is not the purpose of this book to elaborate on the complex background of the art. And though the Bininj descendants of the original artists are reluctant today to pass comment on the stories behind the paintings, a certain amount, however, is generally understood.

as the Tasmanian Tiger) are also attributed to this period. Some believe that certain paintings represent the extinct megafauna species.

When the landscape was inundated to the present sea level, estimated to have taken place between 7000 and 8000 years before the present, the **Estuarine Period** commenced. With the inundation, a new range of animals came into the vicinity of the escarpment, including the saltwater

Annual layers of X-ray style art depicting species of economic value

There are four main periods recognised in the historical development of this art and these correspond with our understanding of the landscape history. These four eras are known as the Pre-estuarine Period, the Estuarine Period, the Freshwater Period and the Contact Period.

The oldest-known art forms were produced during the **Pre-estuarine Period**. This applies to the various art styles known to have been in use prior to the last big rise in sea level. They include hand prints, simple but accurate land animals and the well known stick-like dynamic figures. A small number of paintings of the Thylacine (once known

fish and crocodiles which feature strongly in the art. In this era, the unique X-ray style, highlighting skeleton and anatomy, emerged. As time progressed, it took on a greater complexity. This style is still executed today by Bininj artists, but on bark or paper rather than on a rock surface. It usually features animals which are of economic importance to Bininj.

The **Freshwater Period** involved another time of great environmental change. Increasing rainfall and massive deposition of alluvial material from the Plateau area created barriers to saltwater allowing seasonal freshwater to flood the lowlands. This also brought another change in wildlife species. Again, the species of greatest economic importance to the people are most often depicted in the art, particularly long-necked turtles, Magpie Geese and Arafuran File Snakes.

The **Contact Period** refers to the most recent times when Bininj have had exposure to other races of people, mainly seafarers such as the Macassans and, more recently, white explorers and settlers. Contact objects such as guns can be seen in all the major galleries of the Park. Sailing ships and foreign animals are also frequently depicted. In a few instances, the explorers' parties have been recorded in fine detail in galleries close to their routes.

Bamurru (Magpie Goose)

Life-size monitors (Galawan)

Almangiyi (Northern Long-necked Turtle)

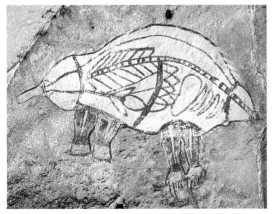

Gowarrang (Spiny Anteater)

Though there are many thousands of art-sites in Kakadu, most of them are not accessible to the general public. Those that are available to the public nevertheless represent fine examples of all art styles in a good state of preservation. There are virtually no Bininj remaining who continue to paint on the sandstone. The galleries which were once repainted each year after the appropriate ceremonies are now slowly fading. What we have is now all we have.

The Australian Nature Conservation Agency has the responsibility of documenting, recording and conserving as many of these artworks as possible.

DANGEROUS ANIMALS

Under normal circumstances, with common sense prevailing, none of the animals in Kakadu should present a threat to human life. Park signs clearly state where caution needs to be exercised. However, it helps to be familiar with the animals that are potentially dangerous. This will help you enjoy them more and lessen the chance of a negative interaction, as these are often the animals that fascinate people most.

Mosquitoes are potentially the most dangerous animals in Kakadu as they are known to carry a range of infectious diseases, some life threatening. Simple precautions however will ensure that you are not put at risk with these creatures.

There are a number of poisonous snakes in Kakadu which can deliver a potentially dangerous bite, although snakebite is rare and in most instances, these snakes are not willing to get involved with humans. Most visitors to Kakadu never sight a snake and this is generally because snakes detect humans first and take evasive action.

Land snakes regarded as dangerous in Kakadu are the King Brown, Western Brown, Taipan and Northern Death Adder. Other venomous species are not regarded as dangerous although they may deliver a painful bite. Seasnakes are venomous but are not normally encountered in Kakadu. Occasional specimens enter the rivers but their inoffensive behaviour does not usually bring them into contact with humans.

King Brown Snakes are large and venomous

Estuarine Crocodiles inhabit tidal and most freshwater reaches of Kakadu's waterways. Although normally not a threat to humans, they are quite capable of attacking and, in extreme circumstances, eating humans. They can be observed with safety, but caution and common sense are needed when using these areas. Park signs give sound advice.

Freshwater Crocodiles are inoffensive to humans and prefer to be left alone. They do become quite unafraid of people in public areas and may bite if provoked or tormented. Areas inhabited by the more potentially dangerous Estuarine Crocodiles are well marked and appropriate advice is given by the Australian Nature Conservation Agency.

Sea Wasps or Box Jellyfish inhabit the inshore waters of Van Diemen Gulf in the wet period between Gunumeleng and Banggerreng. These semi-transparent creatures have long, trailing tentacles armed with lethal stinging cells. It is not advisable to enter the seawater over this period.

Estuarine Crocodiles are not restricted to saltwater

Both the introduced Water Buffalo and the Feral Pig have been known to attack people on provocation. Under normal circumstances, however, these animals will keep to themselves and should not be disturbed. Both animals have been the subject of an eradication program in the Park and buffaloes are now a rare sight. Pigs are more likely to be seen in the vicinity of floodplains and billabongs and are proving to be a much more difficult problem to control.

Feral Water Buffalo are now a rare sight in Northern Australia

A variety of spiders, scorpions and centipedes is found in the Park, although none of these is considered more than a nuisance. Individuals react to bites from these creatures in different ways. By taking the usual precautions when camping, particularly at night, you should avoid any confrontation with these creatures. The relevant medical advice can be obtained through the Health Centre in Jabiru. Contact the nearest ranger in an emergency.

CHOOSING YOUR DESTINATION

A major challenge confronting the visitor to this huge park is 'where do I go ?'. This chapter is designed to save the nature lover time by presenting as many of the available natural history options as possible.

Depending on the season of your visit, it is always wise to become familiar with the habitats first. The Park provides some ideal walks to the habitats covered in this book. Walks and points of interest are described in the following pages, region by region.

Kakadu is divided into five different regions, each with its own ranger staff. Given the marked physical differences between the five regions, separate regional planning and management is required. Each district is unique, offering the visitor a distinctly different experience.

THE ARNHEM HIGHWAY

This is the main access route into Kakadu from Darwin and is regarded by many as 220 kilometres of monotony. However, the journey has much to offer the curious and observant traveller by way of information and scenery.

The trip from Darwin to the Bowali Visitors Centre outside Jabiru takes approximately three hours, with many interesting features along the way. Travelling this highway can be a way of tuning in to the tropical ecosystem. The Darwin region is essentially set in eucalypt woodland or 'bush' as it is locally known. Turning on to the Arnhem Highway from the Stuart Highway and travelling east through the little township of Humpty Doo takes you to the catchment of the Adelaide River. Fogg Dam Reservoir, a failed rice-growing project, has inadvertently created a superb waterbird sanctuary which holds water all year round and makes an ideal introduction to wetland wildlife. Ironically, ignorance of floodplain ecology was the undoing of the rice project but a bonus for the offending birds. Magpie Geese depend heavily on wild rice for breeding success. Their enthusiasm for the cultivated rice could not be suppressed.

In addition to the facilities provided by the Parks and Wildlife Commission of the Northern Territory, an excellent monsoon forest walk has been constructed parallel to the floodplain giving a good view of the structure of both monsoon and paperbark forest. The 'Window on the Wetland' interpretation centre on Beatrice Hill gives a detailed insight into the natural and human history of the surrounding region.

After leaving the Adelaide River Floodplain, the Highway roughly follows the high ground parallel to

Magela Creek floodplain in Yegge

the coast, skirting inland of the various wetland areas until the South Alligator River in Kakadu.

Before the non-tidal Mary River is reached, large termite mounds can be seen in the woodlands from time to time. Some are over four metres high. These mounds are created by one of many termite species of the tropics. Their highly seasonal role in the ecology is only just being appreciated.

The high granite hills of Mount Bundey are part of a geological feature which runs south through the Pine Creek area towards Katherine. Many of the Top End's gold mines are situated in the vicinity of this granite ridge. This is also the site of the proposed Mary River National Park.

Passing through these high, granite hills, you will notice numerous, palm-like cycads growing amongst the rocks. They have been a common feature since the Darwin area, but suddenly stop here and are not seen at all in Kakadu except for a tiny population in the very southern part of Kakadu. Why their distribution stops here is not clear.

Most of the country between here and the South Alligator River falls into the category of tropical woodland and may seem quite repetitive. However, careful observation will show that the composition of trees and plants varies from area to area with the soil type (often visible by colour) and drainage. Ecologists consider this habitat the richest one in the Park. One hectare of these woodlands contains more species of plants and animals than a comparable area anywhere else in Australia. The animals are difficult to see because most of them are nocturnal, avoiding the strong light and heat of the day.

The western boundary of Kakadu is encountered shortly after crossing the West Wildman River. The Park Entry Station is a further 18 kilometres along the highway. The Park is broken into five management districts. These are now dealt with individually.

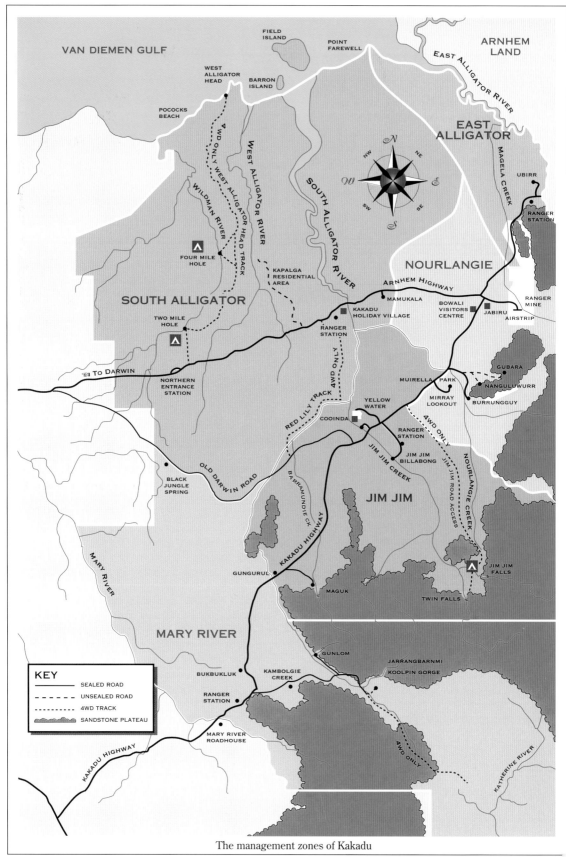

KEY

——————	SEALED ROAD
– – – – –	UNSEALED ROAD
············	4WD TRACK
▨▨▨	SANDSTONE PLATEAU

The management zones of Kakadu

KAKADU REGION BY REGION

SOUTH ALLIGATOR DISTRICT

Shortly after leaving the Park Entry Station, a gravel road leads away from the Arnhem Highway to the north. This is the West Alligator Head Track and is suitable for four-wheel-drive vehicles only.

Numerous creek crossings along the highway show a contrast in vegetation structure from the Stringybark and Woollybutt forests on the higher gravelly soils to the paperbark, Northern Grevillea, pandanus community with thick, scrubby understorey, typical of the more poorly drained soils. Groups of stately Kentia Palms can be seen growing on the sandy soils near the West Alligator East Branch and also Flying Fox Creek.

The only big hill on the southern side of the road is called Bukbuk which is the Bininj name for the Pheasant Coucal. The ancestral bird was born on this hill in the creation era. There are interesting stories associated with many of Kakadu's physical features.

Approaching the South Alligator River you will notice the woodlands increasing in density. These woodlands are particularly rich in wildlife. The Fawn Antechinus has a stronghold in this area and Antilopine Wallaroos are seen crossing the highway early and late in the day.

Off-road driving for Nature Lovers

There are three interesting tracks currently available in Kakadu to the careful four-wheel driver:

West Alligator Head Track
Approximately 78 kilometres from the Arnhem Highway to the coast (Pocock's Beach) via a good range of habitats. Camping is available at a number of points as indicated by signs.

Alligator Billabong Track
Approximately 70 kilometres of track which links the Arnhem Highway with the Old Darwin Road and travels along the western edge of the South Alligator Floodplain.

Jim Jim/Twin Falls Track
Approximately 80 kilometres of track with the last 20 kilometres being arduous. These tracks do not open until well into the dry season and close in early Gunumeleng.

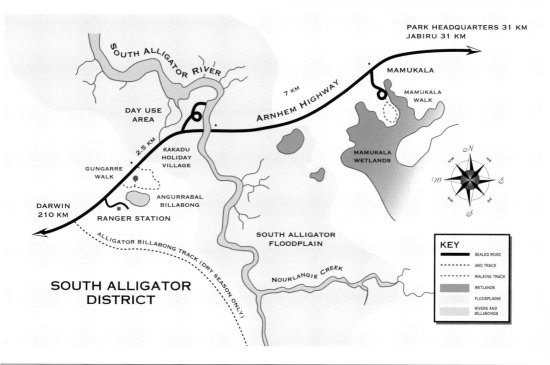

SOUTH ALLIGATOR DISTRICT

PARK HEADQUARTERS 31 KM
JABIRU 31 KM

SOUTH ALLIGATOR RIVER

MAMUKALA

MAMUKALA WALK

7 KM

ARNHEM HIGHWAY

DAY USE AREA

2.5 KM

KAKADU HOLIDAY VILLAGE

GUNGARRE WALK

ANGURRABAL BILLABONG

MAMUKALA WETLANDS

DARWIN 210 KM

RANGER STATION

ALLIGATOR BILLABONG TRACK (DRY SEASON ONLY)

SOUTH ALLIGATOR FLOODPLAIN

NOURLANGIE CREEK

KEY

SEALED ROAD
4WD TRACK
WALKING TRACK
WETLANDS
FLOODPLAINS
RIVERS AND BILLABONGS

Gungarre Monsoon Forest Walk

This provides an ideal opportunity to become familiar with lowland monsoon forest on a 3.6 kilometre loop walk. Quite a diverse mixture of forest trees shades the level pathway, making this an ideal walk in the hotter part of the day. Wildlife is rich in this area, and includes Agile Wallabies, Orange-footed Scrubfowl, Grey Whistlers, Rainbow Pittas and Yellow Spotted Monitors. The track circles back behind the Kakadu Holiday Village and leads back through woodland, where one of the features is the large Bush Apple tree, and returns via Angurrapal Billabong.

★ Allow about 90 minutes.

South Alligator Floodplain

Always drive more slowly across the floodplains because there are many things to see. Stopping is not always easy or safe, but a slow drive will give you the chance to observe wildlife and to avoid animals crossing the road. Large Yellow Spotted Monitors and Northern Long-necked Turtles frequently cross the roads during the day while Water Pythons and Southern Death Adders cross at night. Swamp Harriers, Black-shouldered and Letter-winged Kites, and White-bellied Sea-Eagles frequently fly over the plains and Little Corellas and Magpie Geese feed in the grasses. The geese breed here beside the road in Banggerreng. The mangrove-lined tidal arms which reach across the plains from the river shelter a variety of small birds including occasional Yellow Chats. At night, Barking Owls, Barn Owls and Grass Owls perch near the road and Dingos are a common sight on the plains. The large trees lining the riverbanks are Kapoks, easily identified by the thorns on their trunks. Estuarine Crocodiles may be seen basking on the banks and mudbars or swimming with the tide.

The brown silt in the river comes from the Arnhem Plateau 150 river kilometres or more upstream. It is another 75 kilometres down to the mouth of the river. The rock outcrop on the northern side after you cross the bridge is the story place of Binirrinj, the Mangrove Monitor. Today they live in the mangroves nearby. The road now leaves the floodplain and follows a peninsula of higher ground dominated by spiralling pandanus trees. This transition zone between the plains and the woodland is the home of Yirrbardbard, the Western Brown Snake.

The highway now takes you back into the woodland hills of what was Munmalary Station prior to the declaration of the Park. At a point some 25 kilometres further along the road you enter the catchment of the East Alligator River and catch your first glimpse of the distant escarpment.

Mamukala Floodplain viewing area

This pocket of the South Alligator floodplain holds water longer than most other parts of the plain and attracts large numbers of waterbirds, especially Magpie Geese. The bird numbers reach a peak before the water dries up in Wurrgeng or Gurrung.

 Thoughts for the motorist

★ *Observe all signs.*
★ *Keep vehicles to established roads, tracks and carparks.*
★ *Watch out for wildlife on the roads, especially at night.*
★ *Drive slowly along floodplains and lowland areas to avoid killing wildlife.*
★ *Place rubbish in bins provided or take it with you. Recycle whenever possible.*

This is a magnificent natural spectacle. Excellent bird hides have been provided to make birdwatching an enjoyable experience. This was a traditional hunting area for Bininj who recently decided that visitors should have access to this special area. They now hunt elsewhere.

Old Darwin Road

This was the main northern access road to Arnhem Land prior to the development of the existing Arnhem Highway alignment in 1974. It leaves the Arnhem Highway well before the boundary of the Park and traverses the hills and valleys on the outskirts of the Wildman, West and South Alligator catchments, providing more diverse scenery than the highway. Because of the low-level river crossings, this gravel road is for dry season use only.

Black Jungle Spring (Giyamungkurr)

Set on a spring-fed creek in a fertile valley, this site was an important water point for Bininj in the dry season. Among these hills there are a number of small, natural springs, some supporting monsoon forest communities. Aquatic life associated with these permanent springs is always interesting and dry-season water points act like a magnet to the wildlife. Gouldian Finches are often sighted in this vicinity after the breeding season finishes in Yegge.

South Alligator River & Barramundie Creek Crossings

The Old Darwin Road crosses the South Alligator River well upstream of the tidal influence. The road leaves the woodland and winds across a blacksoil plain which becomes seasonally flooded. Extensive paperbark swamps have formed on these plains and the numerous billabongs represent changes in the course of the river. Magpie Geese, Brolga, Jabiru, Whistling Ducks and numerous other waterbirds can be seen on this floodplain as well as Agile Wallabies, Dingos and occasionally feral pigs.

Barramundie Creek joins the South Alligator from the southeast downstream of the crossing. At the points where the road crosses these two watercourses, corridors of Silver-leafed Paperbarks shade the river channels and Freshwater Mangroves form an understorey. This is the habitat of the White-browed Robin, which is easily located by its loud whistling notes. Shining Flycatchers, Lemon-bellied Flycatchers, Azure Kingfishers, Rainbow Bee-eaters and Black Bitterns all frequent these areas. Pig-nosed Turtles, Estuarine and Freshwater Crocodiles live in the deeper stretches of the river.

Spring Peak Community (Ngurrkdu)

Before the Old Darwin Road intersects the Kakadu Highway, the small community of Spring Peak (Ngurrkdu) is passed. Rather than a destination, this is the private living area of one of a number of groups of the traditional owners of Kakadu. They prefer to remain in close proximity to the lands they own and manage. Further information can be obtained about the traditional owners of Kakadu from the Warradjan Aboriginal Cultural Centre at Yellow Water.

EAST ALLIGATOR DISTRICT

This district takes in the western catchment of the East Alligator River and includes extensive floodplains and examples of all other habitats. Its eastern boundary is shared with Arnhem Land. The East Alligator forms the greater part of this boundary. Access to this district by road may be cut off by water during Gudjewg and Banggerreng.

Merl Campground

This large and well laid-out campground is within comfortable walking distance of the East Alligator River. Situated in rich woodland surrounded by sandstone outliers, the area has much to offer the nature lover. It contains a full variety of habitats and wildlife, including Agile Wallabies, Sugar Gliders

and Northern Quolls, which are all common in the woodland. On the nearby sandstone are Rock Possums, Spiny Anteaters, Sandstone Antechinus and Giant Cave Geckos. Rough Knobtail Geckos live at the base of the sandstone outcrops. Black-tailed Treecreepers, Blue-faced Honeyeaters, Grey-crowned Babblers and Stone Curlews are regularly seen and heard in the campground. Ghost Bats hunt through these woodlands at night. Monsoon forest grows along the river corridor, paperbark forests in the upstream areas and floodplains downstream.

Safety Information

Precautions need to be taken against mosquitoes from Yegge onwards. Black Kites frequently swoop on campsites to snatch food scraps. Rangers advise not to encourage these birds as swooping can result in people receiving nasty scratches.

Cahill's Crossing (Kalarabirr Djowkeng)

This is a traditional crossing point into Arnhem Land and it is 91 river kilometres upstream from the mouth. The correct location of Cahill's Crossing is another 2.7 kilometres upstream of this point. The present concrete causeway was first laid in 1957 by members of the nearby Arnhem Land community of Gunbalanya (Oenpelli). To proceed beyond this point into the Arnhem Land Aboriginal Reserve requires a permit from the Northern Land Council.

The vegetation of the river corridor is mainly monsoon forest and the river supports a large population of Estuarine Crocodiles. As Big Bill Neidjie reminds us, sensible behaviour is required when near the water. Below the Crossing there is an average density of more than 30 individuals per kilometre from Wurrgeng to Gunumeleng. Archerfish, Barramundi, Salmon Catfish and River Sawfish are common species in the river. Schools of Bully Mullet can be seen migrating upstream over the causeway in Gurrung and Gunumeleng. Large upstream migrations of Freshwater Prawns can be seen here from time to time. Flood debris in the trees will give an indication of the height of the annual floodwater.

Man-ngarre Monsoon Forest Walk

This pleasant and easy walk through the monsoon forest features riverine forest made up of Giant Paperbarks, Leichhardt Trees, Cabbage Palms,

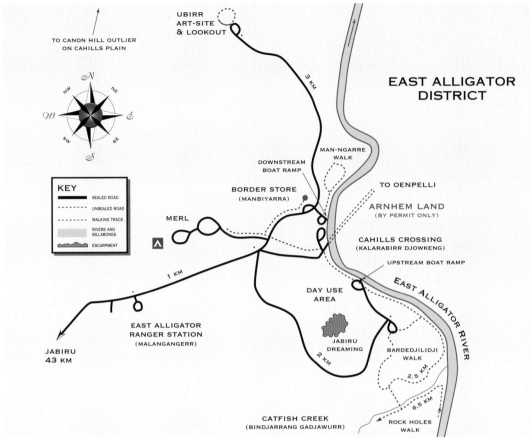

UBIRR
ART-SITE
& LOOKOUT

TO CANON HILL OUTLIER
ON CAHILLS PLAIN

3 KM

**EAST ALLIGATOR
DISTRICT**

MAN-NGARRE
WALK

DOWNSTREAM
BOAT RAMP

TO OENPELLI

BORDER STORE
(MANBIYARRA)

ARNHEM LAND
(BY PERMIT ONLY)

MERL

CAHILLS CROSSING
(KALARABIRR DJOWKENG)

UPSTREAM BOAT RAMP

KEY

— SEALED ROAD
---- UNSEALED ROAD
····· WALKING TRACK
░ RIVERS AND
  BILLABONGS
▒ ESCARPMENT

1 KM

DAY USE
AREA

EAST ALLIGATOR RIVER

EAST ALLIGATOR
RANGER STATION
(MALANGANGERR)

JABIRU
DREAMING

BARDEDJILIDJI
WALK

JABIRU
43 KM

2 KM

2.5 KM

6.5 KM

CATFISH CREEK
(BINDJARRANG GADJAWURR)

ROCK HOLES
WALK

Kapok Trees, Beach Hibiscus, Cluster Figs as well as an extremely large Banyan Tree growing on a rock at the very end. Torres Strait Pigeons, Banded Fruit-Doves and Channel-billed Cuckoos feed in this tree when the fruit is ripe. Orange-footed Scrubfowl, Rainbow Pittas and Rose-crowned Fruit-doves are permanent residents in this forest. The forest is based on the same rich, alluvial blacksoil seen on the floodplains and is inundated each year by floodwaters. There are a number of viewing platforms at vantage points along the river and at quiet times it is possible to observe Estuarine Crocodiles. The rich understorey has regenerated in recent years from serious buffalo and pig damage. A small swamp on the return journey features the native Taro Lilies and other water plants. At intervals throughout the year Black Flying-foxes camp in the canopy of this forest.
★ The return time for this walk is one hour.

Ubirr Art-site

This is a world-famous tourist destination. Set amongst some of the most northerly sandstone outliers of the Park, several galleries of beautifully preserved naturalistic rock art are on display.

Although Kakadu has what is recognised as the best treasury of traditional art in the world, it is not feasible to leave it all on display, nor is it the wish of the traditional owners to do so. Ubirr, however, is one of the best examples of the thousands of known sites and was a tourist destination long before the Park came about. The surrounding area is rich in natural resources and once supported a dense Bininj population. The Main Gallery was used as a wet season residential site until the mid-seventies.

As at the Anbangbang Gallery, the main art-site is accessible to disabled people. A view from the lookout gives a superb 360 degree vista which includes Cahill's Plain (Nardab) and the Cannon Hill outliers (Garrkanj and Nawurrkbil) to the north. An arm of monsoon forest intersecting the floodplain marks a drainage channel from these wetlands to the East Alligator River. The open country to the northeast is all part of the East Alligator River floodplains in Arnhem Land. The course of the river itself, the boundary between Kakadu and Arnhem Land, can be seen on the plains in the middle distance to the northeast. It is marked by a scanty fringe of trees. (Ludwig Leichhhardt passed across these plains and found it

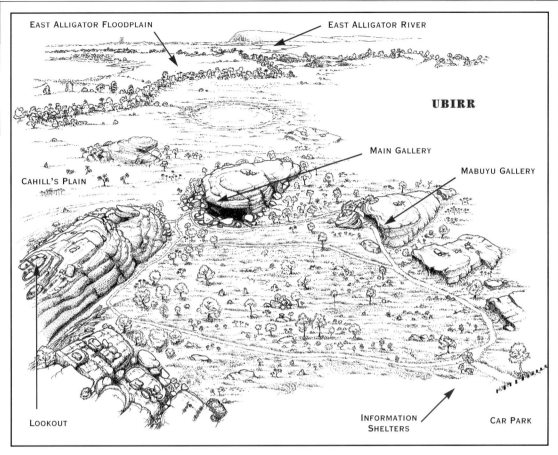

EAST ALLIGATOR FLOODPLAIN

EAST ALLIGATOR RIVER

UBIRR

MAIN GALLERY

MABUYU GALLERY

CAHILL'S PLAIN

LOOKOUT

INFORMATION
SHELTERS

CAR PARK

quite difficult to see over the dense Cane Grass beds.) Until quite recently, thousands of head of feral Water Buffalo grazed and wallowed on these wetlands each night. At the declaration of the Park, Leichhardt's Cane Grass beds were nowhere in sight. Since the removal of the buffalo in the late 1980s, the natural vegetation has made a remarkable recovery and the area is now carrying much greater numbers of native animal species, such as Agile Wallabies, Brolga, Magpie Geese and long-necked turtles. Leichhardt's Cane Grass has also reappeared and is resuming its dominant role.

Animals such as the Common Rock-rat, Sandstone Antechinus, Ghost Bat, Northern Quoll and Short-eared Rock-wallaby frequent the art sites at night. By day, the Black-palmed Rock Monitor, Chestnut-quilled Rock-pigeon and Banded Fruit-dove may be seen in the vicinity of the galleries. Double-barred, Long-tailed, Masked and Crimson Finches, Red-backed Fairy-wrens, Black-tailed Tree-creepers and Forest Kingfishers may be seen in the woodlands between the outliers.

The wildlife motifs which appear in the galleries here are species of economic value to the people. They include Barramundi, catfish, mullet and other estuarine fish which are common in the area, long and short-necked turtles, file snakes, monitors, Magpie Geese, Black Wallaroos and a host of others. An example of a Thylacine ('Tasmanian Tiger') in the very old style can be seen high on an outside ledge of the Main Gallery, but the more recent X-ray style dominates. There are also some excellent examples of sorcery art, as well as the most recent contact art.

One of the main queries of visitors to this place is 'How old is the art?' It is generally accepted that the main art styles reflect the successive changes in the physical environment since the last glacial period. Archaeologists have suggested that human occupation of this region could extend back almost 60 000 years and occupation sites in the vicinity of Ubirr have been dated to about 22 000 years ago. While most of the art in the Ubirr area is of a much more recent nature, some of the early examples could date back at least that far. Many of the galleries in this area were, until the last few decades, seasonally renewed by the appropriate artists. The older paintings become buried beneath a thick layer of ochre, as can be seen on the wall in the Main Gallery.

Bardedjilidji Sandstone Walk

The feature here is the beautifully fine-layered sandstone outliers which have been extensively weathered into many interesting forms.

The name for this pleasant and easy 2.5 kilometre walk refers to the Bininj name for the blue and white water lilies which grow in the nearby Bindjarrang Gadjawurr (Catfish Creek). The creek has a large catchment shrouded in paperbark forest and it drains into the East Alligator River. The track takes you through a group of magnificently weathered sandstone outliers fringed by monsoon-forest trees and returns via the river corridor. White-lined Honeyeaters, Chestnut-quilled Rock-pigeons and Banded Fruit-doves are often seen in the vicinity of the track and Rock Possums feed in the trees at night. Nests of the variety of native bees called Nabiwuh are common in the sandstone walls.

★ Allow at least an hour and a half for this interesting walk.

Rock Holes Sandstone and River Walk

This 6.5 kilometre walk takes you upstream to some picturesque and secluded sections of old river channels beside the East Alligator River. These deep cut-off reaches run beside some beautifully sculptured sandstone cliffs and outliers and, during the wet season, the river floodwaters flow through these channels and down to Bindjarrang Gadjawurr (Catfish Creek) and then back into the East Alligator channel. This is an overlap zone for both Freshwater and Estuarine Crocodiles and also home to the Pig-nosed Turtle. River Whaler Sharks and Freshwater Sawfish can occasionally be seen swimming in the Rock Holes, along with Bully Mullet, Razor-backed Herring and Archerfish.

Care should be taken not to disturb the nests of Freshwater Crocodiles on the sandy banks of the billabongs during Wurrgeng and Gurrung.

The track branches off the Bardedjilidji Sandstone Walk, crosses Bindjarrang Gadjawurr (Catfish Creek) and follows the blacksoil floodway upstream until the Rock Holes are reached. The walk is best undertaken in the cooler times of the day and swimming is not permitted.

★ Allow approximately four hours return.

 ## General Information

Care should be taken not to disturb the nests of Freshwater Crocodiles on the sandy banks of the billabongs during Wurrgeng and Gurrung.

 # Fishing in Kakadu

★ *Fishing with lures is permitted.*
★ *Cast nets, live bait, traps, spear guns and crab pots are prohibited.*
★ *Fishing is prohibited east of the Arnhem Highway including Maguk (Barramundie Gorge), Jim Jim Falls and Twin Falls.*
★ *Release any fish you do not intend to keep.*
★ *Northern Territory bag limits apply.*
★ *Do not clean fish or leave waste at the water's edge as this attracts crocodiles.*
★ *Saratoga, Black Bream (Sooty Grunters) and Eel-tailed Catfish are protected in the Park and must be released if accidentally caught.*

NOURLANGIE DISTRICT

This district occupies the central region of the Park and primarily takes in the Nourlangie Creek catchment. It offers a good cross section of many of Kakadu's unique features, including major escarpment rock art and occupation sites, billabongs and floodplains, as well as the Bowali Visitors Centre and the town of Jabiru.

Bowali Visitors Centre

Featuring some of the latest technology in park interpretation, this Centre has been designed to give visitors a sound briefing in the natural and cultural attributes of this World Heritage Park. A visit here is a good starting point to seeing the Park and at least an hour should be set aside to explore the displays, video theatre, library and audio-visual centre. Additional up-to-date information is available on all aspects from road conditions to specialised research.

Jabiru: a town with no cats

The present township of Jabiru was established in the early 1980s to house the staff of Ranger Uranium Mine which is five kilometres further east in the catchment of Magela Creek. It is the only township in Kakadu. It is situated in typical woodland habitat and an artificial lake has been constructed on the northern side, attracting a variety of waterbirds. One of the conditions for

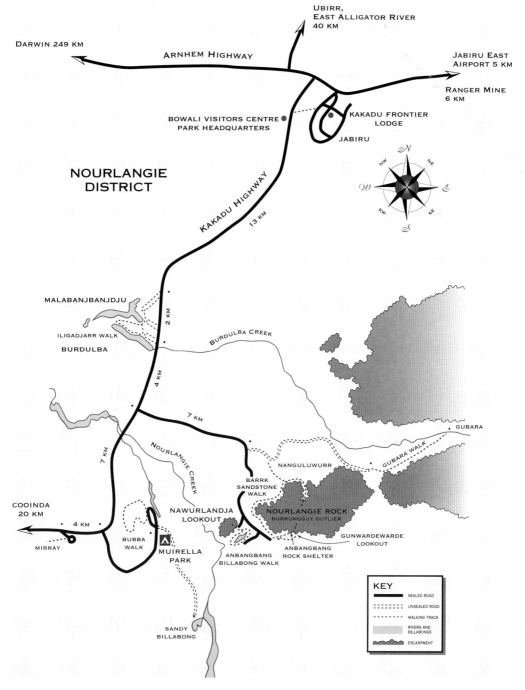

residents laid down by the ANCA since the beginning of settlement is a total ban on domestic cats. This rule has allowed the wildlife to continue living alongside the people and, today, native birds, animals and people co-exist in a unique way. Sugar Gliders, Black-footed Tree-rats and Brush-tailed Phascogales inhabit people's gardens, Long-tailed Finches and Rufous-banded Honeyeaters nest in the shrubbery beside the houses, while Orange-footed Scrubfowl and Black Flying-foxes have taken up residence in the shadier trees of the town. Groups of Partridge Pigeons drink from leaking taps and Antilopine Wallaroos graze on the golf course. A small Estuarine Crocodile has even taken up residence in the artificial lake. This town is the ideal place for the casual wildlife observer.

Iligadjarr Wetlands Walk

This 3.8 kilometre loop walk is part of the Nourlangie Creek drainage system on the eastern side of the South Alligator floodplain. More fish species are found in this creek system than in the entire Murray–Darling system of southern Australia. It is fed by Burdulba Creek and features a billabong and overflow swamp which is an excellent area for waterbirds, including Brolga and Jabiru. It also has a good population of Agile Wallabies and less visible animals such as Water-rats, Dusky Rats and Grassland Melomys. File snakes, long-necked turtles and Estuarine Crocodiles inhabit the billabong. The billabong is also the home of an ancestral file snake called Iligadjarr. It features an intermediate forest dominated by Swamp Box, paperbark forest, billabong and swamp grassland. The walk is accessed from Malabanjbanjdju Billabong or Burdulba Campground off the Kakadu Highway. It is advisable to walk in the cooler part of the day.

★ This walk takes approximately one hour.

Nourlangie Rock (Burrungguy) Art-site

The main attraction here is the superb human history record in both the rock art and the ancient Anbangbang occupation site, which traces Bininj culture through periods of environmental change. These stories are interpreted through brochures and signs as well as by seasonal rangers on duty at the site. Archaeological examination of the occupation site in 1981 revealed a long (over 20 000 years) and close association between the people and the plants and animals of nearby Anbangbang Billabong.

This magnificent outlier gives the visitor a taste of the grandeur of many other parts of the Kakadu escarpment which are too difficult to get to. Facilities here are mainly to provide access to the superb rock art galleries and occupation site from the ancient human history of the region. At quiet times in the cooler hours of the day, many types of wildlife are moving around the escarpment cliffs and overhangs. Banded Fruit-doves are frequently feeding in fruiting forest trees and Chesnut-quilled Rock-pigeons are local residents around the art galleries. Black Wallaroos, Euros, Black-palmed Monitors and Oenpelli Pythons are all sighted from time to time. There is a small water overflow near the information shelter at the carpark. Many bird species drink there throughout the day, including Partridge Pigeons and the endemic White-lined Honeyeater.

The rock art here focusses on a story about Namarrkurn, the Lightning Man, whose elaborate white figure appears here in several places. His activities are said to create the violent thunderstorms for which this region is famous. Using the stone axes which grow from his body, he can split rocks, shatter trees, frighten Mimi spirits and, occasionally, kill people.

Also in the main gallery, large male and female stylised figures in the traditional X-ray style are flanked by legendary heroes and Barramundi. This is one of the few art-sites in Kakadu where a date is given for the artwork. It is known that a man from the Bardmardi clan to the east of this area was the last person to re-touch this artwork in the traditional style. This occurred in 1962 or 1963.

The short optional loop walk at the end of the art galleries (a moderate climb) goes via the Gunwardewarde Lookout. Splendid views of distant Namarrgurn (Lightning Dreaming) to the east and the Burrungguy Massif itself are available from the lookout.

Barrk Sandstone Walk

This is a rugged but beautiful, moderately difficult 12 kilometre loop walk with a climb. It makes a good day walk, has some spectacular views from the top of the Burrungguy outlier and gives an ideal opportunity to observe the endemic plants and animals, particularly Barrk, the Black Wallaroo and Bongga, the Black-palmed Monitor. The haunting calls of the White-lined Honeyeater can be heard at regular intervals along this walk. It starts just beyond the Anbangbang Gallery.

★ The walk takes from six to eight hours.

Anbangbang Billabong Walk

This easy 2.5 kilometre walk is accessible only during the dry months, and is marked by yellow-tipped posts. The Anbangbang area is a shallow overflow zone for Nourlangie Creek and is part of a large paperbark swamp system. In dry years it has been known to dry out completely during Gurrung and Gunumeleng, but since buffalo numbers have been reduced and aquatic vegetation has recovered, this has not recurred. Northern Long-necked Turtles and file snakes inhabit the lily-covered swamp, but there are also many aquatic leeches. A good variety of waterbirds is on show here; in the mornings and, in the evening, Agile Wallabies and Euros come down to drink. Yellow Spotted Monitors roam the fringes of the swamp, even in the hottest part of the day when the other wildlife is resting. By night, Orange Horseshoe-bats and Ghost Bats, which shelter in the caves nearby, hunt over the swamp.

★ Allow about one hour for this return walk.

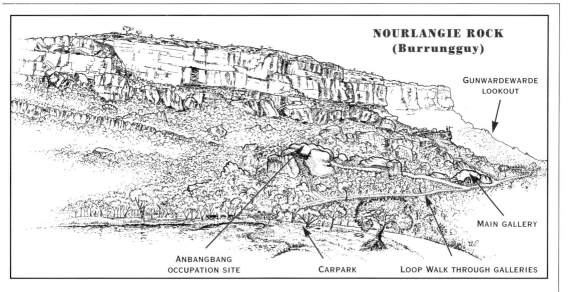

NOURLANGIE ROCK
(Burrungguy)

GUNWARDEWARDE
LOOKOUT

MAIN GALLERY

ANBANGBANG
OCCUPATION SITE

CARPARK

LOOP WALK THROUGH GALLERIES

Nawurlandja Lookout Walk

This is the name given to the tilted sandstone outlier on the western side of Anbangbang Billabong which has also been known as Little Nourlangie Rock. The short walk from the carpark to the lookout, which is open all year, is only 600 metres and involves a moderate climb. This lookout provides an excellent easterly view of Nourlangie Rock (Burrungguy), Lightning Dreaming (Namarrgurn) and the main escarpment in the distance. It is particularly good in afternoon light. It is the home of many sandstone animals, including Badbong, the Short-eared Rock-wallaby, which is part of the creation story of the area. Two large sandstone crevices extending back into Nawurlandja feed rainwater into Anbangbang Billabong and these features were created by two ancestral rock-wallabies. Sandstone Shrike-thrush and Chestnut-quilled Rock-pigeons are often on display. Rock Possums, Sandstone Antechinus, Ghost Bats, both types of rock-rats and occasionally an Oenpelli Rock Python may be encountered after sunset. In the rainy times, all the special sandstone frogs may be found in close proximity.

Late afternoon provides a view of the full magnificence of Burrungguy lit by the setting sun. Listen for the haunting whistle of the White-lined Honeyeater.

★ This return walk takes approximately half an hour.

Nanguluwurr Gallery Walk

This site is situated on the opposite side of the Burrungguy outlier to the Anbangbang Gallery. The sandstone massif is all part of the same giant formation which stretches east and then north almost to Jabiru. This enormous outlier is rich in art, with about 60 known sites. From the carpark it is an easy 3.4 kilometre return walk through open woodland. The nature of the woodlands changes as the track passes through drainage lines where the eucalypts give way to pandanus and Northern Grevilleas. At the foot of the escarpment the trees become more substantial and there are even a few monsoon forest trees under the shelter of the cliffs.

The art-site, depicting a variety of art styles, is situated around a small, permanent spring which trickles out beneath a ledge and provides a watering point for local wildlife. Banded Fruit-doves, White-lined, White-gaped, White-throated and Dusky Honeyeaters, Chestnut-quilled Rock-pigeons, Sandstone Shrike-thrushes and Sandstone Friarbirds all drink there during the day, particularly from Wurrgeng onwards. Olive Pythons are seen sleeping here from time to time.

One interesting feature of this gallery is the contact painting of a white sailing ship and dinghy, thought to depict an early supply vessel to the community of Oenpelli near the East Alligator River. The gallery also features well-preserved sorcery figures. (Sorcery art depicts a variety of malignant spirits which are said to manipulate illness, disease and death among unsuspecting human beings. They are often wildly distorted or grotesque humanoid figures.) There are some fine examples of X-ray fish and these were painted by a Bardmardi man in the early 1960s. The same man, the last of the traditional rock painters, also executed the last known artwork at the nearby Nourlangie Gallery. Smaller, isolated paintings have been carried out in other places since, but essentially the tradition has faded out.

★ This walk takes approximately one hour.

Gubara Pools Walk

A pleasant three kilometre walk into one of the special places of the Kakadu escarpment country, the track winds through the rocky foothills of the outlier and down into the alluvial valley of Burdulba Creek. It then passes through woodland, dominated by Woollybutt and Scarlet Gum on the ridges and Swamp Bloodwood nearer the creek lines. Many of these Scarlet Gums are colonised by the tiny Native Bees. The calls of Silver-crowned and Helmeted Friarbirds are heard in the woodlands, while the ringing notes of the Sandstone Shrike-thrush can be heard from the cliffs.

Nearer the destination are some beautiful examples of Anbinik Trees growing at the foot and on the slopes of the escarpment. Characterised by their dark green foliage, these trees are thought to attain a very great age. As the track joins the creek it enters a monsoon-forest corridor dominated by Native Nutmeg, Calophyllum, Horsfieldia and Anwolbon Trees, which shade the clear pools of Gubara. A wide variety of freshwater fish spends the dry season sheltering here in the spring-fed pools, including the Primitive Archerfish, and Black-blotched Analfin Grunter. Merten's Water Monitors feed on the abundant fish and are often seen basking on the rocks. Banded Fruit-doves, Emerald Doves and Rainbow Pittas are all seen in this forest, and the Escarpment Long-necked Turtle inhabits the creek.

★ This return walk takes about three hours.

Muirella Park & Sandy Billabong

Both Muirella Park and Sandy Billabong are part of the Nourlangie Creek system. Muirella Park was originally the campsite of early buffalo shooter Frank Muir and the remains of his camp can still be seen on the western side of the old airstrip adjacent to Djarradjin Billabong. During the dry months, the river here becomes a chain of long, deep billabongs where both Freshwater and Estuarine Crocodiles live, as well as Pig-nosed Turtles, Northern Short-necks and Snapping Turtles. Azure Kingfishers, Black Bitterns and a good range of freshwater fish are also seen here. Some interesting paperbark swamps can be found within walking distance of both Muirella Park and Sandy Billabong. The one approaching Sandy Billabong often has a good range of waterbirds. The vehicle access track between Muirella Park and Sandy Billabong is four-wheel drive only.

The campsite here between the old airstrip and Djarradjin Billabong offers easy access to all of the features of the region.

Bubba Wetlands Walk

This is a level and easy five kilometre loop walk around an open paperbark swamp area with an extensive Spike-rush marsh in the centre. Here a wide range of wetland birdlife can be observed, as well as an occasional hunting dingo. Between Banggerreng and Wurrgeng there is an extensive display of water lilies in the swamp. From Gurrung to Gunumeleng the waterbird numbers increase as surface water becomes scarce elsewhere. Binoculars are recommended. From the halfway point, a good view can be taken of Nourlangie Rock (Burrungguy) in the distance.

These wetlands are a tributary to Nourlangie Creek system. The walk, guided by yellow-tipped posts, is accessed from Muirella Park Campground.
★ This walk takes an average of one and a half to two hours.

Mirray Lookout

This well-constructed lookout is at the top of a conical hill on the lowlands called Mirray. It offers an excellent 360 degree vista of the central part of the Park, from the escarpment in the east to the South Alligator plains in the west, including Nourlangie Rock (Burrungguy) and Lightning Dreaming (Namarrgurn). This hill is a traditional hunting ground for Gowarrang, the Spiny Anteater. Many woodland birds, such as Yellow Weebills and Black-tailed Tree-creepers, can be seen along the track. Avoid the haze of the middle of the day by visiting this site in the early morning or later in the afternoon.

JIM JIM DISTRICT

This is one of the best known districts of Kakadu and it has a wide range of interest points throughout the year. The name Jim Jim is derived from the Bininj name for the Aquatic Pandanus, Andjimdjim, which is common along the waterways of the area. The district focusses around Jim Jim Creek, from the spectacular waterfalls upstream to the point where it empties into the main South Alligator River channel at Yellow Water.

Jim Jim Falls (Barrhmarlam)

Access to this part of the Park has traditionally been restricted to the dry season and, due to the rugged nature of the latter part of the track, to four-wheel drive vehicles. The major feature of the area is the spectacular Barrhmarlam or Jim Jim Falls, a 200-metre waterfall which channels the massive wet season run-off from the Arnhem Plateau to the lowlands. The waterfall itself is mainly a wet season

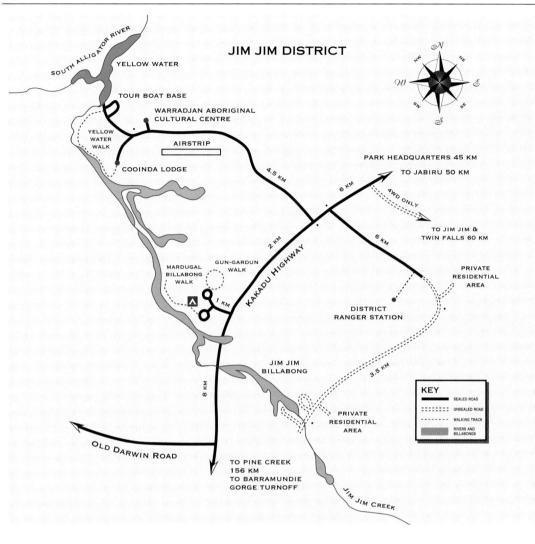

JIM JIM DISTRICT

SOUTH ALLIGATOR RIVER

YELLOW WATER

TOUR BOAT BASE

WARRADJAN ABORIGINAL
CULTURAL CENTRE

YELLOW
WATER
WALK

AIRSTRIP

COOINDA LODGE

4.5 KM

PARK HEADQUARTERS 45 KM

TO JABIRU 50 KM

6 KM

4WD ONLY

TO JIM JIM &
TWIN FALLS 60 KM

2 KM

MARDUGAL
BILLABONG
WALK

GUN-GARDUN
WALK

KAKADU HIGHWAY

1 KM

6 KM

PRIVATE
RESIDENTIAL
AREA

DISTRICT
RANGER STATION

JIM JIM
BILLABONG

8 KM

3.5 KM

OLD DARWIN ROAD

PRIVATE
RESIDENTIAL
AREA

TO PINE CREEK
156 KM
TO BARRAMUNDIE
GORGE TURNOFF

JIM JIM CREEK

KEY

SEALED ROAD
UNSEALED ROAD
WALKING TRACK
RIVERS AND
BILLABONGS

feature, made up largely of run-off water. The flow decreases rapidly as the dry season sets in and may cease altogether in Gurrung. The valley and pools, however, remain a place of beauty throughout the dry months. A shady Anbinik forest shrouds the rocky valley floor through which the one-kilometre return walking track passes from the carpark to the plunge pool. Freshwater Crocodiles inhabit the pools, although they are rarely seen. Allow some hours to explore the valley below the falls. The track is moderately difficult.

There is a strenuous and difficult climb to the top of Barrhmarlam for those who are very fit. A marked walking track leaves the lower falls access track, crosses Jim Jim Creek and ascends the southern side of the Jim Jim Valley.

★ This track takes an experienced bushwalker the best part of four hours and provides a view from the rim of the valley.

Budjmi Walk

For those who particularly enjoy climbing, the Budjmi walking track follows a course up the southern side of a rocky hill from the campground to allow the walker an excellent perspective of the escarpment in the vicinity of Jim Jim Falls. The light on the escarpment is best in the afternoon.

★ The moderate climb takes about 45 minutes for the one kilometre return.

Twin Falls (Gungurdurl)

A ten-kilometre drive beyond Jim Jim Falls brings you to another tributary of the South Alligator River which drains from an area of plateau more to the south. Plunging over the escarpment and into a long gorge at Gungurdurl, it eventually joins Jim Jim Creek ten kilometres further downstream. Access to the spring-fed Twin Falls from the carpark is either by swimming up the gorge (three long pools) with the aid of an air bed or by a difficult scramble along the top of the gorge. It makes a pleasant swim as the first part of the gorge is shaded by monsoon forest trees and some shade is available on the way.

Safety Information

Remember that Freshwater Crocodiles inhabit this and most other sandstone waterways and may be seen basking on rocks from time to time. While generally shy and inoffensive, they can become aggressive if teased or provoked. They, like most wild animals, simply require their own personal space and may be safely admired at a distance. The current swimming policy is under review.

Jim Jim–Twin Falls Campground

The campground on the banks of Jim Jim Creek is an ideal birdwatching location as many species use the shady river corridor. The sandy soil in the vicinity of the campground is home to colonies of Pale Field Rats and their burrow entrances are not difficult to locate. Although rather shy, they may be observed with a torch at night. The large-leafed gum trees are Swamp Bloodwood or Anbamberre and, although the beautiful scarlet flowers mostly occur in the wet season, there may be some in flower at any time. Sugar Gliders feed on the nectar of these flowers at night.

Mardugal Campground

Mardugal is one of the major campgrounds of Kakadu. It is situated beside a billabong system on Jim Jim Creek, upstream of the Cooinda Motel. Mature examples of the Silver-leafed Paperbark are common along the water's edge. The following two walks are available from Mardugal:

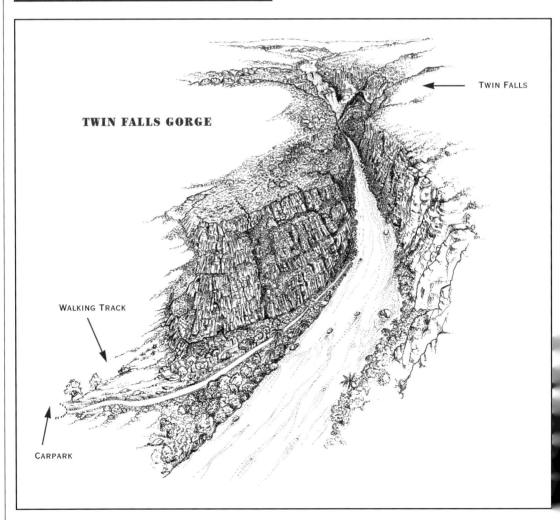

TWIN FALLS GORGE

TWIN FALLS

WALKING TRACK

CARPARK

Gun-gardun Woodland Walk

This is a two kilometre loop walk through eucalypt woodland in the vicinity of the Mardugal camping area. There are good examples of Narrow-leafed Bloodwoods and Liniment Trees (which resemble ti-trees) along the track. Partridge Pigeons, Black-tailed Tree-creepers and Blue-winged Kookaburras are regularly seen in this vicinity, as well as a host of other bird species. Agile Wallabies can often be observed during early and late times of the day.
★ Allow about half an hour for this walk.

Mardugal Billabong Walk

This track winds through a transition zone between the fringing billabong vegetation, dominated by paperbarks and Freshwater Mangroves, and the woodland itself. A few tree species, such as Northern Brush Box and the Liniment Tree, grow only in this zone. Crushing the leaves of the latter tree will release the powerful scent of oils contained within. This track may be inaccessible during wetter times. Precautions need to be taken against mosquitoes here from Yegge onwards.
★ Allow an hour for this return walk.

Yellow Water

This area is one of the best-known destinations in Kakadu as it provides an excellent and easily accessed overview of the world-famous wetlands. Situated on the confluence of Jim Jim Creek and the main South Alligator River channel, several kilometres upstream of the tidal influence, the deep river channels hold freshwater throughout the dry season. The surrounding floodplains also hold surface water longer than most other parts of the catchment, especially between Wurrgeng and Gunumeleng, creating a haven at that time for bird and other animal life. Kakadu has more than 80 species of waterbirds and most of these come and go seasonally from Yellow Water. Many other bird species inhabit the fringing vegetation. Agile Wallabies, Estuarine Crocodiles, Pig-nosed Turtles, Arafura File Snakes and Yellow Spotted Monitors are regularly seen around the billabongs. The area is home to several pairs of White-bellied Sea-Eagles while, at the other end of the spectrum, the brilliantly coloured Little Kingfisher is occasionally seen in vegetation overhanging the water.

Daily commercial boat tours with accredited guides take tourists out on to the billabongs and this is an ideal way to see the wetlands. Bookings can be made from the Cooinda Motel. A well-constructed boardwalk starting at the Yellow Water jetty leads out into the wetlands affording excellent views of the billabongs and paperbark forest. In the cooler times of the day, groups of Agile Wallabies graze in the shady areas while Jabiru, Brolga and flocks of Little Corellas regularly feed in the damper places among the paperbarks. A walking trail links Cooinda Motel with Yellow Water, traversing the fringing woodland and paperbark forest.

Boating in Kakadu

★ *There are boat-launching sites at Mardugal and Jim Jim Billabong camping areas and at Yellow Water.*
★ *Always carry life-jackets, oars, flares, a torch, tool kit and water. For detailed information about safe boating and equipment refer to the Northern Territory Marine Act (1981).*
★ *Know the boating rules. In particular, keep to the right when passing other boats.*
★ *Leave details of your trip with a reliable person.*
★ *Canoes are not recommended.*
★ *If you break down or are stranded and cannot reach land safely, stay in your boat until you are found.*
★ *Amateur fishing in Kakadu is currently allowed in designated areas, but is not seen as being in the best interests of nature conservation.*

Jim Jim Billabong

Limited camping facilities are available for tent campers upstream of Mardugal beside the quiet waters of Jim Jim Billabong. Large, shady paperbarks line the shores and boating access is provided. This is a good area for birdwatching, but mosquitoes can be a problem.

Warradjan Aboriginal Cultural Centre

Ngurrim-rei nguddi-nan dja nguddi bekan ngaddberreh gun-bolk dja culture. This is the welcome to visitors at the Warradjan Cultural Centre at Yellow Water. It means: 'Come, look and feel our culture.' This is an outstanding display by the Bininj owners of Kakadu of cultural materials and information to help visitors to better understand who these people are and how they relate to their land. Local arts and crafts are also available for purchase here. The building is designed in the shape of a Pig-nosed Turtle (Warradjan).

A final message as you leave the centre states: *Gamuk, ngurrdi-nang ngardberre culture. Wanjih ngardberre gun-bolk ngarrdinahna.* 'It is good you looked and felt our culture. Look after our country.'

Barramundie Gorge (Maguk)

Situated where the spring-fed waters of Barramundie Creek leave the sandstone escarpment and flow out through the woodlands, this beautiful and very delicate corridor of monsoon forest, interspersed with Giant Paperbarks, Anwolbon and Anbinik Trees, is home to a wide range of wildlife. In the cooler times of the day, Antilopine Wallaroos can occasionally be seen in the woodlands as you drive along the access track. Rainbow Pittas are often seen in the shadier places searching the leaf litter for invertebrates. The large mauve flowers growing on the silken-leaved shrubs are Native Lassiandra, a water-loving plant of the permanently wet places. They produce a sweet, edible fruit. In the clear waters of the creek lives a range of native fish, including the highly protected Sooty Grunter. Freshwater Crocodiles and long-necked turtles feed on the abundant fish life. The pool at the head of the gorge is a refuge for these aquatic animals. Swimming is currently permitted where it does not interfere with the wildlife. Places like Maguk are of extreme importance to the overall ecology of Kakadu and require a very careful balance with tourism.

MARY RIVER DISTRICT

This is the newest segment of the Park. It was part of the third and final stage of the creation of Kakadu, being declared in June 1987. Roughly comprising about one-third of the total area of the Park, it takes in the headwaters of the Katherine River which then flows south into Nitmiluk (Katherine Gorge) National Park. It is physically different to the rest of Kakadu and completes the protection of the entire South Alligator River catchment.

Gungurul (South Alligator River Crossing) Day Use Area

Picnic facilities are provided at this roadside stop beside the South Alligator River Bridge. A short walking trail leads to a lookout on a rocky hill which gives a good view both ways of the South Alligator River Valley. Volcanic rocks (andesite and tuff) are strewn about the ground surface as a reminder of the ancient volcanic activity which greatly altered the geology of this region. Grey Box Trees are common here and this is one of the few sites where the rare Kakadu Dunnart has been found.

Bukbukluk

This roadside lookout gives a good view to the northeast of the South Alligator River Valley. The location is part of an ancient story about a disagreement between the Frilled Lizard (Gundamen) and the Pheasant Coucal (Bukbuk) over red ochre. A small, spring-fed monsoon forest can be seen beside the lookout. A constant water supply has made this possible. Common Bronzewing Pigeons are often seen in this area. Plans to upgrade and relocate this lookout to provide views to the east, north and west should be completed in 1996. It will be situated on the opposite (western) side of the road to the current site.

Wildlife Information

Between Gurrung and Banggerreng, Hooded Parrots are regularly sighted in the vicinity of Gerowie and Kambolgie Creeks. During the same period, Antilopine Wallaroos are seen south of Gungurul on the Kakadu Highway and in the vicinity of Plum Tree Creek.

Yurmikmik Walking Trail

This walking trail starts from the clearly marked main road carpark 16 kilometres before you reach Gunlom. The following walks begin and end at this point.

Small Gorge Walk is a two kilometre return walk which features a small patch of monsoon vine forest sheltered by the walls of the gorge. You may note the volcanic breccia rocks lying about this area. The black and white butterflies in the monsoon forest are Common Australian Crow butterflies. The melodious Sandstone Shrike-thrush and the Chestnut-quilled Rock-pigeon also frequent the area.

★ Allow about one hour for this return walk.

Yurmikmik Lookout Walk, a five kilometre return, skirts around the rocky slopes to the top of a hill where you can gain an overview of the South Alligator valley. The rather stunted, yellow-barked trees with the small leaves are one of several varieties of Native Gardenia.

★ This walk takes about one and a half hours.

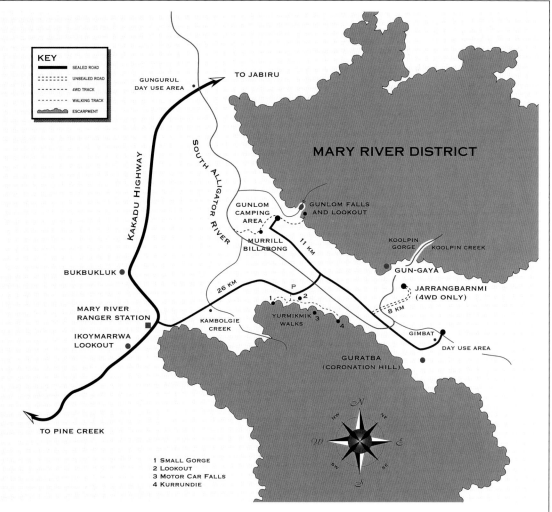

KEY

▬▬▬	SEALED ROAD
▪▪▪▪▪	UNSEALED ROAD
▪ ▪ ▪	4WD TRACK
─ ─ ─	WALKING TRACK
∿∿∿	ESCARPMENT

MARY RIVER DISTRICT

TO JABIRU

GUNGURUL DAY USE AREA

KAKADU HIGHWAY

SOUTH ALLIGATOR RIVER

GUNLOM CAMPING AREA

GUNLOM FALLS AND LOOKOUT

MURRILL BILLABONG

11 KM

KOOLPIN GORGE   KOOLPIN CREEK

BUKBUKLUK

26 KM

GUN-GAYA

JARRANGBARNMI (4WD ONLY)

MARY RIVER RANGER STATION

KAMBOLGIE CREEK

YURMIKMIK WALKS

P

8 KM

GIMBAT

IKOYMARRWA LOOKOUT

GURATBA (CORONATION HILL)

DAY USE AREA

TO PINE CREEK

1 SMALL GORGE
2 LOOKOUT
3 MOTOR CAR FALLS
4 KURRUNDIE

Motor Car Falls Walk is a 7.5 kilometre return walk that passes through more open woodlands from the Lookout Track.
★ Allow three hours.

Kurrundie Falls Walk, an 11 kilometre return walk, is a more strenuous walk on a less well-defined track leading on from Motor Car Falls. Small-leafed Salmon Gums grow on the hillsides. Peregrine Falcons, Black-breasted Buzzards and Grey Goshawks all inhabit this valley, while Banded Fruit-doves and Black Wallaroos are seen on occasions.
★ Allow approximately five hours.

Walking through the open woodland you may observe groups of small burrows excavated in the red soil. These burrow systems belong to the Pale Field Rat which lives in colonies in this area. They are only abroad at night to collect seeds and nesting materials. Keep your eyes open for small flocks of

Hooded Parrots flying or feeding on the ground in these woodlands. Small flocks of Gouldian Finches are also seen occasionally in the area from Yegge onwards. Red-backed Fairy-wrens and Partridge Pigeons frequent the carpark area and Swamp Bloodwoods grow in the alluvial soils of the creek banks.

Gunlom Day Use area and Campground
Formerly known by visitors as UDP Falls or Waterfall Creek, this beautiful tributary of the South Alligator River is well known for its waterfall and plunge pool. Like Maguk, it is a fragile area needing careful management and has much to offer the keen naturalist. The Day Use Area features some splendid examples of the Large-leafed Salmon Gum. Forest Kingfishers and Blue-faced Honeyeaters frequent the lawn area. The short walk to the pool crosses a monsoon forest stream which accommodates an interesting range of freshwater fish as well as crayfish and long-necked turtles.

An even better view may be obtained at night with a good torch. You may see the large female Golden Orb Spider on her strong web over the water. Almost harmless to humans, these monsoon forest spiders snare large prey, sometimes as large as small birds and bats.

The campground, situated below the Day Use Area, is home to a wide range of birdlife, as well as Little Northern Quolls, Black-footed Tree-rats, Pale Field Rats and Northern Brown Bandicoots. These are seen or heard mainly at night, along with Stone Curlews, Barking and Boobook Owls.

Gunlom Lookout

A steep trail leads up the right-hand side of the Falls from the Day Use Area. The effort is well worth the experience. A lookout gives a fine view of the surrounding South Alligator Valley and the track continues on a short distance to the pools upstream. Swimming is permitted. This is another good area to look for endemic flora and fauna, especially White-throated Grasswrens, Chestnut-quilled Rock-pigeons, White-lined Honeyeaters and Sandstone Shrike-thrush. The sticky-leafed Helix Wattle seen in the vicinity of the lookout is also an endemic. Like spinifex, it gives off a strong aroma.

Murrill Billabong

This is a pleasant, almost-level walk from the Gunlom Campground across open woodland past Murrill Billabong to the main channel of the South Alligator River. There is not a lot of shade on the walk, but on arrival at the river, the Silver-leafed Paperbarks offer a cool resting point. The past volcanic activity in this valley is evident in the occasional granite outcrop and the breccia rocks along the track. In the vicinity of the billabong, a wide variety of waterbirds can be seen, as well as Forest Kingfishers, Rainbow Bee-eaters and a range of finches. Antilopine Wallaroos drink here periodically.
★ Allow about one hour for this return walk.

Guratba (Coronation Hill)–Gimbat Day Use Area

Good examples of Ghost Gums and Cluster Figs can be seen here. Sand Monitors and Collared Sparrowhawks are also seen here from time to time.

Koolpin Gorge (Jarrangbarnmi)

There are many beautiful gorges in Kakadu National Park where streams and rivers exit the escarpment country with powerful water action and gradually slow down to cross the lowlands to the sea. This less well-known gorge has restricted visitor use because of its delicate nature, limited carrying capacity and four-wheel drive only access. For these reasons, development here has been kept to a minimum and visitor numbers will continue to be restricted. The region supports all of the endemic wildlife and is the southernmost known limit for some species.

A site of significance exists adjacent to the campground and the traditional owners require visitors to avoid the area. Please observe the on-site signs to this effect.

Gun-gaya (Freezing Gorge) Walk

A tributary stream enters Koolpin Creek downstream of the campground. A six-kilometre return walk follows this creek upstream to a narrow, west-facing gorge known to the Jawoyn as Gun-gaya. This is a strenuous walk on an unmarked track over difficult terrain. For proper appreciation, this walk requires a full day. Camping permits are required, as are permits for overnight bushwalks. These can be obtained from the Mary River Ranger Station or the Bowali Visitor Centre.

 Visitor Information

Conditions are subject to constant development and climatic change in Kakadu and it is always advisable to obtain up-to-date information from the ANCA Darwin Office or Bowali Visitors Centre, Jabiru, when visiting or planning a visit.

ANCA Darwin Office (PO Box 1260 Darwin NT 0801) is located on the sixth floor of the MLC Building, 81 Smith Street, Darwin Phone 089 81 5299   Fax 089 81 3497

Bowali Visitors Centre (PO Box 71 Jabiru NT 0886) is located 1 kilometre south of the junction of the Arnhem and Kakadu Highways, outside the town of Jabiru. Phone 089 38 1100   Fax 089 38 1115

EXPLORING KAKADU'S SPECIAL HABITATS

FOR VISITORS WHO WOULD LIKE TO EXPERIENCE A PARTICULAR HABITAT, WITHOUT VENTURING TOO FAR OFF THE BEATEN TRACK, THE TABLE BELOW PROVIDES SOME EXCELLENT BUT EASILY ACCESSIBLE EXAMPLES. THEY ARE LISTED ACCORDING TO REGION.

STONE COUNTRY	NOURLANGIE DISTRICT	EAST ALLIGATOR DISTRICT	MARY RIVER DISTRICT
	Nawurlandja Lookout Walk	Bardedjilidji Walk	Gunlom Lookout
RIVERS & BILLABONGS	EAST ALLIGATOR DISTRICT	NOURLANGIE DISTRICT	JIM JIM DISTRICT
	Rock Holes Sandstone & River Walk Guluyarnbi Boat Cruise	Iligadjarr Nature Trail	Yellow Water Boat Tour
FLOODPLAINS	SOUTH ALLIGATOR DISTRICT	EAST ALLIGATOR DISTRICT	JIM JIM DISTRICT
	Mamukarla Floodplain Viewing Area	Ubirr Lookout	Yellow Water Boat Tour
PAPERBARK SWAMPS	NOURLANGIE DISTRICT	NOURLANGIE DISTRICT	NOURLANGIE DISTRICT
	Anbangbang Billabong	Bubba Wetlands Walk	Mardugal Billabong Walk
MONSOON FOREST	SOUTH ALLIGATOR DISTRICT	EAST ALLIGATOR DISTRICT	NOURLANGIE DISTRICT
	Gungarre Monsoon Forest Walk	Manngarre Monsoon Forest Walk	Gubarra Pools
OPEN WOODLAND	NOURLANGIE DISTRICT	JIM JIM DISTRICT	MARY RIVER DISTRICT
	Gubarra Pools Walk Nanguluwur Gallery Walk	Gun-Gardun Walk	Yurmikmik Walking Trail
MANGROVES	SOUTH ALLIGATOR DISTRICT	SOUTH ALLIGATOR DISTRICT	
	Pocock's Beach, West Alligator Head (4WD)	South Alligator Bridge (vicinity) Arnhem Highway	
SHORELINE	SOUTH ALLIGATOR DISTRICT		
	Pocock's Beach, West Alligator Head (4WD)		

WILDLIFE TERMINOLOGY OF KAKADU

A selection of frequently used common names of wildlife,
with accompanying scientific and Bininj names.

(G) Gagudju • (K) Kunwinjku • (I) Iwadja

Common English Name	Scientific Name	Bininj Name
Agile Wallaby	Macropus agilis	Gornoboloh
Antilopine Wallaroo (f)	Macropus antilopinus	Garnday
Antilopine Wallaroo (m)	Macropus antilopinus	Garndagidj
Arafura File Snake	Acrochordus arafurae	Gedjebe (K)
		Nawandak
Archerfish	Toxotes chatareus	Nyalkarn
Arnhem Land Crevice-skink	Egernia arnhemensis	Unknown
Arnhem Land Rock-rat	Zyzomis maini	Godjberr
Asian Water Buffalo	Bubalis bubalis	Anabarru
Australian Bustard	Ardeotis australis	Benuk
		Imagirrk (G)
Australian Owlet-nightjar	Aegotheles cristatus	Natjik
Australian Pelican	Pelicanus conspicillatus	Makakurr
Australian Pratincole	Stiltia isabella	Uluruwitj (G)
Banded Fruit-dove	Ptilinopus cinctus	Adjmu
Barking Owl	Ninox connivens	Mobok
Barn Owl	Tyto alba	Mobinj
Barramundi	Lates calcarifer	Namarngol
Black-blotched	Pingalla midgleyi	Unknown
Anal-fin Grunter		
Black Flying-fox	Pteropus alecto	Na-ngamu
Black Kite	Milvus migrans	Buludjirr
Black Wallaroo (f)	Macropus bernardus	Djugerre
Black Wallaroo (m)	Macropus bernardus	Barrk
Black Whipsnake	Demansia atra	Wurrgurduk
Black-winged Stilt	Himantopus himantopus	Amurak
		Nginarrk nginarrk
Black-faced Cuckoo-shrike	Coracina novaehollandiae	Wirriwirriyak
Black-footed Tree-rat	Mesembriomys gouldii	Barrih
Black-headed Python	Aspidites melanocephalus	Madjurn
Black-palmed Rock Monitor	Varanus glebopalma	Bongga
Black-spotted Ridge-tailed	Varanus baritji	Unknown
Monitor		
Blind Snake family	Typhlopidae spp.	Unknown
Blue-winged Kookaburra	Dacelo leachii	Barradja
Brahminy Kite	Haliastur indus	Unknown
Brolga	Grus rubicundus	Algordu
		Gurdurrk
Brown Bandicoot	Isoodon macrourus	Yok
Brown Booby	Sula leucogaster	Unknown
Brown Falcon	Falco berigora	Garrkanj
Brown Flycatcher	Microeca leucophaea	Mayhmayh
Brown Quail	Coturnix australis	Djerndi
Brush-tailed Phascogale	Phascogale tapoatafa	Wumbu
Bush Stone-curlew	Burhinus grallarius	Gurrwirluk
Calaby's Pebble-	Pseudomys calabyi	Unknown
mound Mouse		
Carp Gudgeon	Hypseleotris compressus	Djegert djegert
Carpenter Frog	Megistolotis lignarius	Unknown
Carpet Python	Morelia spilota	Djokbinj
Cattle Egret	Bubulcus ibis	Ngarrgundul
Cave Prickly Gecko	Heteronotia spelea	Unknown
Chameleon Dragon	Chelosania brunnea	Al-walngurru
Chanda Perch	Ambassis spp.	Betem
Chequered Rainbowfish	Melanotaenia splendida	Dilebang
Chestnut Rail	Eulabiornis castaneiventris	Unknown
Chestnut-quilled		
Rock-pigeon	Petrophassa rufipennis	Gurrbelak

Common English Name	Scientific Name	Bininj Name
Claw-snouted		
Blind Snake	Ramphotyphlops unguirostris	Unknown
Coal Grunter	Hephaestus carbo	Dubang
Common Koel	Eudynamis scolopacea	Djawok
Common Northern	Tiliqua scincoides	Gurrih
Bluetongue		
Common Rock-rat	Zyzomis argrurus	Godjberr
Darter	Anhinga melanogaster	Garrabaybay
Common Planigale	Planigale maculata	Unknown
Copland's Rock Frog	Litoria coplandi	Unknown
Delicate Mouse	Pseudomys delicatulus	Mulunjbi (I)
Dingo	Canis familiaris dingo	Dalken
Domestic Dog	Canis familiaris	Durug
Dotted Velvet Gecko	Oedura gemmata	Unknown
Double-barred Finch	Poephila bichenovii	Nirn
Dugong	Dugong dugon	Marndihngunjngunj
Emu	Dromaeus novaehollandiae	Ngurrurdu
		Gurdugadji
		Alwandjuk
Estuarine Crocodile	Crocodylus porosus	Namanjwarre
		Ginga
Euro (m)	Macropus robustus	Galkberd
Euro (f)	Macropus robustus	Worlerrk
Excitable Delma	Delma tincta	Yirrhyirrh
Exquisite Rainbowfish	Melanotaenia exquisita	Dilebang
False Water-rat	Xeromys myoides	Unknown
Fish (general)		Djanj
Flatback Turtle	Chelonia depressa	Alabika (K)
Flying-fox family		Goloban
Fork-tailed Swift	Apus pacificus	Unknown
Freshwater Crocodile	Crocodylus johnstonii	Muwuydjalki
		Gumugen
Freshwater Long Tom	Strongilura kreffti	Galirr
		Wurrgabal
		Burdukkulung
Freshwater Prawn	Macrobrachium rosenbergi	Waagi
Freshwater Whip-ray	Hymentura	Nawarla
Frilled Lizard	Chlamydosaurus kingii	Gurndamen (K)
		Ngarlangak
Frogs (general)		Djati
Galah	Cacatua roseicapilla	Wirliwirli
Ghost Bat	Macroderma gigas	Nabarraminjminj (I)
Giant Frog	Cyclorana australis	Unknown
Giant Termite	Mastotermes darwiniensis	Unknown
Gilbert's Dragon	Amphibolurus gilberti	Matjandemit
Golden Orb Spider	Nephila maculosa	Unknown
Grass Owl	Tyto capensis	Unknown
Grasshoppers (general)		Djadede
Great Bowerbird	Chlamydera nuchalis	Djuwe
Great Cormorant	Phalacrocorax carbo	Barrngudbu
Great Egret	Egretta alba	Gomolo
Great-billed Heron	Ardea sumartrana	Naaburrmi
Green Ants	Oecophylla smaragdina	Gaboh
Green Pygmy-goose	Nettapus pulchellus	Bewutj
Green Tree Snake	Dendrelaphis punctulata	Unknown
Green Turtle	Chelonia mydas	Manbiri
Green Tree-frog	Litoria caerulea	Belkanghmi
		Gortbolbok

Common English Name	Scientific Name	Bininj Name
Grey Whipsnake	*Demansia simplex*	Unknown
Grey-crowned Babbler	*Pomatostomus temporalis*	Ngakngak
Hooded Parrot	*Psephotus dissimilis*	Djikilirritj
Intermediate Egret	*Ardea intermedia*	Mulugumulugu
Irrawaddy River Dolphin	*Orcaella brevirostris*	Bid djurrangkan (I)
Jabiru	*Xenorhynchus asiaticus*	Djagarna
Kakadu Dunnart	*Sminthopsis bindi*	Unknown
Kangaroos (general)	*Macropus* spp.	Gunj
Keelback	*Amphiesma mairii*	Unknown
Kimberley Rock Monitor	*Varanus glauerti*	Unknown
King Brown Snake	*Pseudechis australis*	Dadjbe
Kimberley Rock-monitor	*Varanus glauerti*	Balagadi
Leichhardt's Grasshopper	*Petasida ephippigera*	Aldjurr
Lemon-bellied Flycatcher	*Microeca flavigaster*	Mayhmayh
Lesser Frigatebird	*Frigata ariel*	Unknown
Little Corella	*Cacatua pastinator*	Andel / Ngalelek (K)
Little Egret	*Egretta garzetta*	Gabagaba
Little Friarbird	*Philemon citreogularis*	Mitjpirringu
Little Pied Cormorant	*Phalacrocorax melanoleucos*	Barrakbarrak
Little Red Flying-fox	*Pteropus scapulatus*	Na-gayalak
Long-tailed Mouse	*Pseudomys nanus*	Unknown
Lotusbird	*Irediparra gallinacea*	Demdorrkehdorrken
Magpie Goose	*Anseranas semipalmata*	Bamurru / Manimunak
Magpielark	*Grallina cyanoleuca*	Gubirlibbirlib
Mangrove Monitor	*Varanus indicus*	Binirring
Masked Rock-frog	*Litoria personata*	Unknown
Masked Plover	*Vanelus miles*	Berrepberrep
Merten's Water Monitor	*Varanus mertensi*	Burarr
Mitchell's Water Monitor	*Varanus mitchelli*	Djeli
Mouth Almighty	*Glossamia aproni*	Djabelh
Mud Lobster	*Thalassina squamifera*	Unknown
Nabarlek	*Peradorcas concinna*	Nabarlek
Native Bees/Sugarbag	*Trigona* spp.	Angung
Native Ginger	*Curcuma australasica*	Anbindjarra
Northern Bandy-bandy	*Vermicella multifasciata*	Nayin
Northern Brown Tree Snake	*Boiga fusca*	Bandorl / Rambirambi
Northern Brushtail Possum	*Trichosurus arnhemensis*	Djebuy / Wirk
Northern Death Adder	*Acanthurus praelongus*	Bek
Northern Geebung	*Persoonia falcata*	Andag
Northern Nailtail Wallaby	*Onychogalea unguifera*	Goloindjurr
Northern Quoll	*Dasyurus halucatus*	Djabu / Bakadji / Njanjma (K)
Northern Long-necked Turtle	*Chelodina rugosa*	Almangiyi
Northern Shovel-nosed Snake	*Simoselaps roperi*	Nayin
Northern Snapping Turtle	*Elseya dentata*	Ngarderrhwu
Northern Territory Frog	*Sphenophryne adelphe*	Unknown
Oenpelli Rock Python	*Morelia oenpelliensis*	Nawaran
Olive Python	*Liasis olivaceus*	Alngurruhmanj / Andjurdurrk
Orange-footed Scrubfowl	*Megapodius reinwardti*	Gulguldanj
Ornate Burrowing Frog	*Limnodynastes ornatus*	Unknown
Osprey	*Pandion haliaetus*	Unknown
Oxe-eye Herring	*Megalpos cyprinoides*	Galalbarr
Partridge Pigeon	*Geophaps smithii*	Mimguwuy / Raagu
Pacific Black Duck	*Anas supercilliosa*	Nawangku
Peaceful Dove	*Geopelia placida*	Golobok
Pheasant Coucal	*Centropus phasianinus*	Bukbuk
Pied Butcherbird	*Cracticus nigrogularis*	Djobo
Pied Heron	*Ardea picata*	Miniwalmat
Pig-nosed Turtle	*Carettachelys insculpta*	Warradjan
Plumed Whistling-duck	*Dendrocygna eytoni*	Djalwilimbirr
Praying Mantis	*Orthoderinae*	Djulungudjulungu (G)
Purple-spotted Gudgeon	*Mogurnda mogurnda*	Djagol, Gombo
Rainbow Bee-eater	*Merops ornatus*	Birritbirrit
Rainbowfish	*Melanotaenia* spp.	Dilebang
Rainbow-skinks	*Carlia* spp.	Loklok (generic)
Rainforest Fly		Morl
Red Tree-frog	*Litoria rubella*	Unknown
Red-cheeked Dunnart	*Sminthopsis virginiae*	Unknown
Red-collared Lorikeet	*Trichoglossus haematodus*	Deded
Red-tailed Black Cockatoo	*Calyptorhynchus magnificus*	Garnamarr
Red-tailed Rainbow Fish	*Melanotaenia splendida australis*	Dilebang
Reticulated Perchlet	*Ambassis macleayi*	Unknown
Ring-tailed Dragon	*Ctenophorus caudicinctus*	Madjarndamat (K)
River Saw Fish	*Pristis microdon*	Djanjgurndamen
River Whaler Shark	*Carcharhinus leucas*	Wamba (K)
Rock Pigeon	*Petrophassa albipennis*	Gurrbelak
Rock Possum/ Rock-haunting Ringtail Possum	*Petropseudes dahli*	Djorrgurn
Rockhole Frog	*Litoria meiriana*	Unknown
Roth's Tree-frog	*Litoria rothi*	Unknown
Rough Knob-tail Gecko	*Nephrurus asper*	Belerrk
Rufous Owl	*Ninox rufa*	Warrayangal (G)
Rufous Whistler	*Pachycephala rufiventris*	Mayhmayh
Salmon Catfish	*Arius leptaspis*	Anmagawarre / Ginga
Sand Monitor	*Varanus gouldii*	Djanay
Sandstone Antechinus	*Pseudantechinus bilarney*	Dokun
Sandstone Friarbird	*Philemon buceroides*	Gawolk
Sandstone Shrike-thrush	*Colluricincla woodwardi*	Mayhmayh
Saratoga	*Scleropages jardini*	Guluybirr
Saw-shelled Turtle	*Elseya latisternum*	Bamdurek
Sharp-nosed Grunter	*Syncomistes butleri*	Unknown
Shining Flycatcher	*Myagra alecto*	Mayhmayh
Short-eared Rock-wallaby	*Petrogale brachyotis*	Badbong
Shovelnosed Ray	*Rhinobatos batillum*	Unknown
Silver-crowned Friarbird	*Philemon argentea*	Wurlata
Smooth-handed Ghost Crab	*Ocypode cordimana*	Unknown
Snakes (general)	*Serpentes*	Nayin
Sooty Grunter/Black Bream	*Hephaestus fuliginosus*	Nagertmi / Galarrk
Southern Death Adder	*Acanthophis antarcticus*	Bek
Spangled Grunter	*Leiopotherapon unicolor*	Bort
Spectacled Hare-wallaby	*Largorchestes conspicilaris*	Djoded (K)
Spiny Anteater	*Tachyglossus aculeatus*	Gowarrang / Ngarrbek (K)
Spotted Nightjar	*Caprimulgus argus*	Lablab
Striped Grunter	*Amniataba pericoides*	Mandildi
Sugarbag (low nesting)	*Trigona* sp.	Nabiwuh
Sulphur-crested Cockatoo	*Cacatua galerita*	Ngarradj
Tailed Sole	*Ascleropages klunzingeri*	Bembem
Tawny Frogmouth	*Podargus strigoides*	Djungud'djungud
Tornier's Frog	*Litoria tornieri*	Unknown
Torres Strait Pigeon	*Ducula spilorrhoa*	Manawokwok (K)
Torresian Crow	*Corvus orru*	Wakwak
Varied Lorikeet	*Psitteuteles versicolor*	Djurrih
Wandering Whistling-duck	*Dendrocygna arcuata*	Djurrbuyug
Water Python	*Liasis fuscus*	Borloko
Water-rat	*Hydromys chrysogaster*	Yirrkbard / Yirrku
Wedge-tailed Eagle	*Aquila audax*	Namardol (K)
Western Brown Snake	*Pseudonaja affinis*	Yirrbardbard
Whistling Kite	*Haliastur sphenurus*	Nawurrkpil
White-bellied Sea-Eagle	*Haleatus leucogaster*	Marrawurdi
White-browed Robin	*Poecilodryas superciliosa cerviniventris*	Mayhmayh
White-lined Honeyeater	*Meliphaga albilineata*	Bindjanok
White-necked Heron	*Ardea pacifica*	Gulabakku
White-throated Grasswren	*Amytornis woodwardi*	Yilding
Willie-wagtail	*Ripidura leucophrys*	Djikirdi'djikirdi
Wimbrel	*Numenius phaeopus*	Galarrwidwid
Yellow Oriole	*Oriolus flavocinctus*	Birrkpirrk djolok
Yellow Spotted Monitor	*Varanus panoptes*	Galawan

ABORIGINAL LANGUAGES

Today, throughout the Park, the Aboriginal languages encountered (with some difficulty) by Leichhardt are still in everyday use, in one form or another. Speakers are generally multilingual, understanding all the other languages in the region. The Gagudju language in the north of the Park has largely been replaced by Kunwinjku from further east. Gundjeihmi or Mayali is spoken by the bulk of the Bininj Park residents and Jawoyn is spoken by the traditional owners of the southern region. A number of other languages have faded out since the time of Leichhardt.

The bulk of the knowledge about the Park is preserved in these ancient languages. For this and other reasons these languages need to survive. To our benefit, the traditional owners are finding more ways to convey this knowledge to visitors, as can be seen in the Bowali Visitors Centre and the Warradjan Cultural Centre. A special orthography is in use for recording the languages of the Park. The languages are complex, but the rules are simple and easy. The following examples with the nearest English equivalents have been provided by the ANCA to help visitors with basic pronounciation:

Vowels
a - about, but
e - bed
i - bit
o - pot
u - put
Diphthongs
au - house
ai - ay-ay captain
ei - hey

eu - hell, as pronounced in Adelaide
iu - hill, as pronounced in Adelaide
oi - poise
ou - raw, horde
ui - Nhulunbuy
Consonants
b - bank
d - dog

dj - jump
g- gun
h - Cockney 'wha_' for what
k - cake (end of word)
l - lift
m - mad
nj - canyon
n - nose
ng - sing

nj - canyon
r - rice, carry
rd harder
rl - (Harlem) American
rn - harness
rr - carry (Scottish)
w - wait
y - yell

FURTHER READING

Australian National Parks & Wildlife Service 1985, ed. R. Jones, *Archaeological Research in Kakadu National Park,* Special Publication no. 13, AGPS, Canberra.

Australian Nature Conservation Agency & North Australian Research Unit 1995, *Kakadu: Natural & Cultural Heritage Management,* ed. Press, T. et al., ANU, Canberra.

Breeden, S. & Wright, B. 1989, *Kakadu – Looking After The Country The Gagudju Way,* Simon & Schuster, Sydney.

Brennan, K. 1986, *Wildflowers of Kakadu,* K. Brennan, Jabiru, NT.

Brock, J. 1995, *Native Plants of Northern Australia,* rev., A. H. & A. W. Reed, Sydney.

Chaloupka, G. 1995, *A Journey in Time,* Reed Books, Sydney.

Fox, R. W., Kelleher, G. G. & Kerr, C. B. 1977, *Ranger Uranium Environmental Inquiry: Second Report,* AGPS, Canberra.

Leichhardt, L. 1847, *Journal of an Overland Expedition in Australia, from Moreton Bay to Port Essington,* T. & W. Boone, London.

Miles, Greg. 1995, *Wildlife of Kakadu and the Top End of the Northern Territory, Australia,* 2nd edn, Barker Souvenirs, Alice Springs, NT.

Neidjie, B., Davis, S. & Fox, A. 1985, *Kakadu Man,* Resource Managers, Darwin, NT.

Specht, R. L. (ed.) 1964, *Records of the American-Australian Scientific Expedition to Arnhem Land,* vols 3 & 4, Melbourne University Press, Melbourne.

GLOSSARY

aestivation. A term to describe the period of inactivity that many sandstone animals endure during the dry months.

affinities. Close links between living species.

ANCA. Australian Nature Conservation Agency (formerly called Australian National Parks & Wildlife Service or ANPWS), the Federal Government nature conservation agency responsible for the management of Kakadu.

ANPWS. See ANCA.

arboreal. Tree-dwelling or tree-using animals.

Balanda. A widely used term given by Bininj to fair-skinned races (thought to be an early derivation of the word 'Hollander').

billabong. A deep body of permanent water which was once part of a river channel.

Bininj. The linguistic title for the Aboriginal residents of the Kakadu region.

bio-geography. The study of relationships between living and past groups of plants and animals, populations of which are today isolated by distance.

biomass. Total living organisms within a given natural system.

carapace. Hard upper shell of an animal eg. turtle or hard-shelled invertebrate.

diurnal. Active mostly during the day.

ecology. The study of how living things interact with each other and with their environment.

ecosystem. A dynamic community of living things existing in an area governed by natural factors.

endemic. Originating in, or belonging to a certain area. A term usually applied to living things.

Gagudju. The name of an old language spoken by Bininj in the northern region of what is now Kakadu National Park. It was the dominant language spoken there at the time of European arrival, but has since been replaced by Kunwinj'ku and Mayali. Very few people alive today speak Gagadju.

Gondwana. The ancient super-continent from which Australia and its present surrounding islands are presumed to have originated.

gregarious. Species which live in large social groups.

invertebrate. An animal without a backbone, e.g. insects, spiders and centipedes.

lowlands. Country between the escarpment and the sea.

marsupial. Mammal with no placenta, whose young are born at embryonic stage.

nocturnal. A term to describe animals which are active only by night.

outliers. Islands of sandstone on the lowlands away from the main escarpment.

prehensile. Usually applied to the tail of an animal which has the ability to grip or wrap round an object such as a tree branch.

raptor. A bird that is a member of the eagle or hawk group.

savannah. Tropical or subtropical grassland with scattered trees and shrubs.

saxacoline. Rock dwelling.

sedentary. Usually refers to the lifestyle of an animal which lives in the one place and does not move or migrate.

tadpole. The first free-moving, fully aquatic stage in a frog's life-cycle.

taxonomy. A system of naming both living and non-living things.

INDEX OF WILDLIFE AND PLANTS

Page numbers in italics refer to photographs